ArtScroll History Series®

Rabbi Nosson Scherman / Rabbi Meir Zlotowitz

General Editors

BETWEEN
MY FATHER

Published by

Mesorah Publications, ltd

AND THE
OLD FOOL

A HOLOCAUST MEMOIR

MAIER CAHAN
Adapted into English by
YOSEF NEUMARK

FIRST EDITION
First Impression … July 2004

Published and Distributed by
MESORAH PUBLICATIONS, LTD.
4401 Second Avenue / Brooklyn, N.Y 11232

Distributed in Europe by
LEHMANNS
Unit E, Viking Business Park
Rolling Mill Road
Jarow, Tyne & Wear, NE32 3DP
England

Distributed in Australia and New Zealand by
GOLDS WORLD OF JUDAICA
3-13 William Street
Balaclava, Melbourne 3183
Victoria, Australia

Distributed in Israel by
SIFRIATI / A. GITLER — BOOKS
6 Hayarkon Street
Bnei Brak 51127

Distributed in South Africa by
KOLLEL BOOKSHOP
Shop 8A Norwood Hypermarket
Norwood 2196, Johannesburg, South Africa

ARTSCROLL HISTORY SERIES®
BETWEEN MY FATHER AND THE OLD FOOL
© Copyright 2004, by MESORAH PUBLICATIONS, Ltd.
4401 Second Avenue / Brooklyn, N.Y. 11232 / (718) 921-9000 / www.artscroll.com

ISBN:
1-57819-356-7 (hard cover)
1-57819-357-5 (paperback)

Typography by CompuScribe at ArtScroll Studios, Ltd.

Printed in the United States of America by Noble Book Press Corp.
Bound by Sefercraft, Quality Bookbinders, Ltd., Brooklyn N.Y. 11232

Foreword

This book, which is adapted from the extensive memoirs our father wrote in Yiddish, focuses primarily on the war years. It is not necessary for us to provide background information about him and his family or about his personality, because it is all in the book. Nonetheless, we feel we should say a few words about the father we knew and loved for so many years and through whom we felt connected to earlier, purer generations.

More than anything else, our father was to us an exemplar of a level of *emunah* and *bitachon* uncommon in our generation. It was evident in his *tefilah*, his Torah, his love for *talmidei chachamim*, his *tzedakah* and *chessed*, his business dealings, and his relationship with family and friends. He lived with the *Ribono Shel Olam*; he was a Yid through and through

Our father had a hard life. He lost most of his family during the war and barely survived himself. After the war, he lived for years in anti-Semitic Communist Romania before he ultimately fled to Belgium, a middle-aged, broken man, forced to begin life anew. Through all his hardships, his *emunah* and *bitachon* kept him strong and happy, always with a positive outlook on life. His experiences also gave him a special sensitivity to the suffering of others. He always tried to understand, to help, to give advice and monetary assistance to people who had fallen on hard times.

Our father was a very clever, charismatic person with a deep understanding of people and a special *eidelkeit* and *mentchlichkeit* (two untranslatable words that mean so much) in his dealings with others. He was always the first to greet people, both Jew and Gentile alike, with a heartwarming, gentle smile. Even the janitor of his *shul* commented that things would just not be the same without him.

During the *Shivah*, a friend came all the way from England to pay his condolences. "The encouragement which I got from your father," he said, "the way he treated me with the utmost respect and dignity despite my youth, has remained with me until this very day!"

The honor and respect he showed every individual was unusual, but the honor, respect and sheer deference he showed all Torah scholars, be they Chassidic *rebbes* or Litvishe *roshei yeshivah*, were on a different plane altogether. Before he would enter the presence of a *gadol*, he would put on a Shabbos suit and hat, button his jacket and wash his hands. For a Chassidic *gadol*, he would put on a *gartel* as well.

Our father was a big *talmid chacham* who simply loved to learn. There was no one happier or more content than our father with a *sefer* in front of him. He used to say that he does not understand how he will be rewarded for learning Torah in the next world, since it was so enjoyable for him. He had a special talent for *chiddush* in *drush* (originality in homiletics) and for weaving seemingly disparate topics together into a beautiful, homiletic tapestry.

He was the paradigm of how an *ehrlicher Yid*—an upstanding, faithful Jew—conducts his business affairs. In his deep concern for other people and his desire to spread joy, he would make sure, even when closing a business deal, that all parties involved were completely pleased with the results. If a person later regretted the deal, he was always willing to give back the money and cancel the deal, even if it meant taking a loss. Once, our father brokered a business deal in which one of the parties later declared bankruptcy, causing his investors to lose large sums of money. Although our father was completely innocent of any wrongdoing, being only a broker, he could not come to terms with having innocently and indirectly caused others a financial loss, and over time, little by little, he paid them back.

He was a wise, kind, caring and giving father who taught by example. To us, he was the epitome of responsibility, starting life over several times despite devastating personal losses. Nothing was too difficult for him. His greatest pleasure was waking up before anyone else to shop for everyone's favorite food, or finding just the right gift he knew would mean so much.

He was very serious about life, but somehow he always managed to be the center of entertainment; he loved to make others happy. His robust singing at *simchos* was particularly unforgettable, and the brilliant *grammen* (poems) he composed brought people to laughter and to tears.

Our father passed away with his bed ringed by *rabbanim* and distinguished people engaged in Torah study as his *neshamah* departed. He lived a life that spread light and *kvod shamayim*. Without a doubt he is reaping his just reward now, deriving pleasure from the great and eternal light of the *Shechinah*.

He leaves behind his wife and life partner, our mother, Ila, may she live and be well until one hundred and twenty, and three sons: Meshulam Feivish (Favi) Cahan, his wife Civia (neé Reinman), and their children, Batsheva, Daliah and her husband David Mechlowitz, and Dovid; Yehudah Cahan and his wife Faygie (neé Brezak), and their children, Miriam, Esther, Sora, Moshe and Yaakov; and Menachem (Mendy) Cahan.

Chapter 1

Even with the world exploding all around us, we were not much affected in Lower Vishiva (Unter Vishiva). Hitler came to power in Germany. Tensions rose. Armies massed. The Germans invaded Poland. England and France declared war. What did this all mean to us? Not very much. Judaism and poverty were the only factors that affected the cadence of life in our little village tucked away in the hills of northern Romania, and they remained unchanged despite all the convulsions on the international scene. All the people in our village, most of whom were staunch *chassidim* of the Vizhnitz dynasty, were uniformly and unwaveringly observant. And just about all of them were also uniformly and unwaveringly poor.

Lower Vishiva was famous throughout the entire region for its outstanding poverty. We had one supposedly rich man, who owned a lumberyard and even had a telephone. All the rest struggled, pushing through each day with great effort and courage but very little success. Even my father, who was fairly prosperous by Lower Vishiva standards, would walk around with worry lines on his face before the holidays, when household expenses accumulated quickly. "The Passover Haggadah instructs us to get wine and eggs," people would remark before the holiday, "but it doesn't tell us how to get the money with which to buy them." And yet, somehow or another, people managed to usher Shabbos and the holidays into their homes, and as soon as the sun set and the holy days began, there was only carefree joy in every heart. Of course, all the misery returned with a vengeance the moment the holy days passed. Still, the periodic respites provided by the Torah, made life bearable. We managed to survive and even flourish, but only in a spiritual sense of course.

The Nazis terrified all Jews, even those living across the ocean, but there was no sense of immediate danger in Lower Vishiva. Although we had originally been part of Hungary, an ally of the Nazis, we had become part of Romania when the Austro-Hungarian Empire broke up after the First World War. For the time being, at least, we were out of reach. But in 1940, things changed. In the Second Vienna Decree the Germans rewarded their loyal Hungarian allies with a huge chunk of northern Romania. We were included in the package.

The Hungarians, enthusiastic allies of the Nazis, closed the vise of persecution around us and tightened it continually, notch by painful notch. When they decreed, in the summer of 1943, that Jews must wear the yellow Star of David, we could practically smell the stench of burning flesh drifting over the Carpathian Mountains from Poland to the north.

My father a month before the Holocaust   *My younger brother Yehudah*

On March 19, 1944, with their eastern flank being pulverized by the Red Army, the Germans invaded Hungary and installed a puppet government. Then they sent in killing squads called *Einsatzgruppen* to organize and carry out the massacre of the Jewish population. You would have thought that with the fall of the Reich staring them in the face, they would forget about the Jews for a while and worry about their own defenses. But you would have thought wrong.

In April, ghettos were prepared in every city and town in Hungary. All the Jews in the countryside were concentrated into these ghettos, and the deportations began. In our area, the ghetto was prepared in Upper Vishiva, which was a fairly large town. On April 14, Hungarian gendarmes appeared in our village to announce the relocation of all Jewish families to the ghetto. They ordered up transport from the countryside and gave us one day to get ready.

The next day, April 15, was a Shabbos. It was also the last day of Passover, and for most of us, the last Passover on this earth. On the festival celebrating our redemption from Egyptian exile, we were about to be plunged into an exile more frightening than any our people had ever endured before. The Nazi goal was not enslavement. It was extermination.

The gendarmes arrived in force early in the morning. Through a crack in the curtains, I saw them spreading through the village. I heard them coming down our street, banging on the doors of our neighbors. I heard them shouting, "Everyone out! Off to the ghetto! March!"

The door burst open, and two husky gendarmes stomped into our house. My father, my forceful, resourceful, charismatic, courageous, wise father, the illustrious Reb Meshulem Favish Cahan, the sun and stars of my universe, the man I had obeyed unquestioningly and idolized all my life, my poor father shrank back, face pale, hands trembling, eyes defeated. The young children cowered in a corner. My stepmother went to stand beside them. As for me, a feisty twenty-year-old just back from managing a rough logging crew in the forest, I had to put on a meek face and slink back against the wall. I knew that at the slightest sign of defiance, these brutes would tear me to pieces and enjoy doing it.

"All right, where's the money?" one of the gendarmes, a tall man with a red mustache, said to my father.

"There is no money. Just a few *pengos*," my father said quietly.

The gendarme sneered and turned to my stepmother. "Give me your jewelry. Right now!"

My stepmother handed him her gold watch, her pearl necklace and a few other small pieces of jewelry she had treasured for so many years. The gendarme stuffed the jewelry into his pocket. Then he grabbed her hand and ripped the gold wedding band off her finger.

He laughed. "You won't be needing these where you're going. I'll take care of them for you."

I saw a flash of anger in my stepmother's eyes, but it was gone in an instant. We were beyond anger. All winter long, we had been reading the handwriting on the wall. We had expected this. And worse.

The shorter gendarme reached into the recesses of one of the lower shelves in the large cupboard. "Aha! What have we here?"

His hand emerged with my stepmother's heirloom silver candlesticks gripped tightly in his hairy fist. My stepmother burst into tears and covered her face.

"Don't cry, Ethel," my father soothed her. "If only they would take all our things and leave us and the children alone, I would laugh with joy and thank the Almighty all the days of my life. Don't cry for things, Ethel. They're only things."

The tears subsided, and she looked up at my father and then at the children. There was a look of such sadness on her face. Then she managed a miserable smile and nodded.

The gendarmes finished their search and prepared to leave with a sack full of our belongings.

"Why are you people wasting time?" the tall gendarme with the red mustache demanded. "You should be loading up your wagon and be on your way to the ghetto. Where's the wagon? It's not even here. Weren't you assigned a wagon driver?"

"Yes, we were," said my father. "His name is Gavrila. We're packed and ready, but he hasn't come yet."

The gendarme's face turned such a deep crimson that his mustache paled by comparison. "What do you think this is?" he screamed. "A picnic? If the wagon's not here, the driver is probably drunk. Go get him!"

I sprang forward. "I'll get him, Father. I know where Gavrila lives."

The gendarme gave me a speculative look, obviously considering if he had the time to give me a good thrashing. Apparently, he didn't. "You do that, Jew," he snarled. "Right now!"

They stormed out and slammed the door behind them. The sharp sound reverberated in my ears long after they had gone, as if a door had slammed shut on my entire life up until then. The past was over, the future too dreadful to consider.

My father and stepmother with Chaya, me, Alta, Sarah and Rickel.

"Go quickly, Maier," my father said. "We should get moving as soon as possible. There are the little children to consider. Who knows when and where they'll get to sleep tonight?"

In a strange way, I was happy to go searching for Gavrila. The house was too depressing, and in my exuberant youth, I wasn't quite ready to succumb to despair. The only problem was that the scenes in the street were even more depressing. Wagons laden with the pathetic accumulation of bare necessities and little pieces of life that simply could not be left behind, along with ashen-faced fathers, weeping mothers, and wailing children, with hopelessness and resignation on the faces of old people who knew they would never survive this ordeal.

I could hear Benzion Ganz screaming even before I turned the corner and saw his house. I hung back in the shadows, mesmerized.

A wagon piled high with bundles and children stood out front, and Mrs. Ganz stood trembling alongside. Benzion, however, was struggling mightily with three gendarmes who were trying to get him onto the wagon. His face was covered with cuts and bruises, and blood streamed from a gash on his forehead, into his matted beard.

"No!" he kept screaming as they continued to beat him mercilessly. "I will not go! Never in my life have I violated the Shabbos, and I won't do it now. Never!"

"Get on the wagon right now, you filthy Jew," one of the gendarmes shouted, and he kicked him in the groin.

Benzion doubled over in pain, his eyes bulging, his mouth moving without emitting a sound. But his wife's hysterical shrieks and the wails of the children immediately filled the sudden silence.

"Benzion! Benzion!" Mrs. Ganz pleaded between sobs. "What are you doing? Please come into the wagon. We need you. You must come with us. Don't let them kill you. Please, please, don't let them kill you. Please, Benzion, don't you see that we have no choice?"

Her words seemed to galvanize him, and he found his voice. "No choice? No choice? I do have a choice. I will remain here, and if they want to kill me, let them kill me. I am prepared to sacrifice my life to sanctify the Name. I want to die *al Kiddush Hashem*. Right now, right in front of my own house. Right now on the holy Shabbos which I have never violated in my whole life." He tore himself from the gendarmes and surged toward the house. "Kill me. Kill me. I am prepared to die right here."

One gendarme spun Benzion around and punched him full in the face, knocking him senseless to the ground.

"You'll get your chance to die, Jew," said the gendarme with a chuckle. "Only not just yet. Not . . . just . . . yet. Janos! Tomas! Tie him up and toss him onto the wagon."

By the time, Benzion's head cleared he saw that he had been deposited on a pile of bundles, trussed up like a calf being shipped to slaughter.

"Untie me, you monsters," he began to scream. "It's Shabbos! Oh, what has this world come to, that pious Jews are forced to desecrate the holiest day? Let me off! Kill me! Kill me!"

The old mare hitched to the wagon pawed nervously at the ground, but the driver, a droopy-eyed Hungarian peasant, slouched on the bench, smoking languidly, oblivious to everything. Now he turned slightly and cast a disdainful look at Benzion out of the corner of his eye.

The gendarme spit on the ground and signaled to the driver. "Move!"

I waited till the wagon had rounded the corner and the gendarmes were gone, and only then did I emerge from the shadows. I didn't know how to deal with what I had just seen. Where was justice? Where was the grandeur and power of the Almighty? Benzion's father, Reb Leibish Ganz, had suffered poor health all his life, yet he had given every moment to the study of the Torah. Even while walking down the street, he would murmur chapters of the Psalms or the Mishnah under his breath, so deep was his love for the Almighty and His Torah. Was it right that the son of a man like this should be beaten bloody, because he refused to desecrate the Shabbos? Something was seriously askew in the world.

My eager young mind grappled with the awesome inscrutability of pure evil. I could still hear the cries of Benzion's anguish fading in the distance, and I shuddered. Even today, fifty years later, those terrible cries still ring in my ears in the stillness of the night. As do the cries of Shosha Chanah.

Shosha Chanah was an older woman who lived in the next street. On that day, when I approached her house, she lay on the ground dressed head to toe in white burial shrouds and surrounded by gendarmes. The rooster feathers in their caps quivered in the air.

It was not the first time I had seen her shrouds. Every Yom Kippur, she wore those shrouds in the synagogue, freshly washed and starched, her way of reminding herself and the Almighty that life was ephemeral, a passing shadow, a dream that flies away. But now the shrouds were not there for the symbolism.

"Bury me here!" she screamed. "This is where I was born, and this is where I want to die. I want to be buried in a Jewish grave right here in our own Jewish cemetery. Look, I'm ready. Look at what I'm wearing! Kill me and bury me. Kill me and bury me. I'm staying here!"

I didn't have the time to watch this dismal drama play itself out. I ducked between two houses and cut across to a different street. Gavrila lived a short walk beyond the metal bridge that spanned the small but swift river at the edge of the village. Bowing my head and hunching my shoulders, as if that would help me block out the sounds and sights of the destruction of my village, I hurried towards my destination.

I don't know how long she had been walking beside me trying to get my attention. Her voice finally penetrated the invisible shell I had drawn around me. "Maier! Why don't you answer me? Why are you ignoring me?"

I looked up, surprised. It was Sarah Malik. When I was a young boy, my friends and I used to go to the Malik house every Shabbos, and Sarah's father, Reb Aharon Malik, would test us on our studies of that week.

Sarah was close to my age, maybe a little younger. She stood there twining and untwining her fingers nervously. Her face was white, and her eyes were red.

"I'm sorry, Sarah," I said. "I simply didn't hear you."

She nodded. "I wish I could escape into my own head like that."

"What were you saying?"

"I wanted to ask you a question."

"Ask."

"This happened years ago so I'm not sure you'll remember." She cleared her throat. "Do you remember telling us about the destruction of the Holy Temple in Jerusalem?"

"Remind me."

"The part that really stuck in my mind was the story about the four hundred Jewish girls who were taken prisoner and sent by ship to Rome. Do you remember telling us about it?"

"I'm not sure," I said guardedly. "But I do know the story."

"They asked the rabbis whether they would be held accountable in the Next World if they took their own lives. They didn't want to have their souls defiled by what the Romans planned to do with them. The rabbis assured them that, although suicide was a terrible sin, they would not be penalized under the circumstances. Do you remember what those girls did?"

"Yes," I whispered.

"They jumped into the sea! All four hundred of them." She paused to give me a chance to respond, but I had nothing to say. She took a deep breath and continued. "A group of us girls here in Vishiva have made a pact to die before we allow ourselves to be violated. We are not afraid of death, but we don't want to come to the Next World with tainted souls. What do you think, Maier?"

"What do you want me to say, Sarah? What are you asking me?"

"You know perfectly well, Maier. Is it the right thing to do? Do we have a right to do as those four hundred girls did two thousand years ago?"

"You can't ask me a question like that, Sarah. Do you expect me to answer questions of life and death? Why don't you ask your father? He is a great Torah scholar. We have a rabbi here in Vishiva; why don't you ask him? Why are you asking me such questions?"

"I did ask them."

"Oh. And what did they say?"

"They said, 'Have faith. G-d's salvation comes in the blink of an eye.' They said, 'We will definitely be delivered from this misfortune.' That is the most they will say to me. But it's not enough. What if, Heaven forbid, we are not delivered? What if He turns His face away from us in this terrible, terrible time? Didn't the people in Jerusalem have faith when the Romans were battering down the walls? Didn't the Jewish people in the towns on the Rhine have faith when the Crusaders were coming? Faith is no guarantee, Maier, is it?"

"No," I said quietly. "Of course it isn't."

"Exactly. So I think I am entitled to an answer to my question, but they won't give me one. You're no ignoramus, Maier, and you are a clever fellow as well. You have to give me an answer, Maier. You must!"

I chewed on my knuckles and looked at the ground for a minute or two. What was I supposed to say to this girl? Was I supposed to give her and her friends permission to commit suicide? Out of the question. But I couldn't brush her off either. She was entitled to an answer, and I was simply the one whom she had managed to back into a corner.

Oh G-d, I thought desperately, what should I say to her? Oh G-d, look at your pure Jewish girls. What are they worried about right now? Not survival. Not a little food to still their hunger. Not safety. They're worried about coming before You in the Next World with untainted souls. Oh G-d, haven't we suffered enough? Do we really deserve to be crushed like this? Do You really want these girls to commit suicide?

"Listen to me, Sarah," I said. "There is a great difference between the Romans and the Germans. To the Romans, we were just the enemy, but to the Germans, we are the scum of the earth. Their propaganda for the last ten years has convinced them that we are slimy insects, subhuman creatures that have to be exterminated. I don't think it is very likely that a German would want to touch a Jewish girl, not after everything that's been drummed into his head for the last ten years. And even if one German here and there would get such an idea into his head, would he risk embarrassment and even punishment if he should be discovered?"

"So you think it wouldn't happen, Maier?"

"Look, we can't fool ourselves. There are no guarantees in this world, and anything can happen. But I think it would be the exception rather than the rule. Most Germans would look at a Jewish girl with disgust, no matter how beautiful she is."

Sarah shivered. "I hope you're right."

"I think so."

"But still, it could happen, couldn't it?"

"It could," I replied. "But we're talking about a suicide pact here. Does it make sense for a group of Jewish girls to take their own lives because something out of the ordinary will maybe, maybe happen?"

"No, I suppose not," she said. She sounded almost disappointed. I gave her a quizzical look, and she turned away and stared down at the ground. "I'm really grateful to you, Maier. You were really a big help. Maybe we'll meet again someday when all this will be only a bad memory."

"I'm sure we will. Be strong."

"I'll try," she said in a voice suddenly gone limp. "And you, Maier, take care of yourself." Her eyes met mine for an instant, then she ran off to join her parents.

What had I heard in her voice? What had I seen in her eyes? I was almost sure it was disappointment. She had come to me all fired up with her resolve to take her life. Bad as things were, she would rise above everything in a moment of blazing glory. She would be a shining heroine remembered in story and song, like the female captives of the Romans, for at least two thousand years. She would be an inspiration and a role model, triumphant in her tragic death. But I had stolen this from her and condemned her to the sordid reality of hopelessness and despair. What had I done? I had given her back her life, but I had taken the life out of her. Perhaps it would have been better had I left her question unanswered.

I looked back in the direction toward which she had run, but she was already out of sight. Too late to try and repair the damage. Too late to do anything about anything except submit to the will of the Almighty. That was the only avenue that offered even the slightest bit of hope. The Almighty was allowing this to happen; it was all part of the divine plan, and we were His instruments. Only faith and acceptance could give meaning to the bitter last moments of our lives.

Easier said than done, I told myself as I went off to find Gavrila.

Two older men were coming toward me as I stepped onto the bridge. They walked with heads lowered and shoulders bent, but I immediately recognized them as David Genuth and Zalman Unger. They glanced at me and mumbled a greeting as they hurried past.

Memories suddenly flooded my mind, triggered by the bridge, the rushing river swollen by spring rains and the two men who had just passed by. I was carried back just a few short years. Once again, it was Passover, but two nights earlier. It was the eve of Shevi'i shel Pesach, the Seventh Day of Passover, the day on which, three thousand years ago, the Jewish people emerging from slavery in Egypt had stood on the shores of the sea, the day on which the sea had split open to give them safe passage, the day on which the sea had closed behind them and drowned their Egyptian pursuers.

I was back in my father's house. It was midnight, and the men of our village were gathering in our large front room. They had long since returned from the synagogue. They had enjoyed the festival meal with their families and had sent them off to sleep. It was now time for serious celebration.

The table was piled high with fruit, hard-boiled eggs and an assortment of other Passover delicacies. My father circulated around the room with a large bottle of brandy, filling everyone's glass again and again as he led the people in boisterous festival songs.

Mild-mannered men, who ordinarily moved through the village like so many gray shadows, raised their glasses and their gleaming faces and shouted with joy. Ragged *shtreimels* and long black *kaftans* were flung off. The room, pungent with the aroma of brandy, reverberated with the inspired singing and dancing. It was all pure and holy and intensely spiritual.

As the dancing and drinking intensified, David Genuth jumped onto the table, thrust his arms high into the air and began to dance, graceful, passionate, light as a floating feather. His long *tzitzis*, the fringes on his rectangular garment, swung through the air in every which direction, never quite able to catch up with his own gyrations. Finally, hands reached up and pulled him down into a circle of dancers who were literally running around the table as they sang at the top of their lungs.

In the midst of all this pandemonium, Zalman Unger, meek, soft-spoken Zalman Unger, burst through the crowd and launched himself onto the table. He lay down on his back, stretched to his full length on the wine-stained white tablecloth, opened the two top buttons of his shirt and lifted his head until his beard jutted straight up and his throat was bared.

"Look at me!" he shouted. "I'm ready to die *al Kiddush Hashem. Shecht* me! Slaughter me! Help me show Him my love and devotion. I want to die right here to sanctify His holy Name."

A simple, unlearned man, Zalman did not know how to give expression to the religious frenzy being generated in the room. He did not know how to achieve an expanded state of consciousness and transcend the physical world. He could only express his zeal by offering to give his life for G-d, but only in a symbolic way, of course. The dancers smiled at him indulgently without even slowing their pace.

"Hey!" Zalman shouted. "Didn't anyone hear me? Slaughter me right now. Please! I want to die al Kiddush Hashem and go straight to my reward in the Next World. Who cares about this world? What does it all mean? Nothing! Slaughter me now so that I can go up to my Creator as a pure, unblemished sacrifice."

The dancers laughed and slapped him affectionately on the thigh.

"What's this? No one is taking me seriously?" Zalman screamed, suddenly angry. He groped though the debris on the table until he found a sharp fruit knife, which he brandished aloft. "Here, take this knife. Cut my throat. I want to die to sanctify the Name. Help me, if you are my friends."

My father leaned over and gently removed the knife from Zalman's hand before anyone thought to accommodate his wishes. "We have to be careful, Zalman," he said. "Someone may get hurt. Come off the table now and dance with me. The Almighty has definitely taken notice of your willingness to sacrifice your life for Him, and He will not forget it."

Just before the break of dawn, the men retrieved their shtreimels and kaftans and put them on, but the celebration was far from over. Now it was time to go to the river to sing the songs of praise the Jewish people had sung during the Exodus, when the waters of the sea parted before them.

The soft pink tinges on the horizon took the edge off the darkness as we strolled through the village, singing wake-up songs to rouse the sleeping villagers to join us on our trek to the sea:

Beloved brothers, dear brothers,
why are you still asleep?
It's time to purify yourselves,
time to go to the study halls.
What? No purification? No study?
Then what are you doing in this world?
From what will your soul draw life?
Beloved brothers, dear brothers,
why are you still asleep?

It was a full kilometer from our house to the bridge, and by the time we were halfway there, most of the villagers had joined us. Women and little children watched from the windows along the way. There was a slight chill in the early morning air, but that only added to the delicious excitement of the moment.

We all packed onto the bridge, end to overflowing end, and my father led the crowd, verse by verse, in the recital of the Biblical song of praise, "Then Moses and the people of Israel sang . . ."

Suddenly, David Genuth pushed to the railing and shouted, "Nachshon ben Aminadav!"

Instinctively, I knew what was coming. Moses had told the Jew to go forward, but whereto? The sea blocked their progress. Nachshon, the heroic prince of the Tribe of Judah, took the initiative. He plunged headlong into the sea, and then it split open before them. David Genuth was about to do a Nachshon ben Aminadav.

And he did. He flung off his *shtreimel* and *kaftan* once again, clambered over the railing and leaped into the rushing river several meters below.

"Nachshon ben Aminadav!" he yelled as he plummeted through the air.

"Father!" his son Shloimele screamed in terror as our heroic Nachshon disappeared from sight.

But there was no harm done. After a few heart-stopping seconds, our own Nachshon surfaced and climbed out onto the riverbank.

Now, in the midst of calamity, I stood on the deserted bridge, looked down at the turgid river and thought about the men who had just passed by. David Genuth and Zalman Unger, heroes of the night, hearts aflame with love for the Almighty, how they had inspired us with their readiness to sacrifice their lives for His greater honor and glory! But what about now?

I glanced over my shoulder and caught sight of them in the distance, two frightened old men hurrying back to their families to share the suffering that awaited them, and perhaps a morsel of hope that might be found in some forgotten corner.

Chapter 2

Gavrila was already hitching two oxen to his wagon when I arrived. He grunted several times as I explained to him the urgent need for his prompt arrival, but he didn't seem to find it necessary to say a single word. Seeing no purpose in staying there, I headed back home.

Along the way, as I passed near the Jewish cemetery of Lower Vishiva, I felt drawn to it as if by a magnet and thought it must be my mother summoning me to bid her farewell. Being a Kohein, a member of the priestly caste, I was forbidden to enter the cemetery or come into any other kind of close contact with dead people. Instead, I climbed up to the small rise upon which I usually stood when I came to pay my respects to my mother. From this vantage point,

My paternal grandfather,
R' Yaakov Cahan

I could get a good view of the cemetery, although I couldn't actually see my mother's grave.

My mother, Alta Etieh Cahan, and my father had been first cousins; their fathers were brothers. She passed away in 1924, within a year after I was born. Chaya, my older sister, was two years old at the time. Left with two small children, my father soon remarried.

I remember my father waking me early one morning when I was just three years old. "Come, Maier," he said. "Today you must go to the synagogue. It is your mother's yahrzeit, the date on which she passed away, and you must say Kaddish."

"What should I say?" I asked.

"Don't worry," he reassured me. "I'll help you with every word."

I remember standing on a chair to say Kaddish. I remember people crowding around to gawk and say Amen at all the appropriate places. I heard one of my friends ask his father, "Why is Maier saying Kaddish?"

"Sh, not so loud," his father replied. "Maier is a poor orphan. That's why he has to say Kaddish."

Well, I certainly didn't feel like a poor orphan. My stepmother was a wonderful woman who loved me no less than if I had been her own child, and I could not have loved her more had she given birth to me. We were very close, with a deep sensitivity to each other's moods and feelings. My stepmother always honored and respected the memory of my mother, and I was grateful. Every year on my mother's yahrzeit, she would bake a little cake for me to distribute to the men in the synagogue after I said Kaddish. I would carry it proudly, a symbol of my bond to both my mothers.

Much as I loved my stepmother, I always felt a special closeness to my natural mother, perhaps because of all the time I spent in my maternal grandparents' home. My grandfather, Reb

My stepmother with her mother, her brother Yaakov and her sister Hentsha

Herschel Cahan, was witty and warm, and my grandmother Chantze never failed to fuss over me and speak to me about my mother, her much lamented daughter who had passed away in the bloom of youth. So it was little wonder that I would often think about my mother and speak to her in my thoughts. She was my confidante, always sympathetic, never disapproving, and occasionally quite helpful.

Standing on the rise near the cemetery, I now spoke to her aloud, as if the breeze would scoop up my words and carry them to her. "Dearest mother, this may be the last time I ever stand here. We're in terrible trouble, your parents, your husband, your children, and even your tiny granddaughter whom you've never seen. We are powerless to resist, and the Almighty seems to have turned away from us. Help us! Call all the mothers and fathers, all the grandmothers and grandfathers, and storm the gates of Heaven. Plead for us. Fight for us! What have we done? How have we sinned? Why do we deserve this? If you don't do something right away, most of us will soon be dead. Mother, I have to go now. I love you and will never forget you, but please don't you forget us either."

Back in the village, everything was ugliness and horror, but here, among the graves, it was just another beautiful spring morning. The birds sang in the trees, the flowers blossomed in the fields, and the sun glowed softly through the silken air. I looked at the cemetery in the distance, and I was struck by how peaceful it looked. In Ecclesiastes, King Solomon declares, "And I praise the dead for they have already died." I could now sympathize with that point of view. But still, I was not quite ready to join them. With a sigh, I turned and went to join the living. Or at least, those who were still just barely alive.

After informing my father that Gavrila was on the way, I ran off to see my maternal grandparents. They were old and infirm, and I was sure they could use some help and moral support.

My grandparents lived with my mother's sister Sarah and her husband, Uncle Favish, the rabbinical judge of Lower Vishiva. We were all related, and therefore, there were many men named Favish in my family. A wagon hitched to a pair of oxen waited in front of their house. There were bundles piled inside the wagon and other bundles strewn on the ground near the front door. From inside, my grandmother's Yiddish lamentations blended incongruously with the harsh Hungarian commands of a gendarme. I knocked on the door.

A cadaverous gendarme with a shaven skull flung open the door. A cigarette dangled from his lips. "Who are you? What are you doing here?"

"My name is Maier Cahan," I said, staring down at my shoes. "My grandparents live here. I've come to help them load up the wagon."

The gendarme rubbed his nose with his thumb as he considered this information. Finally, he nodded and waved me in.

In order to get to my grandparents, I had to navigate around the piles of books, clothing and all manner of household items. I wasn't sure if these were being left behind or taken along. The gendarme remained near the door. He surveyed the room, then he pulled a small notebook from his pocket, licked the tip of his right forefinger and began to turn the pages.

My grandfather was sitting at the table hunched over a large volume of the Talmud, his head in his hands. He looked up when I came in, rolled his eyes, gave a fatalistic shrug and returned to his studies. My grandmother was sitting on a chair, holding my Aunt Sarah's infant son in her arms, covering his little face with kisses wet with tears. She greeted me with a pained smile, and then smacked her forehead as if she had forgotten something. She struggled to her feet and walked over to the large cupboard. She opened one of the bottom drawers, pulled something out and slipped it into her pocket.

"All right, old lady," said the gendarme, and in two strides he was by her side with his hand outstretched. "I saw that. Hand it over."

"It's nothing of value," she replied.

"Let me decide that."

Reluctantly, she reached into her pocket and pulled out an envelope half-disintegrated with age. "It's just a letter," she said. "In Yiddish. From my dead daughter."

He dropped his smoldering cigarette butt on the polished floor and ground it out with his boot. "Hang on to your letter, old lady. I'll be back soon to give the order to get moving. Make sure you're ready."

As soon as the door closed behind the gendarme, my grandfather came over and embraced me. He glanced over at my grandmother and her tear-stained cheeks, then he said in an almost conspiratorial tone, "Such terrible times. But if this is G-d's will, we have to accept it with love. Did Abraham complain when G-d told him to abandon his home and land? Of course not. And look how he was rewarded! Our own situation can also turn completely around, Maier, but only if we accept. That is the key. Acceptance." He lowered his voice. "Women don't understand these things."

I gave him a knowing look, and my grandfather returned to his studies. My grandfather is a fortunate man, I thought to myself, if he can think this way with full conviction. But what about my grandmother? I went to sit beside her. I could think of nothing to say.

"You know the letter, Maier," she said. "It's the one I showed you, the last letter I received from her. My poor, poor child. How I miss her! Do you think a day goes by that I don't cry for her? Here, hold the baby. I want to read from the letter. There's one part I want you to hear again."

She deposited the child in my arms and pulled out the letter. With trembling fingers, she opened it.

"Dearest mother and father," she read. Her wrinkled lips quivered with each word. "I am so sorry for all the pain I'm causing you. I know how terrible it must be for you to lose your daughter, especially because we love each other so very, very much. But at least, I am leaving behind my two little children to help you remember me, my Chayala and my Maier. Believe me, parting from my husband, my children and the both of you is very painful. But I know that if the Almighty had asked me to sacrifice my life for Him I would gladly have given it. Well, this is no different. This is how I look at it now. The Almighty is asking me to sacrifice my life for Him, and I give it up gladly. Please look at it the same way, and it will hurt less."

She folded up the letter reverently, kissed it and slipped it into her pocket. "Your mother. Ach, your sainted mother. What can I say? I miss her so much. Oh, the pain in my heart. It never goes away."

The baby stirred in my arms and began to cry. I tried to shush him, but he paid no attention. I looked imploringly at my grandmother.

She shook her head wearily. "Go give him back to his mother. I need some time with my thoughts."

My poor grandmother, I thought, my poor broken-hearted grandmother. I touched her lightly on the back of her hand, but she was oblivious. She was probably back with my mother in a better time and a better place.

Aunt Sarah was in a state when I came into the other part of the house. She snatched the baby from my arms and placed her lips on the baby's forehead. Then clutching the baby tightly in her arms, she began to pace back and forth, arguing vehemently, while my uncle sat silently by. It took me a moment to realize she was arguing with G-d. "What is this? What's going on? My poor child is running a high fever, and we're being thrown out of our home? Is this fair? You know we didn't have children for years after we were married, and then You gave us these little precious ones. Didn't I thank You enough for giving them to us? So what's happening now? Are you taking back Your gift? Is that right? Why are you abandoning us? Aren't we Your chosen people any more?"

Uncle Favish jumped to his feet, scandalized. "Sarah! Are you out of your mind? How can you talk like that? How can you accuse the Almighty of abandoning His children? Would you abandon your children?"

"I would never abandon my children," she said, eyes flashing fiercely. "My heart is pierced by every bit of pain my children suffer. I would give my life for them. But He doesn't seem to have any more need for us. He doesn't love us any more, otherwise, how could He let us suffer so?"

Uncle Favish clapped his hands over his ears. "Sarah! Watch what you're saying. It is forbidden to speak like that.

Did it ever occur to you that we've brought this upon ourselves by our sins? Did you ever think about that?"

"Sins! Come on, Favish, don't make me laugh. What sins? What have I done? What have you done? What have my poor father and mother done? What have our poor innocent babies done? What has any of the people in our village done? Sins? Don't talk to me about sins!"

My uncle's face turned beet-red. "Oy! Oy! Sarah, what are you doing? Such terrible talk! You are going to make us lose our share in the next world. How can you, a good Jewish daughter, talk like this? If your parents heard you, they would be ashamed."

My aunt buried her face in her baby's stomach and started to cry, great heaving sobs that shook her shoulders and terrified the child so that he too began to scream. My uncle seemed to notice me for the first time. He shook his head in frustration. There was no arguing with tears.

"Don't be angry, uncle," I said softly, hoping that my aunt's weeping would prevent her from hearing me. "You know it's not like Aunt Sarah to talk like that. It must be her grief speaking out from inside her. She is not herself. Don't hold her responsible."

Uncle Favish took a deep breath and sighed. "Yes, I suppose you're right. All we have is our faith, Maier. If they can destroy our faith, we will have nothing left. Nothing at all. We have to accept without question. We have to go with absolute faith in the Almighty's perfect justice. Just as our fathers did on so many occasions, even when it meant certain death. There is justice in whatever is happening to us. I have no doubt about it."

I was sure he didn't, and I admired him for it. But my own sympathies lay with Aunt Sarah. I could not begin to fathom what terrible sins and transgressions the good people of Lower Vishiva had committed.

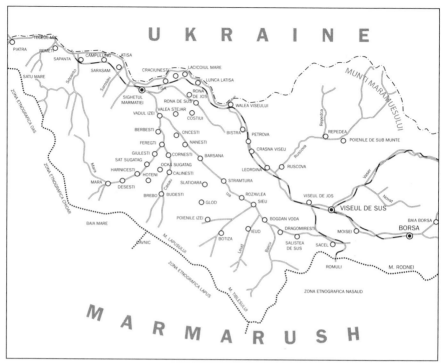

The Marmarosh region

I understood that G-d was allowing this to happen and that, therefore, it was unquestionably just. But it was a brand of justice I did not recognize, a brand of justice that took into account nations and empires and thousands of years of history, a brand of justice that would forge a better new world on the ashes of the old. The simple people of Lower Vishiva could not conceive of such a brand of justice. They only knew that their children were crying and that their hearts were breaking.

Chapter 3

The order to evacuate came while I was still in my grandparents' house. I waited until the wagon was fully loaded just in case they would need my help. My grandmother was the last to leave the house, walking slowly on stiff and swollen legs. She grabbed my arm for support and started to walk in the direction of Upper Vishiva, where the ghetto was located.

Instantly, a gendarme was at her side. "Where do you think you're going, old lady?" he asked.

"Why, to Upper Vishiva, of course," she replied. "To the ghetto."

"Then get on the wagon. Hurry!"

"It's all right. I can walk there. It's not so far."

"Really?" The gendarme laughed harshly. "At the rate you're going, you won't get there till next week. Get on the wagon!"

"It's Shabbos. I can't ride on Shabbos."

The gendarme threw up his hands and rolled his eyes. He called to three of his comrades, and together, they lifted my grandmother and tossed her into the wagon.

I walked along beside them for a short while. Uncle Favish and Aunt Sarah were busy with their children. My grandfather sat in the opposite corner, stone-faced, absorbed in his thoughts. My grandmother lay where she had been flung, tears streaming down the flaccid folds of her cheeks. I tried to soothe her, but she wouldn't speak to me. She just kept bemoaning her fate to G-d. "Oy, Gottenyu, you are putting me through such terrible troubles in my old age. After all these years, I have been reduced to a Shabbos desecrator. Oh, the misery. The shame!"

"But, Grandmother," I interrupted, "are you responsible for this? They forced you to ride. They're the desecrators, not you."

She groaned. "It's not so, Maier. If I had really had proper respect for the sanctity of Shabbos, this wouldn't have happened to me."

"I don't believe it. Your Shabbos has always been perfect."

"Believe it, Maier. The Almighty controls the world, and He doesn't allow things to happen for no reason. Remember that, no matter what happens. Only the wisest people have open eyes; the rest of us are blind. Blind. Oh, who can understand anything? After all, what is this world? It's really nothing. One day you're here, the next you're dead and buried. Before you know it, it's over. The main thing is the next world, the eternal world of souls. Be careful, Maier. Don't do anything that will cause you to lose your share in the next world."

"I won't, grandmother," I said. "I'm going to go to my parents now. They probably need my help. I'll check on you later. Will you be all right?"

She didn't answer. She had slipped back into her lamentations. "Oh, the misery. Oh, the shame! The humiliation!"

Despite the diligence of the gendarmes, moving an entire village street by street, including many old people and young children, was a painstakingly slow process, and so, when I got home, there was still a little time before we, too, would have to leave.

My father gave me a quizzical look when I came in. My stepmother gave me a weak smile.

"I was at Grandmother's house," I said.

My father nodded sadly. "I wanted to say a few things to the children, but I was waiting for you. In the meantime, I removed all the *mezuzos* from the doorposts. We cannot let them fall into the contaminated hands of our enemies. Maybe G-d will take pity on us and let us return soon and put the *mezuzos* back up. Wouldn't it be wonderful if a few weeks from now we could look back on all this as a bad dream?"

"It certainly would," I said, although I did not for a moment believe it would happen. Neither did he; it was just a wistful thought, a fleeting escape from the hellishness of the here and now.

We sat together in silence. There was nothing more to do, nothing more to say. All we could do was wait for the next stage of our ordeal, which could only bring us more and even greater suffering. Presently, the children came back, somber and subdued, and deposited the *mezuzos* on the table in front of my father. He wrapped them in a cloth and put them in his pocket.

"All right," he said. "Maier is here. I want to talk to you."

Altogether, we were seven children, eight if you count my married sister Chayala who lived in Grossverdan. My sisters, Alte Sarah, Rikel, Charna Rachel and Esther, crowded around their mother. My two little brothers, Hersch Meilech and Yidel Eber, came to stand beside me.

My father took a deep breath and let it out very slowly. "Listen carefully, my dear children. In a matter of minutes, we will be leaving our home and going to the ghetto in Upper Vishiva. Who knows where we will end up? Who knows if we will ever return? All we know is that we are suffering, and that there is much more suffering in store for us. They say we are being sent to labor camps. Perhaps this is true, perhaps not. But of this I am sure, only the hardiest will survive. It is likely that we will be separated from each other. Even if you find yourself alone, do not give up. No matter what happens, never show any signs of weakness. If you are sick, if you are injured, if your body is wracked with pain, never let on. Be strong and suffer in silence. Never tell the truth about your age. Add some years. Don't let anyone know how young you are."

He paused for a moment. My stepmother had buried her face in her hands and was weeping silently.

"Listen, my children, and this is very important. You may suffer terribly. You may see the face of evil, and you will wonder why this is happening to you. Accept it all without questioning the Almighty, without complaint. It is not a very great achievement to be G-d-fearing in good times, but it is times like these that show who we really are. Never forget your family, your background, your home, or the upbringing you received. Every year, we shed tears for the destruction of the Holy Temple in Jerusalem and the slaughter of our people by the Romans. Those were also terrible times. Terrible! And yet . . . and yet . . . we never questioned the Almighty when we cried for the tragedies of our past. Now that we ourselves are faced with tragedy, we must also be strong in our faith. Above all, we must keep our souls pure. Remember what your mother and I have always taught you and—"

A sharp rap on the door interrupted him. The tall gendarme with the red mustache opened the door. "Move! Right now!"

My father quickly got to his feet. "Come, children. It's time to go."

As we filed out, we all kissed the *mezuzah* on the outer door, then my father took it down and put it into his *tallis* bag together with the rest of the *mezuzos*. He was crying silently, and I watched him in my own silence.

Gavrila was waiting with the wagon, and the young children climbed in among the bundles. Gavrila cracked his whip over the oxen, and we began to roll.

I glanced back at the house, the touchstone of my childhood and my youth, stripped of its people, stripped of its vitality, stripped of its *mezuzos*, and I felt an unbearable sadness. This, I thought, is the moment when the nightmare truly begins.

I stole a glance at my father. He was staring straight ahead. I thought about his final instructions, and I marveled at his clarity, his wisdom, his exalted spirit. He had articulated with quiet sophistication the ideals to which all the people of our village, in their innocence and simplicity, clung so tenaciously. How terrible that my illustrious father should have his life shattered to pieces right before his eyes. How terrible that on the holy Shabbos, on the last day of Passover, he should be walking alongside a wagon piled high with bundles and staring at the back of a Hungarian peasant wagon driver. I wondered what might be going through his mind, but I didn't dare ask.

Darkness had already fallen when we finally staggered into Upper Vishiva. Gavrila deposited us in front of the Great Synagogue where we were to spend the night, before being billeted with local families, and we were immediately engulfed in a sea of misery. Wagons were streaming in from towns and villages in the surrounding countryside. All I could hear were the sounds of wretchedness, screams, shouts, groans, and children crying. Total confusion, total bedlam. The men came together for evening prayers, bidding farewell to Shabbos and the festival, and then prepared to settle in for the night.

Inside the synagogue, the scene was even more horrendous. Hundreds of people and their belongings were jammed into the main sanctuary, covering just about every inch of floor space. There was practically no place to sit, let alone lie down. Who even thought of sleep amid the noise and the jostling?

Hour by hour, conditions deteriorated. The cries of children and the groans of the old and the sick were unending. The overtaxed lavatories broke down, and the stench sat heavily on the stifling air. My own family bore their privations better than most, but I couldn't bear to watch. Conversation was impossible. All we could do was count the miserable minutes until morning, which would bring a small measure of relief. No matter how cramped the quarters assigned to us, we thought, nothing could be worse than this.

Late at night, I noticed for the first time that the windows high up on the wall had small protruding sills, just deep enough for a slender person to lie on his side if he pressed his back against the pane. It did not occur to me to try to sleep on such a narrow ledge, but perhaps I could find a small modicum of peace and sanity two meters above the crowd. With great difficulty, I managed to climb up onto one of these windowsills. It was much narrower than I had thought. Nonetheless, by wedging myself into the frame, I was able to secure a precarious perch and keep myself from falling.

After a while, my arms and legs began to ache, but it was still better than being down below. My stomach growled with hunger, and I felt lightheaded. My eyes began to droop, and a heavy lethargy flooded my brain. I glanced at my watch. It was twelve minutes before three o'clock in the morning. I fell asleep.

I dreamed that I was standing on a mountaintop leaning against a tree trunk and looking up through the branches at the night sky. Something seemed very strange. I grasped a thick branch and leaned forward to get an unobstructed view of the sky. A few meters in front of me, a precipice fell away into a dark void, and I held tightly onto the branch. I stared up in absolute amazement for a very long time. The heavens glowed with a light more brilliant than any I had ever seen, and wonder of wonders, the sun, the moon and thousands of stars all shone together in the same unmistakably nighttime firmament. How could such a thing be?

It dawned on me as I stood there looking at the eerie night sky, that I was in the midst of a dream, and that somewhere in it there was a divine message for me. The stars, I decided, represented the Jewish people, the brilliant moon was the Messiah, and the dazzling sun was the celestial light that will suffuse the world in the End of Days. Surely, this meant that even in the night there was hope. Even in the darkness, the world was saturated with pure light. Even in the deepest despair, the Jewish people would glow like diamonds in the sky. I felt a surge of happiness, and in this beatific mood, I gazed at the sky for what seemed like hours.

Suddenly, wispy clouds appeared out of nowhere and obscured the sky with a gauzy film. I strained to see the lights, but they were fading quickly. A strong wind arose, and I breathed a sigh of relief. The wind would surely sweep away the cloud cover and expose the heavenly lights once again. But quite the opposite was taking place. The winds blew in new clouds, angry black thunderheads that spread across the sky and blotted out every last flicker. My newfound hope drained from my tormented heart, and I prayed with a fervor born of extreme desperation.

The winds grew stronger, howling through the branches of the trees on the mountaintop. The clouds parted momentarily, and I caught another glimpse of the heavenly lights. Then the cloud cover closed again, and all I could see was the faint afterglow of a handful of stars.

The force of the wind lifted me off my feet, and I grabbed the branch with both hands to keep from being carried away into the inky nothingness. The wind clutched at my feet, while my hands gripped the branch with every ounce of strength I possessed. We struggled mightily for a seemingly endless time, the wind and I, then I heard the sickening sound of splintering wood. The branch came away in my hands, and I plunged into the void.

I broke my fall with a bone-jarring thud, and I heard a loud cry. But it had not come from my throat. My eyes flew open. I had landed on top of Moshe Ruchels Stern, a good friend of the family who was sitting on the ground with his back against the wall right below the windowsill on which I had pitched my camp. His wife was sitting beside him, too dazed to take notice of what had just happened. I looked at my watch. It was five minutes past three. The entire dream had transpired in seventeen minutes.

"Maier, what's going on?" he said.

"I am so sorry. Believe me, I didn't mean to fall asleep. It just happened. Did I hurt you?"

"Nah," he said. "Things are so bad that I can't be disturbed by little things like people falling on my head."

Mrs. Stern gave me a baleful stare. "How are your grandparents, Maier?"

I could not blame her for her despondency. Her husband had been drafted into a Hungarian labor battalion and sent off to the Ukraine, where Jewish men died like flies. She had prayed and waited and prayed and waited, hoping against hope that her husband would return from the land of the living dead. A few weeks before Passover, her prayers had been answered. Moshe had indeed come back, injured and sick but at least alive, and she was overjoyed. And now this.

"My grandparents are as fine as can be," I replied.

"Yes," she said. "As fine as can be. What else is there?"

I wished them a good night and climbed back onto the windowsill, this time determined to stay awake at all costs. The side of my head ached, undoubtedly bruised by the fall, and my body was covered in a cold sweat. I spent the rest of the night reviewing my dream and groping for an interpretation. Did it portend that all the lights in my life would be blotted out leaving only a handful of dim stars? Was it a harbinger of unspeakable tragedy? Was there no hope of a reprieve?

In the morning, all the new arrivals were crowded into the living quarters of residents of the Upper Vishiva ghetto, regardless of the size of their apartments. People slept on the floor and were thankful that they were spared another night in the Great Synagogue.

My stepmother's cousin Basha Marmor, who lived in a tiny apartment with her two small children, took in our family. Her husband, Shmiel, was off at labor in the Ukraine; he never returned. Her husband's parents and their children, six more people, also shared the apartment.

In my pocket I had an order to report to Banya for induction into a labor battalion of the Hungarian Army, which I had not yet shown to anyone. I was not supposed to be in the ghetto, but when I saw the condition of my parents, broken in body and in spirit, I decided to remain with them and help them as best I could.

That evening, after the children had gone to sleep, I told my parents about the induction papers and my decision to ignore them. My stepmother smiled with something that resembled joy, but my father scowled.

"I don't agree," he said.

"But, Favish, why?" my stepmother protested. "Having Maier here with us would make such a difference."

My father shook his head. "Believe me, Ethel, it is just as difficult for me to part with Maier. But he is young and strong. Right now, we are still alive, but who knows what tomorrow will bring? Who knows which path is more likely to lead to safety and survival, labor or the ghetto? Of one thing I'm sure. The Germans will not tolerate people who eat bread but do not produce. Those who are still young and strong, those who can be exploited for their labor, have a better chance of making it through this hell."

Her eyes opened wide. "You think we're all going to die, don't you?"

"I don't know, Ethel. I really don't know. No one knows. Only the Almighty. Let's hope this terrible time comes to an end quickly and we can all go back to a normal life. But in the meantime, each one should follow his own destiny. Let's not try to outsmart fate. I'm sorry, but Maier doesn't belong here."

She bit her lip and nodded slowly, almost imperceptibly.

My father turned to me. "Maier?"

I felt the words choke in my throat. "I will do as you say, Father. I'll leave tomorrow."

The next morning, the men gathered in a hallway for morning prayers. Among them were my grandfather and my Uncle Favish. Afterwards, I told them that I would be leaving, and they both nodded gravely. A tear appeared in my grandfather's eye, but he brushed it away quickly. I kissed his hand, and he embraced me. Then he sat down, opened his Tehillim, and his lips began to move silently.

"How is your baby?" I asked Uncle Favish when we were alone.

"Thank Heaven, a little better," he said. He looked around and lowered his voice. "And your Aunt Sarah has also come around. She now regrets all those things she said on Shabbos."

"Really? That's wonderful. I think I'll go say good-bye to her and the children before I leave."

Uncle Favish seemed taken aback. "Oh no! I don't think that would be such a good idea."

"Why not?"

"It's just better. She'll just get upset."

My eyes narrowed. "Is she all right, Uncle?"

"As well as can be expected under the circumstances."

"What's really the matter, Uncle? Is she sick?"

He nodded. "And she's convinced it's her punishment for

speaking out so strongly. She cries all day and pleads with the Almighty to forgive her. She has even undertaken to fast Mondays and Thursdays to atone for her sin. I try to calm her down, but she's inconsolable. I told her what you said—that it wasn't her speaking, but that it was her grief speaking out from inside her. I think that calmed her down a little bit, but seeing you will just set her off again. If only this would come to an end. If only we could live again."

"I understand," I said. "Give her my best regards and wish her a speedy and complete recovery. And kiss the children for me. I'll go say good-bye to Grandmother."

"Take care of yourself, Maier. Perhaps one day . . ."

He shrugged his shoulders and went to sit beside my grandfather.

My grandmother greeted me with a broad smile and a plate of cookies. I didn't want to take any, because I knew she would need them in the days to come. But I couldn't embarrass her, so I took one, the smallest on the plate. I told her I would be leaving.

"Come sit beside me, Maier," she said. "Let me take a good look at you. Who knows if we will ever see each other again."

"Grandmother! Don't talk like that. Nothing is beyond the power of the Almighty. Let's hope we will soon be home together again. Maybe the Messiah will come! There couldn't be a better time than now."

"Let's hope," she agreed. "You know, your grandfather and I, we are old people. Whatever we live now is just a gift. Ah, but your mother, she never really lived, did she? Twenty years already she's gone. Twenty years. So young. Oh, I'm not complaining, Heaven forbid. I accept everything, even if they kill us. I accept it, as long as I can return my soul as clean and pure as I received it. I ask for nothing more." She paused for a moment and drew a deep breath. "So. You're going away."

"Yes, Grandmother. My father insists."

"And he's right, of course. Just remember, Maier. No matter what happens, no matter where you find yourself, always be a faithful Jew."

"Of course, Grandmother. What's the question?"

She gave me a sharp look. "Oh, I've no doubt that you'll follow the Torah. But what about a *shtreimel* and *kaftan*? When all this is over and you get married, will you wear a *shtreimel* and *kaftan* on Shabbos? According to our traditions, you know, that is what a faithful Jew wears, not some kind of modern clothing. Well, Maier?"

Her suspicions were well founded. A few years earlier, I was on my way to visit my grandparents on Shabbos when I saw a local man named Shloime leading his horses to the river. He was barefoot but wearing his *shtreimel* and *kaftan*. I was not surprised, because he was a very ignorant fellow. Later, my grandparents and I were discussing an upstanding young man named Reb Ezriel Apter, a learned man of fine character who had a beard and *peyos* but no *shtreimel* and *kaftan*.

"I pity his family," my grandmother remarked. "It must cause them so much heartache that Ezriel doesn't wear a *shtreimel* and *kaftan*."

"I wonder who is more deserving of pity," I responded, "the learned Ezriel who doesn't wear them or the ignorant Shloime who does?"

My grandmother jumped to her feet as if bitten by a snake. "What! Maier! Does this mean you don't intend to wear them?"

"Heaven forbid, Grandmother. I was only saying that Ezriel without a *shtreimel* and *kaftan* stands higher than Shloime with them. Nothing more."

"Oh," she said.

But the seeds of suspicion were planted. And now as I stood beside her in the Upper Vishiva ghetto, she wanted reassurance on this issue that was so important to her.

"Well, Maier?"

"Don't worry, Grandmother. Of course, I will wear a *shtreimel* and *kaftan*, as my father and everyone else in my family does."

"I'm so happy, Maier."

I took my grandmother's withered hand in mine and kissed it. "Good bye, Grandmother."

"Good bye, Maier, and may the Almighty watch over you always."

My stepmother before her marriage

When I got home, I immediately began to throw my things together. My stepmother came to sit beside me. She handed me the best blanket we had. The love and sorrow on her face were so strong, I had to turn away.

"I can't take the blanket," I said. "You'll need it more than I will."

"No, I insist. Please take it. Do it for me."

I took the blanket and stuffed it into my bag. Then she gave me a parcel of food for my journey.

"I can't take the food," I said. "Don't worry about me. I'll be fine. Save it for the children."

This time she didn't protest.

"Mother," I said, "before I go, I want to ask your forgiveness for anything I may ever have done to cause you pain or heartache. You deserved only gratitude from me for bringing me up with such love and devotion even though you didn't give birth to me. I could not have wished for a more devoted mother than you."

These words burst the dam, and my stepmother broke down and wept. "Oh, Maier," she said when the tears subsided a little. "You have nothing for which to ask forgiveness.

You have always been a wonderful son to me, and I hope I was a good mother to you. From the first moment that I saw you, a little one-year-old boy, and you gave me that sweet smile, I loved you with all my heart. From that moment on, I was your mother and you were my very own precious child. That is how it always was, and that is how it will always be. No matter what happens, I will love you forever."

"And I will love you forever."

I closed my bag and went to take leave of the children. My sisters were young ladies already, and our parting was warm but solemn. Not so with my little brothers. They grabbed my legs and wouldn't let go.

"Maier, don't go," they pleaded. "Don't leave us. We love you."

I crouched down and hugged and kissed each of them. We cried together for a few minutes, then I soothed them and kissed them some more. I picked up my bag and left, turning back for a final glance. My father was waiting for me outside, and we walked together in silence toward the train station.

Doubts about leaving plagued me. Was is right to leave them alone at such a time? My father was not yet fifty years old, yet he looked like an old man. My stepmother was heartbroken. How would they cope?

"Maier, don't worry about us," my father said, as if he had read my mind. "You are not leaving us alone. The Almighty is here with us. We will share the destiny of all the other Jewish people, because we are certainly no better or worse than the rest. We're doing the right thing. Do you believe me?"

"Yes."

"Good. Now there is one more thing I want to say to you before you go. You must do anything to survive. You will probably have to eat food that is not kosher. But one thing I ask you. If you must eat non-kosher meat, at least don't suck out all the marrow from the bones. Just do what you have to do and no more."

I nodded. "I understand, Father. But believe me, I don't intend to eat anything that is not kosher. One way or another, I will try my best."

He thought for a moment. "I believe it," he said.

We did not speak of our love for each other as I had with my stepmother. Nonetheless, the thoughts and the feelings passed unspoken between us, no less powerful for not having been expressed aloud.

As we approached the station, an officer of the gendarmes blocked our way. "Where do you think you're going?"

I took out my induction papers and showed them to him. "I have to report to Banya," I said.

"And you?" he said to my father.

"I'm his father. I'm escorting him to the station."

The officer scrutinized my papers. "You were supposed to report a week ago. Why are you still here?"

"I was sick," I said.

"Do you have a doctor's note?"

"There are no doctors in our village."

He gave me an appraising look. I had suffered a great deal during the past few days, and I must have looked quite sick.

"Very well," he said. "You can go." He turned to my father. "And you, get back to the ghetto."

I covered my father's hands with kisses, and then, for the first and last time in my life, we embraced. His lips moved, as if he was about to say something more, but then he turned and walked away. I remained standing at the entrance to the train station, watching his back recede until he disappeared completely from sight.

Chapter 4

When my father told the gendarmes he had no more than a few *pengos*, he was not being entirely truthful. But he couldn't very well turn over all his money to those thieves. Without any money, we would all have been doomed from the very beginning.

As I stood before the ticket booth in the train station, I worried about keeping possession of the money my father had given me before we parted. The two wads of bills strapped to my abdomen exerted a cold, brittle pressure against my skin. My mouth felt clammy, and I thought I was going to gag. I reached into my pocket for a crumpled bill and bought a ticket to Sighet.

Passengers were already boarding the train when I reached the platform. Ordinarily, the train would have been crowded with Jewish people of all kinds, portly businessmen, itinerant beggars, black-garbed *chassidim* traveling to their wonder rabbis, along with matrons and children. Ordinarily, the cars would have resounded with a cacophonous blend of singsong Hungarian, voluble Yiddish, good-natured laughter and children chattering or crying. But now, it was half empty and eerily silent. I found a seat easily.

Two hours later, the train pulled into Sighet. I got off and bought a ticket to Satmar, which lay about halfway between Sighet and Banya. The transfer involved a wait of several hours, and I settled down to wait.

As a child of nine, I had been sent away to study in a *cheder* in this big, bustling city on the Czechoslovakian border, where I remained until I was eleven years old. In spite of my young age, I had been forced to fend for myself but, nonetheless, it was a good and exciting time. Being in Sighet now, if only in the train station, brought back many fond memories. I don't know how long I drifted along in my happy reverie, but when I looked up, the platform was quite full. Among the passengers nearby, I discerned about twenty young Jewish men, wearing caps and carrying backpacks, all of whom were apparently also heading to Banya for induction into the Hungarian Army's labor battalions.

"Which of you nice Jewish boys can help us out?"

I turned around and saw that we had been joined by a frail old woman who could not have been a day less than eighty years old. She was carrying a heavy pack on her shoulder and holding a severely handicapped young fellow by the hand.

"This is my grandson," she said. "His name is Benny."

Benny could not have been more than eighteen or nineteen years old. He stood with a corkscrew posture that bespoke spinal deformation and crippling of the legs. His hands were shriveled, and he had sores on his face and neck. One of his eyes was sealed shut, obviously useless. The other was glazed over and unfocused. The boy was practically blind.

A few of us murmured an unenthusiastic "Hello, Benny." The others simply looked at the old lady and her grandson with suspicion.

"Please, boys," the old lady pleaded. "I need help. Who will help me?"

There was only silence.

"We can't answer you," a short fellow with a sharp nose finally said, "until you tell us what you want. You don't really expect anyone to offer help without hearing what you have in mind, do you?"

The old lady's eyes narrowed into slits. "And would that be such a terrible thing to ask of fine Jewish boys?"

The short fellow shrugged. "I can only speak for myself, but I make no offers until I know what it's all about. I don't think anyone else will either."

"All right," she said. "Benny here has received induction papers. He has to report in Banya for labor in the Hungarian Army. The poor boy has no mother, and his father is in the Ukraine—if he is still alive, that is. I'm all he has in the world, but I'm too old and feeble to take him to Banya. I need one of you to take him under your wing and make sure he gets to Banya safely. Who wants to help me?"

"You've got to be kidding," said the short fellow. "Benny is being inducted for labor? Is this some kind of a joke?"

"You don't think he is a candidate for labor?"

"No, I don't."

"Neither do I," said the old lady, "but the government does. They know his name and his age, and they know he is Jewish. Poof! Send him off to labor. My poor baby. What will happen to him?" She began to cry.

"I'm sorry, lady," said the short fellow. "This is just too much for me."

The others nodded in agreement, and they all shuffled away to a different part of the platform. The old lady cried even harder. Benny whimpered. Mucus bubbled under his nostrils, and saliva ran from the corner of his mouth.

Perhaps it was the very repulsiveness of his appearance that made me take pity on Benny, that and his grandmother's tears. I stood up and approached them.

"I would like to help you," I said, "but there is one problem. I'm only traveling on the train as far as Satmar. If you want I can take him until Satmar."

The old lady clapped her hands; the tears vanished. "Oh, would you? That would be absolutely wonderful. May the Almighty bless you for your kindness. Take him as far as you go. When the others see what you've done, I'm sure you'll find someone to take over when you get off in Satmar."

Dusk was falling, and the train would be arriving any minute. I reached for Benny's bag. "Here, I'll take this," I said to the old lady. "Leave Benny with me. He'll be fine. You might as well try to get home before dark."

"Oh, thank you, thank you. How can I ever thank you enough?" She paused. "There are just a few things I have to tell you about Benny before I leave. One, you have to keep an eye on his feet. If he's not careful when he's walking he can twist his feet badly and really hurt himself."

"All right. I'll watch his feet. Good night."

"No, no, wait a minute. Just a few more little things." She pulled a bottle of liquid from her pocket. "These are Benny's eye drops. You have to put them in his good eye every half hour. Very important."

She handed me the eye drops, and I put them in my pocket.

"Just two more things," she said. "He has to drink a cup of water every hour or so. There's a bottle of water in his backpack. When that runs out, you can refill it anywhere. And of course, you must take him to the bathroom at least once every other hour. Other than that, you won't even notice that he's there."

She gave Benny a hug and a kiss. A moment later, she was gone.

I didn't know if I should laugh or cry, so I did neither. Benny, on the other hand, seemed to be very much on the verge of tears.

I patted him on the shoulder and said, "Well, Benny, I guess it's just you and me until Satmar. Come, I'll carry your bag."

He looked at me. "I don't even know your name," he said.

"My name is Maier."

"That's funny. My uncle's name is also Maier. He's a nice man." I couldn't see what was so funny about that, but after all, I wasn't privy to the strange world of Benny's childlike mind. Surprisingly, his words were just the least bit slurred. Other than that, he sounded fairly normal.

"Are you afraid, Benny?"

"A little."

"Well, you don't have to be. I'll take good care of you."

"Oh no. I'm afraid about my grandmother. She is such an old lady." He gave me a secretive look. "I think she's already a hundred years old, and she's not even dead yet. I'm afraid something is going to happen to her."

The train for Satmar was announced. I strapped on my backpack, lifted Benny's bag in one hand and took his hand in the other.

"Come on, Benny," I said. "That's our train. As for your grandmother, let's hope nothing happens to her. If she made it to a hundred, she'll figure out how to make it a little further."

We spent a few minutes in the bathroom, as his grandmother had instructed, then we got on the train. We found seats, and I put our bags on the overhead rack. I put a few eye drops in his one functional eye, then I leaned back and pulled my cap over my eyes.

"Are you going to fall asleep?" he asked. I detected a note of nervousness in his voice. Not that I blamed him.

I pushed my cap back and sat up. "Are you all right, Benny? Are you afraid? I don't mean for your grandmother. For yourself."

He rubbed his eye with the back of his sleeve. "No, I'm not afraid, Maier," he said quietly. "I know I'm going to die. I'm just a little nervous."

"What are you talking about, Benny?" I protested. "Don't say things like that. Why are you going to die?"

"I'd be lucky to stay alive if there was nothing wrong with me."

I couldn't argue with his reasoning. He was probably right. The poor boy. Without his grandmother, he was lost.

"No one knows when he is going to die, Benny," I said gently. "No one. You can be strong and healthy and dead the next day. Or your life can hang on a thread for years and years. If I were you, Benny, I wouldn't give up just yet. You may just surprise us all."

Something resembling a smile appeared on his face. "Yeah. Maybe."

The cap came back over my eyes, and in a minute, I was asleep. I was just sliding down into the sweet softness of deep slumber, when I felt Benny's birdlike hand on my knee. I groaned and shook it off, but he would not let go. I opened my eyes and was instantly wide awake.

The train was standing in a dark station of some town whose name I could not make out. The lights had come on in the car, and four gendarmes were at the other end, talking to the conductor. One of the gendarmes turned and blew three piercing blasts on a whistle. If anyone was not yet awake, he was up now.

"Everyone up! All Jews, unpack all your bags, and prepare for inspection. Spread everything out on the floor. Right now!"

The gendarmes worked their way down the car, scrutinizing documents and inspecting the belongings strewn across the floor.

"What's going on here, officer?" a burly Hungarian complained. He looked like a carpenter. "Some of us are trying to sleep. Why do we have to be woken up because of these dirty Jews?"

"We'll be finished soon," said the gendarme. "It's important."

"Then why don't you just take these filthy swine off the train and search them on the platform of some town or other?"

"That's right," a well-dressed Hungarian matron chimed in. "Why do we have to go through this? You're not interested in searching us, are you? It's bad enough we have to sit in the same car with these disgusting Jews."

"I assure you, madam," said the gendarme, "that we will do our best not to disturb you more than is necessary. Rest assured, soon there won't be any more Jews in your train cars. Nor in anyone else's."

The gendarme's words chilled my bones, although I can't really say they surprised me. The hatred on the faces of the Hungarian passengers, so strong I could actually feel it hot against my cheeks, was typical of what most Hungarians felt in their hearts. The German propaganda over the last ten years had fanned the flames of anti-Semitism in Hungary, and now that Hungary had become a German ally, the Hungarians had become part of the German killing machine.

Five minutes later, the gendarmes reached us. We were at the end of the car, and I had needed every bit of the extra time to unpack both my bag and Benny's and to arrange our things neatly on the floor. I stood near the aisle. Benny cowered behind me.

The gendarme in charge extended his hand. "Papers!"

I handed them to him. He glanced through my papers quickly. Then he poked through my belongings.

"Late reporting, aren't you?"

"I was sick."

"Are you ready for work now?"

"Oh, yes."

"I'm so pleased to hear that." He paused to enjoy the snickers his sarcasm had elicited. "Are you feeling better now?"

"Much better, thank G-d."

"Don't be so quick to thank G-d." He handed me my papers. "Next!"

I handed him Benny's papers. "My friend is not well," I said, trying as hard as possible to obscure his view of Benny.

"Get out of the way! Let him speak for himself."

He shoved me aside, and there was Benny. The gendarme's mouth fell open. He looked at the papers in his hands, then he looked at Benny, then back to the papers again. He grabbed Benny by the shoulder and jerked him forward into the aisle. Benny spun to the ground with a cry of pain, which he immediately stifled.

"Get up, you piece of scum!" shouted the gendarme.

Silence had fallen throughout the car. All eyes were fixed on poor Benny. I reached down to help him up, but the gendarme kicked me in the knee. Benny whimpered and twisted himself around until he managed to get a grip on the edge of the seat with his crippled hand. Slowly, he pulled himself to his feet. Two of the sores on his neck were oozing blood, and his face was wet with mucus and tears.

"What are you doing here, you miserable Jew?"

"I am g-going t-to Banya," Benny managed to stammer. "To w-work."

"This is insanity," said the gendarme. "Work? What kind of work can you do? Take your things and get off the train. Now!"

"Sir, I am responsible for him," I said. "He can't get off the train by himself. If you must send him off, please let me go with him."

The gendarme gave me an angry look. "What are you, his brother or something? Your papers say Banya, and that's where you're going. Nowhere else!"

"But, sir, Benny's papers also say Banya."

"Shut up, you insolent worm, before I break both your arms. Pack up this . . . this . . . this specimen's belongings. He is getting off."

One of the other gendarmes looked worried. "Hey, Milos," he said in a low voice which I could just barely hear. "Maybe we should let them worry in Banya about what to do with this cripple. We're not authorized to remove him from the train. When the records show he never showed up in Banya, they're going to check it out and find out we took it on ourselves to throw him off the train. We could get into trouble."

The gendarme named Milos accepted his friend's reasoning, but he clearly wasn't happy about it. He kicked at a pile of Benny's underclothes and scattered them in every direction. Then he turned and walked away, tossing Benny's papers over his shoulder without looking back.

As soon as the gendarmes were gone, the Hungarians crowded around and started to badger Benny.

"Hey, lamebrain, are you going to build us some bridges?" the carpenter wanted to know. "Remind me to stay off them."

The matron laughed maliciously. "Who knows, maybe Cyclops here has special powers."

Others joined in the fun, and all the while, Benny cried silently.

I stood up and blocked their view of the sobbing boy. "Why don't you all just leave him alone? Don't you have anything better to do than start up with a poor cripple? You should be ashamed of yourselves."

I don't know where I got the audacity to speak like that to these rabid Jew-haters, and it immediately became clear I had made a big mistake. The carpenter slapped me hard across the face, and two others grabbed my arms and pinned them behind me.

"We're going to teach you a little respect," said the carpenter, "before we toss you off this train. Everybody, step back! Give us some room."

Benny let out a high squeal. "Leave him alone. Take me instead."

The carpenter laughed. "You'll be right behind him, you miserable excuse for a human being. Don't you worry."

"All right, enough of this," said a new voice, resonant with authority.

It belonged to a tall, muscular man who had kept to himself throughout this whole episode. I had noticed him sitting near the front of the car with his nose buried in a newspaper. He pried me loose from the grip of my captors and turned to face the angry crowd.

"All of you, calm down," he commanded. "You can't just take matters into your own hands and beat up an able-bodied young Jew whose been inducted for labor. The army needs good workers, and this fellow seems to fit the bill. Everybody, go back to your seats. I'm taking charge here."

The passengers grudgingly obeyed the man. The train started to move, the lights were dimmed once again, and soon, all that had transpired was no more than a bad nightmare. The man took a seat across from Benny and me.

"People can get a little out of hand sometimes," he said good-naturedly, "wouldn't you agree?"

"This whole country is a little out of hand," I replied.

"Watch how you talk. Some people may take offense at such a remark."

"But not you?"

"Nah, not me. Personally, I tend to agree with you."

"Really?" I stuck out my hand. "My name is Maier Cahan. What's yours?"

He took my hand and shook it. "Pleased to meet you. My name is Hahn, and I am a lieutenant in the Hungarian Army. I'm actually on my way to Banya myself."

"You're a rare Hungarian, Mr. Hahn," I said. "Very rare."

"Well, I may be a lieutenant in the Hungarian Army, but I'm not quite Hungarian. My father is a Serb, and my mother is Czech. They moved to Hungary and took Hungarian names. I was born here."

"That explains your kindness and tolerance," I said. An idea suddenly sprouted in the back of my mind. "Lieutenant Hahn, I believe you may be the answer to a prayer. You see, I don't really know Benny. I met him and his grandmother at the station in Sighet, and she asked me to keep an eye on him. The problem is, I have to get off in Satmar. Would you make sure that Benny gets to Banya safely?" I pulled a twenty-*pengo* note from my pocket and handed it to him. "Please accept this for your troubles."

He glanced at the money and at Benny, and he shrugged. He took the money and slipped it into his pocket. "Sure, why not? I'm going that way anyway." He yawned. "Time to sleep."

He closed his eyes and was snoring in no time at all. Next to me, Benny had also fallen into an exhausted sleep. As for me, I was too troubled to fall asleep so easily. But eventually I did. When next I opened my eyes, we were pulling into Satmar in the gray dawn.

Benny and the lieutenant were both asleep. I didn't wake them. I just took my bag and slipped off the train.

Chapter 5

I t did not take me long to find the address I needed. I knew my way around Satmar, because I had come there often enough on business. Now, however, I was here on urgent business of a different kind. I had to meet with Reb Shmiel Hersch Weiss, the husband of my father's sister Chava Yitte. He was also my beloved sister Chaya's father-in-law.

My sister Chaya and I were about as close as brother and sister could be. Perhaps if our mother had not died so young, we might have grown up more independent of each other. But as it was, we always had a very close bond that set us apart from the rest of our family. Only the two of us shared our own private mother. Only the two of us had a special set of grandparents in our village who doted on us and told us

My sister Chaya

stories about our mother. Only the two of us instinctively felt the pain or the gladness in each other's heart and could communicate without words. As children we used to chase the roosters together alongside the river, then plop down exhausted under a tree and talk for hours.

In later years, our closeness took on different forms but did not diminish. As a boy descended from a prominent rabbinical family, it was my responsibility to excel in Talmud studies, and my father believed, as did many others, that this could only be accomplished away from the distractions of home. So I was sent away when I was nine years old to study in Sighet, coming home only for holidays. My experiences and exploits during those three years really taught me to be independent and resourceful. At twelve, my father sent me to study with his first cousin, Rabbi Tzvi Hersch Cahan, who had an excellent *yeshivah* in the village of Strimtura, not too far from Sighet. My father's brother Ephraim Fishel, who also lived in Strimtura, made all the arrangements. That put an end to my youthful adventures. The next five years of my life were devoted to serious study.

During these years, I did not see my sister as often as I would have liked. We did exchange letters often, however, and when I was home for the holidays, we spent a lot of time together. By this time, Chaya was already blossoming into a young woman and I was a *yeshivah* boy from a *chassidic* family. Although we were brother and sister, chasing roosters by the riverside was a thing of the past, and even going for long walks together would have been immodest and unseemly. Still, we talked and laughed and loved every moment spent in each other's company.

When I was seventeen years old, my father started making very serious efforts to find a husband for my sister Chaya, who had already turned eighteen. While I was home for the holidays, there was much talk about a cousin of ours named Yosef Maier Weiss, the son of Reb Shmiel Hersch Weiss of Satmar and my father's sister Yitte Chava, who was no longer alive. Uncle Shmiel Hersch was a brilliant man, a respected *chassid* of the Spinka Rebbe and one of the leading members of the Satmar community. His son Yosef Maier, whom we did not have occasion to meet very often, was a handsome and personable young man. The match was appealing to both sides, but there were money issues. I returned to Strimtura with the issues far from resolved.

One day, I received a message in the *yeshivah* to go to my Uncle Ephraim Fishel's house. It was unusual for my uncle to summon me in middle of a study session, and I was somewhat concerned as I turned into his street. There in front of me, I saw my father and uncle walking back and forth in front of the house, deeply engrossed in conversation. They didn't see me. My uncle looked pensive and reserved, and my father had a strained and perturbed look that instantly told me he had come to my uncle for financial assistance. It did not take a great leap of the imagination to connect my father's appearance with my sister's proposed match. Money was needed for her dowry, and it hurt me that my father had to humiliate himself to get it, even if only before members of his own family.

I cleared my throat to announce my presence. My father gave me a broad smile and shook my hand. We went inside for a glass of tea, then my uncle left us alone.

"Maier, I came here because I need your help," my father began. "I feel terrible asking you this, but I have no choice."

"Don't, Father," I said. "I would do anything for you. Just ask."

My father gave me a quizzical look. "Are you really sure you would do anything, Maier?"

What a question, I thought. Of course I would do anything for my father. I would sell myself into slavery if that would give him the money he needed to set his mind at ease. But then another thought struck me. Was I really prepared to do anything? It was not uncommon for a young man to marry a rich but homely girl and then give a portion of his dowry to his sister so that she too could get married. What if my father asked me to marry some drooling, hunchbacked, rich girl so that there would be some money for Chaya's dowry? Would I do it? I didn't think so. Anything was obviously not a good choice of words in this case.

"Well, let's say almost anything," I said with a sheepish grin. "Tell me, Father, what I can do for you."

Close to tears, my father took a document from his pocket and put it on the table. "Maier, we never spoke about this, but now we must. You know that the house in which we live was part of the dowry your mother, may she rest in peace, brought with her. The house was registered as her own property in her own name. After your mother passed away, it wasn't easy for your grandmother to see me living with a new wife in the house they had given their daughter. Your grandmother especially has never come to terms with the death of your mother, whom she loved desperately, and my continuing to live in the house has always been a particular sore point with her. The only thing that pacified your grandmother a little bit was that you and Chaya were also living in the house. We agreed to register the house in your name and Chaya's name, and that settled the matter. Otherwise, the house would have been dragged through the rabbinical courts. So you see, we are all living in a house that belongs to you and your sister. Are you aware of all that?"

I shifted uncomfortably. "A little. We never really discussed it, and I don't see any reason to do so now. You can continue to live in the house without a care in the world until one hundred and twenty years. It means nothing to me."

"I appreciate that." He started speaking very quickly, as if the words were painful and he had to get them out before they lodged in his throat. "Now let me tell you what I came about specifically. The match between your sister and Yosef Maier Weiss is close to being sealed, but money is the issue. We have agreed that Chaya will receive the house as her dowry, which is a very handsome dowry by any standard. But in order for it to happen, I need you to sign over your half of the house to her. I feel terrible to have to ask you such a thing, but I have no choice. I've brought the document."

I glanced at my father, but he wouldn't meet my eyes. I took the document in my hand. "Do you have a pen?"

My father seemed to be holding his breath. "Please read it through before you sign it."

"What for? I don't want anything more than my other brothers and sisters. As far as I'm concerned, the house has been yours all along, and if you want to give it to Chaya for her dowry, I couldn't be happier."

I signed quickly and passed the document back to him. He smiled with relief and pleasure, but then his face clouded over again. He reached into his pocket and took out a second document. Several times, he attempted to speak, but each time he only sighed miserably.

"What is it, Father?" I asked. "It also relates to money, doesn't it?"

He swallowed hard and nodded.

"Tell me," I coaxed. "How bad can it be? It's only money!"

He took a deep breath and released it slowly. "I am ashamed to do this, but I have no choice. Your mother left quite a bit of personal jewelry which her parents gave her as a bride. All the jewelry is being held in safekeeping by the Rebbetzin of Petrova, the wife of Rabbi Yeshia Cahan, your Uncle Favish's mother. Your mother specified clearly which pieces go to Chaya and which go to you. The gold wristwatch, the heart-shaped earrings and a few diamond pieces are set aside for you to give to your future bride. Unfortunately, however, I see no way to pay for the expenses of Chaya's wedding other than to sell off your mother's jewelry. This document authorizes the Rebbetzin of Petrova to release the jewels to me. Chaya has already signed it. What choice did she have? It's her wedding. But why should you agree? What right do I have to ask you to sign this document? Only the extreme pressure I'm under can make me ask you such a thing."

I have to admit that the jewelry posed more of a dilemma for me than the house. These were the jewels my mother had worn; they had touched her skin. My grandmother had spoken to me about them countless times. She had even taken me once to show them to me. They were indeed beautiful and probably very valuable. But their sentimental value to my sister and me was inestimable. These jewels were our only tangible link to the mother we knew only from photographs and stories. Now my father was asking us to forfeit that final link for the sake of the wedding. It was a hard thing to do, but I had to do it. How could I refuse?

I reached out and took the paper from my father's hand. "I will sign this document," I said, "but on one condition."

"I'm listening," said my father.

"You can sell all the jewels,," I said, "but I keep the gold wristwatch for myself. I want to give it to Chaya as my wedding present."

He smiled. "I accept your condition, Maier."

When the wedding took place several months later, no one could have known how much anguish was invested in the atmosphere of pure happiness that reigned in our family and village that day. My grandmother danced with both of us, and I actually felt as if my mother's spirit was there, rejoicing with her beloved children. My sister must have thanked me over a thousand times, and whenever she caught my eye from afar, she raised her wristwatch-adorned hand triumphantly. I had never seen my sister so radiant and happy, and with all my heart, I wished her many long, healthy and blissful years and a better life than our mother had known.

The young couple lived with us in Lower Vishiva for about a year, and then moved to Grossverdan. Soon after, Chaya gave birth to a beautiful little girl, whom she named Etieh, in honor of our mother. Meanwhile, my brother-in-law tried several different businesses, all without success. My heart went out to Chaya, living as she did so far away from home and finding life such a struggle. My brother-in-law began yet another business, and this time, it seemed promising. But after a brief surge of hope, he was inducted into a labor battalion and sent off to the Ukraine. My sister was heartbroken, and I along with her. I could just picture her in the apartment in Grossverdan, holding her baby in the still and lonely night and crying until her eyes were red.

My poor beloved sister—beautiful, vibrant, full of hope and love and joy, young wife, young mother, reaching out to embrace the future and finding her arms full of emptiness. Her husband condemned to a living death, unlikely ever to return, her parents and family expelled from their homes and condemned to a fate I dared not even contemplate, and me, her devoted brother, on the way to Banya to join my own labor battalion. How my heart ached for her.

And so here I was in Satmar, spending a few stolen hours to organize a little help for my poor sister before I submitted to my own uncertain fate.

Uncle Shmiel Hersch welcomed me with his usual aplomb and warmth. Technically, he was no longer my uncle after my aunt passed away, but the family bond between us remained strong, especially since my sister was his daughter-in-law, the mother of his young granddaughter. I went into a room to pray. Afterwards, my uncle's wife served us a nice breakfast. Their four young daughters came in to say hello to me, then she gently shooed them away so that my uncle and I could speak in private.

"Have you heard from Yosef Maier?" I asked before anything else.

"Not a word." He shook his head sadly. "What's going to happen with you in Banya, Maier? You're going for labor?"

"Yes."

"Are they sending you to the Ukraine?"

"No one gets sent to the Ukraine any more. The Russians have taken back most of it."

"Of course. Some men have come back, here and there. I should have heard from Yosef Maier, shouldn't I?"

"Don't give up hope."

"My heart still hopes," he said, "but my head doesn't."

"I understand." I allowed a moment of silence to hang between us before I continued. "We have to do something for Chaya and the baby."

He nodded. "Yes, we do. But what?"

I reached under my shirt and pulled out a thick wad of bills. "Count it. Here are ten thousand *pengo* for them. I want you to add ten thousand *pengo* of your own. Twenty thousand *pengo* will help her get through this time. Maybe help her get away. Will you match this money?"

Uncle Shmiel Hersch stroked his beard, his brow furrowed in thought. "Yes, I will match it. It will be very hard, but I'll do it. Of course, I'll do it."

"Wonderful. I'll write to her to tell her you have the money for her. Between the two of you, you'll figure out a way to get it to her. What's happening here in Satmar?"

My uncle scowled. "It's bad—like everywhere else. They're preparing a ghetto. It's only a matter of time. Deportations have begun in other places already. People are being sent to Poland and Germany. We are doomed."

"We're not doomed until we're dead. In the meantime, we have to do what we can. Hungary is a death trap. The only answer is to cross the border into Romania." I reached into my pocket and pulled out two tightly folded pieces of paper. "These are two copies of a list of guides who help people slip across the border. For a hefty fee, of course. I'm going to include one with the letter I send to Chaya. I'm leaving the other one with you. Please, I'm begging you, help her escape from Hungary. It's her only chance."

My uncle patted me on the shoulder. "Don't worry, Maier. I'll get the money to her, and I'll help her make the arrangements. I also have a few contacts of my own. We'll try to go as soon as possible."

"It can't be soon enough. The Germans are losing the war, and it looks like they're going to try and kill as many Jews as they can before the end."

"We're in God's hands."

I bit my lip. In God's hands, I thought bitterly. Why didn't He put a stop to all this death and suffering? Why did He let innocent people be tortured? What would happen to my beloved sister and her little child? In spite of all my questions, my faith was strong. My parents and teachers had done a good job.

After breakfast, I sat down to write to Chaya. I told her about the money, and I urged her not to waste a moment in making arrangements to get to Romania. I told her about what had happened to Lower Vishiva. I described the events in the gentlest terms possible, but when I reread what I had written, my eyes misted over. I had no doubt that my sister would soak this letter with her tears, but I had to tell her the truth. I concluded the letter with words of encouragement and hope. Someday, I assured her, we would sit together under a tree and watch the river flow by, and down near the water, her little daughter would be chasing roosters with her cousins.

I placed the letter and a list of border guides into an envelope and wrote her address on it. Frangipan Street 12, Grossverdan. Then I brought the letter to the post office myself to make sure it was properly mailed; I would not entrust it to a street corner mailbox.

An hour later, I caught the bus to Banya. The train would take much longer, and I had already stretched my liberty time to the limit. I arrived in Banya before nightfall and was inducted into the Hungarian Army. My rank? Forced laborer.

Chapter 6

There were literally thousands of us on the military review field of Banya the next morning, the flower of young Jewish manhood skimmed off for exploitation before we would be sent to share the fate of our families. Most were strong and vigorous, but there were also a number of one-armed and one-legged men and assorted walking wounded. I even saw Benny from afar, and he waved to me excitedly. The Hungarian Army, trawling with a wide net, had scooped up many derelicts along with the prime fish.

I wondered what would happen to these derelicts. Would they be given gainful employment or would they be cast back into the roiling sea? I never did see Benny again after that morning, and I do not know what became of him. We were thrown together for one intense afternoon, and our paths never crossed again. I do not even know his last name.

Among the inductees, there were hundreds of young men like me who were determined to eat only kosher food. I was assigned to a brigade of two hundred men, over fifty of whom were kosher eaters. When our brigade was further divided into four squads, we asked the officers to allow all kosher eaters to join the same squad. Since we shunned food from the main kitchen and sought other arrangements, we explained to the officers, it would be more efficient if we were all in this together. They agreed.

Two months later, our brigade was transferred to a labor camp in Margaretten, and we were put to work repairing the city's drainage system. There were no Jews left in Margaretten when we got there, exept for two families of veterans wounded in the First World War who had received special permission to remain in their homes. From time to time, the daughters of these families would bring some food for the younger Jewish laborers.

Those of us who were kosher eaters managed to get by, for the most part, on the water and bread provided by the army, supplemented by fruit, vegetables and dairy products brought to the camp by farmers from the surrounding countryside. Most of us had a little money, and a brisk little business developed between the farmers and the kosher eaters. It did not take long for the gendarmes to take notice.

One fine morning, we received an order to take all our belongings and assemble in the main yard of the camp. We were arranged in a large quadrangle, hollow in the middle. A large number of gendarmes appeared on all sides and ordered us to unpack our belonging on the ground. Then we were ordered to empty our pockets. All our possessions were inspected in the minutest detail and anything of value was removed.

Next came the personal searches, during which our bodies and clothing were meticulously probed and examined. All the money I had sewn into my pant legs was discovered and confiscated. Most of the others suffered a similar fate. This was a devastating blow to all of us; without money, we felt naked and vulnerable. To the kosher eaters, the confiscations were doubly cruel, because we could no longer pay the farmers for food. Fortunately, a few of us had managed to secrete some money where it could not be found, and the whole group was able to subsist on it for a while.

After the drainage system in Margaretten was repaired, our brigade received orders to transfer to Siklos near the Bulgarian border, where we were to restore an old bat-infested fortress to functionality.

We were all packed onto an army train and sent off to our destination. Railroad schedules were very sporadic at this time however, and it took us about two weeks to reach Siklos. Sometimes, we would sit on a siding for two or three days waiting for clearance to proceed. We, of course, didn't mind the leisurely pace of our journey. Security was fairly slack, and whenever the train was at a standstill, we were able to range some distance from our train without reprimand from the officers. We enjoyed the respite from work, and we spent as much time as possible resting and sleeping in the boxcars.

One day, we pulled over into a siding near a main route and sat there for most of the day as train after train rumbled by. There was something eerie about these trains, but I couldn't quite place my finger on it. Overcome by curiosity, I climbed out of the boxcar and walked along the tracks for several hundred meters until I came to a sharp bend which would slow the train down enough to give me a better look. It was a warm day, and I wiped the sweat from my brow. I sat down to wait behind some bushes, where I could see without being seen. Minutes later, another train came screeching around a bend, and from my vantage point I got a very good look.

I couldn't believe my eyes. The train consisted of a long string of cattle cars, each crammed to capacity with human cargo. I saw them. I saw their hollow-eyed faces in the cracks between the boards, sullen fathers, frantic mothers, terrified children, and disheartened old people. I saw hands groping through the boards, clutching out into the emptiness as if they could snatch a fleck of freedom from the passing wind. Through the cracks between those boards, I saw all the Jewish faces of Vishiva, of Sighet, of Strimtura, of Satmar, of Dragomiresti, of Banya, of Grossverdan, of my brothers and sisters all over the world and all through the ages, and I knew in my heart that I was also seeing the face of death.

The train gathered speed as it came out of the bend, and as it receded into the distance, I felt as if the gates of Hell had opened and released a gust of pure evil into the world. Despite the warmth of the day, my innards turned to ice.

My brain had been so overloaded by the sights of the train that I could not recall hearing even the slightest sound. All my other senses seemed to have shut off. I don't know how long I sat there mesmerized by the lingering images in my mind, but eventually, the sound of another approaching train penetrated my consciousness.

I had to force myself to look at the train as it came slowly into the bend. There they were, the same faces, the same eyes, the same outstretched hands. Only this time, I could also hear. This time, I could also smell. I heard moans and groans and wails. I heard heartbreaking pleas for a little water; to whom they were directed, I do not know. And the awful smells, the choking smells of unwashed bodies, of stagnating feces and puddled urine; the harsh smells that steal the very oxygen from the air.

I instinctively drew back into the bushes in which I was hiding, partly repelled by the smell, and partly out of shame that I could watch such a scene from relative safety. My shifting position must have caught someone's attention, because I suddenly heard a voice call out, "You!"

I looked up and saw a hand reach through the boards. There was a blur of movement, and a black object came flying through the air.

"Give it back to G-d," the voice shouted. "I don't need it any more."

The slipstream of the train grabbed the object and flung it back against the wheels. A moment later, the train was already gathering speed and streaking away. I bent down to look at the object the wretched soul on the train would no longer be needing, and I felt my stomach turn over.

There on the ground lay a small black box connected to leather straps that had come loose and lay spread-eagled on the ground. It was the *tefillin shel rosh*, the phylactery worn on the head. The wheel of the train had crushed one side of it, exposing the holy scrolls inside, like pale intestines spilling through a fatal wound.

I picked it up gently and kissed it, as if to soothe its pain. And I cried. I slumped to the ground as the tears gushed from my eyes and great heaving sobs wracked my body. I cried for the poor, miserable passengers of the train, innocent victims of the unspeakable evil that had broken loose from the nethermost bowels of Hell and was running rampant among my people. I cried for my father, my stepmother, my beloved brothers and sisters, my grandparents, my uncles and aunts, my cousins, for all the people that had populated my life and were now stuffed into these cattle cars on their way to an unthinkable destination.

Oh, my poor father. What was he thinking? What was he doing? Was he keeping the children calm? Was he helping my stepmother find the courage to face the unfaceable? A bizarre thought struck me. My father had always been such a fastidious man. I remembered that once, when I was three years old, I had climbed onto his lap after eating onions in my neighbor's garden. My father had gagged at the smell and put me down. And now he would have to endure the fiendish stench of the cattle cars for who knows how much time.

I thought about the man who had thrown the *tefillin* from the train. Who was he? Was he alone or with his family? I ventured to guess that he was alone, because he would probably not have wanted his family to see such an act of defiance. I did not fault him for what he had done, and I had no doubt in my mind that he would regret it, should he survive this nightmare. I did not see his act as a denial of G-d. Rather, I saw it as a desperate call to Him for help, like a child who tells his parents, "I don't like you any more." If he denied G-d's existence, how could he be angry at Him? I felt only pity for this poor man who had inflicted spiritual wounds upon himself even as others were tearing at his physical existence.

For a long time, I sat on the ground, hugging the crushed *tefillin* to my chest and crying like a little baby. Then I kissed it again with great sadness. This damage could not be repaired, and the best I could do was bury it with dignity. With my bare hands, I scraped out a hole in the ground fifteen centimeters deep. I wrapped the leather straps around the box and placed it solemnly into the grave. Then I closed the grave and smoothed the ground over it. Unsure about what to say in such circumstances, I chose the safe route and recited a few Psalms. The ground above the buried *tefillin* seemed to glow warmly, and I felt strangely comforted.

That night, I lay in the boxcar for a long time unable to fall asleep. A cool breeze teased my nostrils with the sweet smells of spring. I had bread in my stomach and a warm blanket over my shoulders. And I felt incredibly guilty. I should never have listened to my father. I should have stayed with the family. I should have been there on the train with my family. I should have been there to help my grandmother who could barely walk. What good was being alive when I had turned my back on my family, in their hour of direst need?

I fell into a troubled sleep. I dreamed that I was in a dark field in the dead of night. A light rain was falling. I could hear a strange blend of moans and sobs, ghostly echoes off in the distance. I began to run towards the sounds, stumbling through the darkness without thought of my own safety. I ran as fast as I could, until I was forced to stop for a moment to catch my breath. Suddenly, right there in front of me, I saw a single cattle car standing in the field. The sounds were emanating from within, and I now recognized them as the voices of my own family. I was gripped by a terrible fear. Who was that crying? Could it be my strong father whom I had never seen cry in all my life? Then I heard the voices of my little brothers calling to me, "Maier, come help us. You always took such good care of us. Why have you abandoned us now?"

Overcome by shame and rage, I picked up a stout piece of wood from the ground, which I brandished over my head like a club, and ran towards the cattle car with a cry of defiance on my lips.

A figure holding a rifle materialized out of the rainy night.

"Who are you?" a voice demanded in Hungarian. "Stop or I'll shoot!"

I swung the club at his arm, and it deflected the rifle just as it went off. The gendarme fell to his knees from the force of the blow, but he was already beginning to struggle to his feet. I swung my club again, this time across the back of his neck. He fell to the ground and moved no more.

I pried open the doors of the cattle car and saw all my family trussed in iron chains, but my father, stepmother and two little brothers were wrapped in chains of red fire that was slowly consuming their hands and feet.

Desperate, I ran outside to fill my mouth and hat with the rain falling from the sky. It seemed to take forever for the raindrops to accumulate, but at last, I had enough to douse those angry red flames. It was dark inside the car, and I bent closer to look at my parents and brothers. To my horror, I saw they were all black as charcoal. I had to help them quickly, but where was I to begin? My father told me to take care of the little ones first, and I quickly unbound them. They lifted their blackened faces and gave me an ethereal, macabre smile. We tried to embrace and kiss, but they screamed in agony when I touched their charred skin. Their limbs began to twitch spasmodically. I recoiled in shock, and then I turned to unbind my parents.

"Does anyone here have any salve for wounds?" I shouted to my relatives, who were trussed up in their iron chains. "Please! Hurry!"

Blank stares were the only response I got.

I recalled hearing somewhere that saliva was a palliative for wounds, and I immediately got down on my knees and began to lick the wounds on my brothers' arms and legs. Soon, the twitching subsided, and they seemed at peace.

My tongue was dry as parchment, and I took a sip of rainwater from my hat to replenish my supply of saliva. Then I bent over my father.

My father's whole head was black—his skin, his lips, his hair, his beard. Only his eyes and teeth were still white. He looked at me with a peculiar detachment. "Maier, Maier," he said.

From outside, I heard the tramp of heavy boots and the barking of dogs. The soldiers were coming closer. There was no time.

"My dear Maier," he said, his voice emanating from those disembodied eyes and teeth. "There is danger. Leave us here, and go take care of yourself. You have done enough. More than enough. You honored us in our lifetime, and now you have honored us in death. G-d bless you."

Death? Death? Was this the face of death? Were all these people dead? Was this car a charnel house?

I looked at my father's blackened face. "Father, are you dead?"

He did not answer me. He just continued to look at me with that same peculiar detachment.

"Father!" I screamed. "Father, don't leave me!" I knew it was useless, but I continued to scream hysterically until I thought my heart would break and all my blood would burst through my skin and splatter all over me.

My father extended his charred arms, from which minuscule wisps of smoke still rose, and wrapped them around me in a grisly embrace. The smell of death was acrid against my nostrils. I gagged, but at the same time, I was loathe to let go. The charred cadaver embracing me was all that remained of my father.

My eyes flew open and I found myself back under my blanket in the army boxcar. I was disoriented at first, my mind an utter blank, and then the dream flashed back into my consciousness. At that moment, I was overcome with a terrible fear that my father was no longer among the living. I buried my face in my bedclothes and moaned, "No! No! No!"

The noise caught the attention of my sergeant, and he came over. "What's the matter, Cahan? Why all the ruckus?"

"It's nothing," I said. "Just an ordinary nightmare. A meaningless nightmare."

I tried to stand, but my knees gave way. My face felt as if it were on fire. I was suddenly afraid I would be deemed unfit for labor and deported.

"I think I'm a little sick," I said. I tried to stand again, and this time I was more successful. "A little fresh air, and I'll be fine."

The sergeant shrugged. He looked tired. "Go get some air for a while," he said, "but don't get lost."

I wrapped my blanket around my shoulders and stepped outside. It was a fine spring night, the air soft and warm, the sky brilliant with stars. But the dream was still vivid in my mind, and I shivered and pulled the blanket tighter. My heart throbbed with a pain sharper than any I had ever known before, and I wept uncontrollably. I wept for my revered father, for my beloved stepmother, for the innocent little brothers I adored. I wept for my grandparents and all my unfortunate relatives who had joined my family in death. But most of all, I wept for myself.

Chapter 7

The fortress at Siklos was enormous; there must have been more than a hundred rooms, chambers and hallways of every size and description. It was also thoroughly dilapidated. Apparently, it had been fighting a long and losing battle with nature, like a sunken ship overgrown with coral and teeming with aquatic life. Bats, rats, snakes and other vermin had long taken up residence in every corner of the fortress. Many parts of the roof had caved in. Wild vines clambered over the walls and into the windows. The courtyard was overgrown with weeds and choked with garbage, fallen plaster and other debris.

The fortress was well away from the corridors of the war, and we weren't sure why the Hungarian Army considered it important to restore it to military use. But all that mattered to us was survival, and we actually considered ourselves quite fortunate in Siklos, and we were in no immediate danger. The Americans and British apparently didn't consider the fortress significant either, and, although Budapest was pounded almost daily, no bombs were addressed to Siklos. As for the work, it was convenient and not unbearably hard. We did not have to walk far from our barracks to the work site, and we usually stopped at a reasonable hour. None of the officers seemed to be driven by a sense of urgency, which didn't surprise anyone. We were all perfectly content to play out the war in this remote backwater.

Our first assignment was to prepare ten rooms for our own immediate occupancy, which was accomplished rather quickly. My own room, which also housed twenty-five other kosher-eaters, was dank but spacious. In the evenings, many of our friends, kosher-eaters and otherwise, would join us for long sessions of commiseration and reminiscence.

A few weeks after we arrived in Siklos, we observed the fast day of Tishah b'Av, the Ninth of Av, the date on which both the First Temple and the Second Temple were destroyed in ancient Jerusalem some five hundred years apart. Traditionally, we would assemble in the synagogues on this solemn day and read from the Kinos, lamentations composed by the great poets of our history. But we had no synagogue in Siklos, nor did we have any copies of the Kinos. Instead, I took it upon myself to compose some original lamentations that focused more on the destruction of our own world, than on the destruction of ancient Jerusalem some two thousand years ago.

I had never considered myself a writer. The most I ever did was write impassioned letters to my family from time to time. But elegiac poetry? Never. Nonetheless, the despondent atmosphere touched a chord deep in my heart, and I filled pages and pages with Yiddish poems of sorrow and hope. We gathered in my room that night, and we all wept as

I read aloud the lamentations I had composed. By popular demand, I read them several times, and afterwards, when I was too emotionally exhausted to continue, others took over the readings. Unfortunately, only the memory of these compositions survives.

The weeks passed slowly but uneventfully in Siklos. The kosher-eaters faced the biggest problems, because we were running low on funds with which to buy produce from the local farmers. The news that trickled in from Budapest was encouraging. Regent Miklos Horthy, relegated to the role of figurehead when the Nazis occupied Hungary in March, had appointed a new cabinet and instructed them to seek an armistice with the Russians. According to what we heard, Horthy had already suspended all deportations of Jews, and he had also promised there would be no deportations from Budapest itself. Although the countryside had already been virtually emptied of Jews, there was now at least a reprieve for the many tens of thousands crowded into the capital city. Furthermore, these developments seemed to signal that the end of the war was in sight.

Towards the end of August, we received notification from Army headquarters that, since Siklos did not require such a large contingent of laborers, one hundred men were to be transferred to Budakalasz outside Budapest immediately. What sort of work would be required there? No one knew. Regardless, the kosher-eaters, myself among them, were eager to be included in the group being sent to Budakalasz. By this time, dwindling funds and malnutrition had reduced our number to about thirty. It wasn't easy to forgo the nourishing food provided by the army kitchen and subsist on bread and vegetables, assuming there was enough money with which to buy them. In Budapest, we hoped, the large Jewish community would provide us with the food we needed. Moreover, since Horthy had pledged not to deport Jews from Budapest, we felt we would be safer there.

Our friends pleaded with us to remain in Siklos, but we were determined. We put in our request, and it was accepted. In retrospect, it was a poor decision. The Siklos contingent was liberated six months early, and most of them survived. We did not fare as well.

In Budakalasz, we were stationed in a former coffee-house, a large building which had been converted to a barracks. True to our expectations, the food situation was much improved for us there. We all had friends and relatives who brought us food, and we even got furloughs from time to time to leave camp and visit them in Budapest, where we were served hot meals and made to feel at home. My cousin Tzili Weiss, my brother-in-law Yosef Maier's sister, lived in Budapest and took me under her wing, as did the Pollack family from our village.

The work details, however, could not have been more hazardous. We were assigned to the antiaircraft defenses of the capital city. Budapest was an important target of the Allied warplanes, who mounted bombing runs over the city every day. The Hungarians returned fire from a ring of anti-aircraft batteries around the city. Budakalasz was the site of one of these installations.

On our first day in Budakalasz, we were awakened at dawn, given shovels and marched out to the installations. The long barrels of the guns were half lowered, and the gunners sat on the ground smoking and exchanging lewd jokes. Stacks of shells were arranged in pyramids within a meter or two of each gun emplacement. More shells sat in boxes in a bunker twenty meters away. The sergeant ordered us to start digging and piling up earthworks around each emplacement so that nothing but a direct hit would knock out the guns.

The morning turned out to be unusually magnificent. The sun shimmered incandescently in a clear and brilliant blue sky, and a gentle breeze took the edge off the end of summer heat. For hours, we dug and piled, dug and piled, while the artillerymen smoked and watched us. Finally, we were allowed a break, and we slumped to the ground to rest.

"Hey, would you like a drink of water?" one of the gunners asked me. "You look like you could use one."

"Very kind of you," I said. "This is hard work."

He handed me his flask. I took a deep swallow and handed it back.

"First day here?" he asked.

"Yes."

He smiled. "Wait till the show begins."

"Show? You mean a bombing raid?"

"Yeah. Just about every day." He shaded his eyes and scanned the western sky. After a minute, he lifted his finger and pointed to three tiny specks on the horizon. "There they are! They're coming. These are Americans. The British come at night."

"What are their targets?" I asked. He seemed friendly enough, and I took the liberty of asking him my question. I was concerned about my friends and relatives in Budapest.

"All kinds," he replied. "Factories. Fuel dumps. Ammunition dumps. Troop concentrations. But you know what their first targets are?"

I shook my head.

He laughed. "Air defenses! First, they're going to try and knock us out, then they'll go after their targets."

I didn't find that so amusing. In fact, it seemed quite frightening to me. I warned my comrades about what to expect, then I began to recite Psalms from memory.

A short while later, the air-raid siren sounded, and everyone sprang into action. The gunners loaded their shells into the breeches and ratcheted up the barrels until they pointed almost straight up at the sky. All the artillerymen and the officers of our labor battalion donned flak helmets, but there apparently weren't enough helmets for the Jewish laborers.

The drone of the bombers drew ever nearer. I saw waves of broad-winged planes flying in formation; no enemy fighter planes rose to intercept them and contest their mastery of the skies. From a distance, I saw the bombs released from the bomb bays, like tiny matchsticks tumbling down from above. I saw the bombs strike the ground a few kilometers to the west with flashes of silver light and a thud like dull, rolling thunder. I saw tall sprays of earth rise into the air, and here and there, I saw real explosions with flames and dense clouds of smoke.

When the first bomb hit near us, I was taken completely by surprise. The bomb struck the ground more than a hundred meters away, but the explosion was so loud and violent, I actually felt the earth tremble. I was thrown to the ground, and my eardrums felt as if they had been pierced with sharp nails.

I glanced up and saw my friendly gunner laughing at my discomfiture, but I could barely hear him because of the persistent ringing in my ears.

"Here goes!" he shouted. He slammed the shell into the breech, sighted along the barrel and fired. The barrel recoiled, and fire belched from its mouth. I looked up at the sky and could not recognize it. The American planes were very high up in the sky, obscured by a smoky mist peppered with puffs of flak. Gone were the incandescent sun and the brilliant sky.

Suddenly, a force like a giant hand slammed into my back and flung me face down into a pile of loose earth. I felt a searing hot wind across my neck, and I heard loud screaming. It took me a moment or two to realize that the screams were my own. I covered my head with my hands and tried to burrow deeper into the soft piled earth while I took mental inventory of my limbs to make sure nothing had been removed by the blast.

A hand gripped my shoulder and spun me around. It was my sergeant.

"What do you think you're doing, Cahan?" he shouted into my ear. "Taking a beauty rest? Get up right now and start bringing more shells from the bunker. Quick! They're running out of ammunition!"

I struggled to my feet and ran stumbling toward the bunker. Along the way, I passed the body of one of our group, a young Jewish boy from Szeged. He lay on his back, neck bent at an impossible angle. His eyes stared up sightlessly at the planes overhead. I doubled over and vomited, but I knew I could not afford to stop and indulge my agony. With a surge of adrenaline, I ran into the bunker and grabbed an ammunition box. I could not lift it. It was much too heavy. With all my might, I maneuvered it out into the open where one of my comrades helped me carry it to the gunners.

The gunners' faces were black with discharged powder, and sweat poured down their backs. I collapsed on the ground to catch my breath and watched them reload and fire, reload and fire, reload and fire. My eyes were glazed over from shock and fatigue, but a loud shout shook me out of my stupor. The gunners were pointed excitedly at the sky. One of the American bombers had been hit and was plummeting down in a slow spiral, flames and black smoke streaming behind.

I felt a momentary surge of triumph. These bombers had almost killed me, and now, the ammunition I had lugged with my last ounce of strength might very well have brought one of them down. But then I caught myself. How stupid of me! What an ironic twist to the bitter tragedy my life had become. Here I was, risking life and limb to help my mortal enemies. Should I also rejoice with them when my liberators were shot down? I felt ashamed.

This became an almost daily routine. We worked for hours in the emplacements, often right in middle of air raids, with bombs exploding all around us. At night, we were occasionally awakened by air raid sirens and had to run to the shelters half-dressed. One near miss ripped a huge hole in the barracks not far from where I slept. After a while, we developed a sort of sixth sense that made us dive for cover just before an explosion nearby. Was this the safety we had sought when we asked to be transferred from Siklos? Oh, if we could only exchange these bombs for the bats and rats of the old fortress!

One of the unexpected consequences of our work in the gun emplacements was its effect on our clothing. Before long, our clothes were reduced to shreds and tatters, and they had to be replaced. The Hungarian Army was not prepared to absorb the expense of providing us with replacement garments, especially in Budapest where there were plenty of Jews who could be expected to clothe their less fortunate brothers. And so, one day after work, our lieutenant took a group of us, myself included, to the Jewish community center to procure some clothing for our contingent.

The president of the Jewish community of Budapest, Dr. Frankel-Cahan, was a distant relative of mine, and when I introduced myself to him, he wept as he hugged and kissed me. He asked me about different members of my family, in particular about Rabbi Yeshia Cahan, the Rabbi of Petrova, my Uncle Favish's father. What could I tell him? What I knew was terrible. What I surmised was even worse.

Dr. Frankel-Cahan's office was a beehive of activity, and he asked the lieutenant to wait just a few minutes until he would be able to take us down to the room which served as a warehouse for old, but still serviceable, clothing. A long line of people waited to speak with him. In a corner, a secretary huddled over a typewriter, filling out forms for an elderly man.

A well-dressed, clean-shaven, middle-aged man caught my eye. He was accompanied by his wife and a young daughter about seventeen years of age. The three of them seemed to be there only to assist others, without as much as a thought for themselves. The man saw that the lieutenant was becoming impatient but that Dr. Frankel-Cahan had his hands full and was far from finished.

"Doctor," he asked in formal Oberlander Yiddish, "would you like me to show these gentlemen to the warehouse?"

Dr. Frankel-Cahan looked immensely relieved. "It would be a great favor, Miklos. Thank you so much."

The man approached the lieutenant. "Follow me, if you would be so kind. The warehouse is downstairs."

As we walked down the stairs, he turned to us and bowed slightly. "Let me introduce myself. My name is Miklos Gaspar. Moshe in Hebrew. This is my wife Bella, and this is my daughter Lily. We are here to help you in any way we can. It will be our pleasure."

He then made a special point of shaking everyone's hand and asking his name. My name, of course, he already knew, as did everyone else who had been in Dr Frankel-Cahan's office when we met.

We spent several hours going through the piles of clothes in the warehouse. Mrs. Gaspar and her daughter Lily stayed with us throughout the entire time, helping us sort and pile the clothing. Mr. Gaspar was needed in other parts of the building, but he looked in on us, every once in a while, to make sure everything was going smoothly. He also made a special point of asking me if I needed any help. His wife and daughter were equally solicitous. I attributed my special status to my familial relationship with Dr. Frankel-Cahan. A few times, I saw Mr. Gaspar exchange odd looks with his wife and daughter after speaking with me, but I did not make much of it. They probably had all sorts of things on their minds which were really no business of mine.

We finished with our selections and bundled them up. Mrs. Gaspar and Lily surveyed the results of our efforts with satisfaction and asked if there was anything else they could do for us. Then they bid us a good afternoon and left.

One minute later, Mr. Gaspar came rushing into the warehouse. "Hold everything," he said, his hand outstretched in front of him. He turned to the lieutenant. "Sir, there has been a new development. We've just gotten word that tomorrow morning we will receive a shipment of clothes in excellent condition. In fact, it may even come tonight. These garments are probably far superior to those your men have picked out here. I would recommend that you stay here in Budapest overnight so that you'll have first crack at the shipment tomorrow morning."

"Well, I don't know . . ." said the lieutenant.

"There's no problem, sir. We'll put you all up comfortably. You'll get a hot meal and a good night's rest, and tomorrow morning you'll have you pick of the lot. What do you say?"

The lieutenant was obviously tempted to agree, but he still hesitated. "Sounds good, but I'm not authorized to make such a decision. My captain's orders were to bring the men here, pick out the clothes and come right back. There was nothing about an overnight stay in my orders."

"Of course, sir," said Mr. Gaspar. "I understand perfectly. But this is an unexpected development. Surely, you have some flexibility for unexpected developments, don't you?"

"Well, I do and I don't." The lieutenant fidgeted a little. "I don't think a new shipment of clothes warrants my deviating from my orders."

"So why don't we call your captain?" persisted Mr. Gaspar. "We have a telephone right here on that table by the door. Feel free to use it."

The lieutenant shrugged. "Sure, why not? Let him decide. I wouldn't mind staying overnight."

It took about ten minutes to get a connection with the captain. The lieutenant spoke to his captain for several minutes, but it was clear that he was making no progress. Mr. Gaspar asked for the telephone, which the lieutenant gladly surrendered.

"Captain, sir, my name is Gaspar Miklos," he said. Hungarians always give their family name first. "As I was explaining to your very fine lieutenant, we are getting a new shipment tomorrow. The clothes are much better, and your men will have first choice. The clothes they have selected now are leftovers from the pickings of many other people. They are not the finest quality. If you let them stay till tomorrow, you will get first quality."

Mr. Gaspar listened for a while, nodding his head.

"I understand, sir. By quality I meant durability. The clothes in the new shipment are of stronger, longer lasting material. You will not have to come back here so often to replace them. They will last and last."

Mr. Gaspar listened again, a slight frown on his face.

"Of course, sir. You are undoubtedly right. Who knows how long any of us will last? Still, durable clothes are important. Besides, you can also take additional clothing for some of the other men in your battalion who will be needing replacements before long. It will be in the best interests of your battalion to have the men stay over until the morning. . . . Yes, sir, I understand. . . . Of course, sir. . . . Thank you very much. We will take good care of them. . . . Yes, sir, I will put him on right away."

With a broad smile on his face, Mr. Gaspar signaled to the lieutenant to take the telephone.

"Oh, one more thing, captain," he said into the telephone before handing it to the lieutenant. "If I could perhaps ask you for a personal favor. It turns out that one of the men you sent here is a nephew of my wife. His name is Maier Cahan. Would you give him permission to stay with us tonight in our apartment? . . . Of course, sir. Just for tonight. We will take good care of him and return him to you in the morning along with the rest of the men. . . . Thank you so much, sir. It is very kind of you. . . . Yes, I take full responsibility. . . . The lieutenant is right here. Thank you, again."

Mr. Gaspar gave the telephone to the lieutenant. Then he looked at me and smiled. Tonight I would be his guest.

So, I thought, Mrs. Gaspar is my aunt? Since when?

Chapter 8

My newly acquired aunt and cousin were waiting in the street when the lieutenant brought our group outside. They smiled at me and waved, and I smiled and waved back.

"Maier, I heard the good news," Mrs. Gaspar called out in Hungarian as we approached. "I heard you're coming to us for the night."

"Yes, I am, Aunt Bella," I replied, also in Hungarian, keeping up my part of the charade. "I am so grateful to you for inviting me. And of course, to you, too, Lily."

"We're so glad you could come, Maier," said Lily. "We have so much to talk about."

We did? Oh well, I shrugged inwardly. What did it matter? I would find out what this was all about soon enough. In the meantime, I would have a night off from the labor battalion, a night of unexpected normalcy.

Mr. Gaspar spent a few more minutes making sure the lieutenant and the group would be well fed and comfortable for the night. Then we left.

The Gaspars lived fairly close by. We crossed a few small streets and one large avenue, and we were there. Their apartment was on the fourth floor of a building that had seen better days. The apartment itself was modest in size and modestly furnished, but it was immaculate. There was not a speck of dust anywhere. The tablecloth and curtains were freshly laundered and ironed, and the kitchen fairly gleamed.

Lily brought me a glass of water. "Please sit down, Maier, and have something cold to drink while Mama and I prepare dinner. Are you tired?"

Even in the house, the Gaspars spoke Hungarian, which was apparently their first language. My Hungarian was passable but not nearly as fluent as theirs. Yiddish was my first language.

"A little," I admitted.

"Would you like to lie down for a little while?"

"That would be nice," I said. It had been a long day, and every bone in my body ached. "I can just sit down on the couch over there and put my head back. That would be wonderful."

"Ach! I wouldn't hear of it," said Lily with a toss of her head. "We have a comfortable bed for you. You can nap for a half-hour or an hour, and then you'll wake up feeling refreshed. You'll feel like a new person. Come!"

I followed Lily past the bathroom and down a short hallway with three doors clustered together at the end.

"These are our bedrooms," she explained. "This one on the left is my parents' bedroom. The first bedroom on the right is mine. You can use the second one. The bed is made."

She opened the door with a reverence that struck me as exceedingly odd. The room was bright and airy, but it had the faint musty smell that comes with not having been used for a long time. The lace coverlet on the large bed, which matched the lace curtains on the window, was perfectly folded. There was a small escritoire with a high-backed chair in a corner and a massive, highly polished armoire against the opposite wall. A framed picture of a handsome young man sat on the escritoire next to a pile of books. There was another picture on the armoire alongside a small clock.

Lily turned down the coverlet and fluffed up the pillows. "Make yourself comfortable, Maier," she said in a low voice, almost a whisper, as if not to wake anyone. "We'll call you when dinner is ready."

Without another word, she turned and left, closing the door gently behind her. I sat down on the bed. It was deliciously soft.

Still seated, I considered the questions piling up in my mind. The Gaspars seemed to be wonderful people, but something strange was going on. Why were they so intent on having me spend the night with them? Why had they felt compelled to represent themselves as my family in order to get permission from the captain? Why had Lily entered this room as if she were stepping into a shrine? What was going on?

The questions agitated me, and I began to pace around the room like a caged lion. Most of the books on the escritoire were about mathematics and science. There was also a Hungarian translation of Tolstoy's *War and Peace*. The eyes of the young man in the framed picture followed me around, and I stopped to get acquainted.

A slender, good-looking fellow, probably no more than twenty or twenty-one years old, he had wavy dark hair, intelligent dark eyes with laugh lines at the corners and a slightly prominent nose. Who was he? Probably a son of the Gaspars and clearly not living at home. I wondered where he was now. Perhaps he was also in a labor battalion. Or perhaps he had emigrated to America or Palestine before the war.

A thought suddenly struck me. If the Gaspars were my aunt and uncle and Lily was my cousin, then this gentleman here was also my cousin. In fact, we even had a certain ambiguous resemblance. "Hello, cousin," I said aloud, and I laughed.

After ten minutes, I decided time was too precious to waste on idle speculation. I prayed quickly, then I took off my shoes and slid under the covers. Seconds later, I was fast asleep.

The delicious smells emanating from the kitchen woke me even before Lily's light knock on the door. The clock on the armoire told me I had been asleep for an hour. Lily was right. I did indeed feel like a different person. I decided to laze in bed for a little while, but after a few minutes, I felt strangely uncomfortable, as if I were trespassing on another man's life. I left the room.

Mr. Gaspar was reading a newspaper on the couch when I came out.

"So how was your rest, Maier?" he asked. "Was the bed comfortable? Did you like the room?"

"The room is nice, and the bed is just wonderful. I haven't slept this well since I left home. It was perfect, just like home."

A happy smile spread across his face. "Bella, Lily," he called out to the women whom I heard puttering in the kitchen, "our honored guest is ready to join us."

He glanced at me and then at his wristwatch. "It is getting a little late, Maier. Let me go lend a hand in the kitchen. We'll only be a moment. Make yourself comfortable."

There were four place settings on the dinner table. Although the surroundings and furnishing were simple, almost spartan, the table itself was elegantly appointed with white linen, china, silver and crystal. Mr. and Mrs. Gaspar, I assumed, would occupy the head and foot of the table, while Lily and I would sit at the sides. For the first time, I noticed that an oil painting of the young man, undoubtedly the Gaspars' son, adorned one of the walls of the dining room. I sat down in the chair directly across from the painting, because I wanted to study it.

The women came in, Mrs. Gaspar carrying a tureen of steaming soup and Lily a platter of roasted potatoes. Mr. Gaspar trailed behind with a basket of fragrant bread. Courteously, I stood up.

"Oh, Maier," Mr. Gaspar said rather hastily, "would you mind coming around and sitting on this side? Lily usually sits where you're sitting now."

Lily gave me a lame smile but seemed somewhat relieved.

"Not at all," I said. Yet, it seemed odd. What did it matter to him or to Lily where I sat? I had actually wanted to sit where I could get a good look at that painting, but now I would be sitting directly under it. Still, I went to the proffered seat without making an issue of it.

The next hour passed pleasantly. The food was excellent, the conversation even better. The Gaspars told me many stories about how they had secured documents and other necessities for refugees who had come to Budapest from other places. The stories were told with such a lack of pretentiousness and bluster that I could not help but marvel at the sterling character of these people. I recalled how they had bustled about the community center earlier that day helping everyone in sight, and I was convinced I had never met people who had such a profound love for any and all Jewish people.

The Gaspars were not the kind of Jews to whom I was accustomed in Lower Vishiva. Although Mr. Gaspar wore a *yarmulke* on his head, he shaved his beard and dressed in modern garb. Mrs. Gaspar did not cover her hair. Lily wore her long hair in a stylish wave, and her sleeves did not quite reach her elbows. My grandmother would not have approved. But they were good people, and I held them in the highest esteem.

The women cleared the table and brought in cakes, and Mr. Gaspar poured some of wine, which we sipped slowly. The warm glow induced by the wine and the minuscule touches of luxury carried us far away from this time and place. They asked me many questions about my family and my life, and I found myself talking freely about my childhood experiences and all the people I loved and admired. As I spoke, I noticed that each of them glanced up at the wall behind me every once in a while, but I paid little mind to it. The breathless attention with which they hung on my every word had opened a floodgate of memories, and my words came out in a rush. When I told them about the eviction from our homes, the transfer to the ghetto and my sorrowful parting from my parents, they all wept openly. I did not tell them about my dreams. They were far too intimate.

The hour grew late. The wine bottle was drained, but the conversation continued to flow. By this time, we had formed a real closeness, and we bared our souls to each other as only close friends do. We spoke about the cabinet moves by Regent Horthy, and the hope that soon Hungary would withdraw from the war and our nightmare would come to an end. We cried and we laughed, and we were happy for a little while.

None of the Gaspars had mentioned the young man in the painting on the wall and the pictures in the bedroom, but I thought it would not be inappropriate for me to ask. And so I did. "Would it be rude of me to ask about the young man in this painting? Is he your son?"

Lily's eyes quickly brimmed over, and her lips began to quiver. Then she buried her face in her hands and burst into hysterical weeping. Mrs. Gaspar lowered her head and cried softly. Mr. Gaspar looked down at his hands.

"I am so sorry," I said. "I didn't mean to pry. Forgive me."

"Don't be sorry, Maier," Mr. Gaspar told me, his voice solemn and subdued. The weeping subsided a little as he began to speak. "Yes, that is our son, and we really do want to tell you about him. We just couldn't bring ourselves to begin. Our son has been dead for four months now. His name was Shloime. Shloime Gaspar, may he rest in peace."

These last words sparked a renewed outburst of weeping by both mother and daughter. Mr. Gaspar waited until they calmed down before he continued. "Shloime was only nineteen years old. He was such a wonderful boy." The words caught momentarily in his throat, and he sighed deeply. "He was bright, lovable and so very, very kind. There was nothing he wouldn't do for another Jew. He cared. He really cared."

Just like his parents and sister, I thought.

"One day, about four months ago, he was walking home in the evening. We were waiting for him to join us for dinner. A few blocks from here, he saw five Arrow Cross hoodlums beating a Jewish man. There was nothing he could really do, was there? But it wasn't in Shloime's nature to abandon a Jew in distress, no matter how hopeless the situation. As soon as he joined the fray, they abandoned their first victim, who was already half dead from the beating, and turned on Shloime. The boy fought valiantly, but it was no contest. Because he had dared stand up against them, they beat him mercilessly and left him for dead."

Mr. Gaspar was silent for a moment as he gathered his thoughts. The image of Shloime being brutally beaten by those hoodlums made me shudder. Founded and led by Ferenc Szalasi, the Arrow Cross Party, the Nyilaskeresztes, was Hungary's most rabid fascist party. Although excluded from Horthy's coalition government, Arrow Cross was still an evil presence throughout Hungary. Arrow Cross paramilitary units, the most vicious anti-Semitic thugs in Hungary, did whatever they pleased, which was usually some form of mayhem and death.

"Shloime was still alive when we found him," Mr. Gaspar continued, "but just barely. We tried to nurse him back to health, but his injuries were just too severe. For four weeks, we watched him writhe in agony. We struggled to keep him alive, but he kept slipping away. We tried so hard."

He closed his eyes and bit his lip.

Mrs. Gaspar took up the thread of the story. "Maier, those four weeks were unbearable. I wanted to die right then and there. I couldn't bear to see my Shloime suffer. But we don't die, do we? We just go on. Crushed and heartbroken, we just go on. That is the Almighty's will, isn't it? Maier, you know how we felt. You went through the same thing with your family, may Heaven have mercy on all of us."

"Yes, I did," I said. "I know what you are saying."

"I remember that last night," she continued, "when Shloime lay on his deathbed. I knew it. We all knew it. We said good-bye to each other. I bent over him, and I kissed my poor baby good-bye. His eyes fluttered open, and he looked at me with such serenity I was sure he had already stepped across into Heaven. 'Don't cry, mother,' he whispered to me. 'One thing. . . . After I die, continue helping every Jew . . . If you do . . . I will live on through you . . . oh, mother . . . I feel . . .' He was dying, right there in front of our eyes." She dabbed at her eyes. Lily wept silently. "Miklos said Shema with him. And then he died. Just like that. He died. My Shloime was gone. My poor Shloime, such a beautiful young boy senselessly snuffed out. And . . . and . . . that's it. What more is there to say?" She picked up her wineglass and put it to her lips, even though it was empty.

"So, Maier," said Lily, "now you know about Shloime. Now you've shared our pain."

I saw that a response was expected, and I waited a full minute doing so. "Yes, I have shared your pain," I said gravely. "These days, tragedy and sorrow have no bounds. Everyone has lost family. Everyone has pain. But to watch a loved one slip away before your eyes despite all your desperate efforts, that's a rare and horrible tragedy. My heart goes out to all three of you. You are such good people. Shloime was fortunate to have you as his family during his brief nineteen years on this world. I feel honored and privileged that you have opened your home and your hearts to me. If I survive, I will always cherish the memory of this evening."

Mr. Gaspar came over and embraced me.

"So will we, Maier," he said, his voice hoarse. "So will we."

"And now, everyone," said Mrs. Gaspar with artificial brightness, "it's time to go to sleep. Maier, you know where your room is. Good night and pleasant dreams."

I found it hard to sleep that night. It was still dark outside when Mr. Gaspar knocked on my door, but I was already awake.

"Come, Maier, we have to leave right away," he said through the closed door. "I must go to the synagogue to say Kaddish for Shloime."

Without another word, I swung out of that delicious bed and got dressed. To my surprise, Mrs. Gaspar and Lily were also dressed and waiting for me.

"I don't understand," I said to Mr. Gaspar. "I thought we were going to the synagogue."

"I am going, not you," he replied. "It would not be prudent for a labor conscript to move about the city unless he is under guard. Aunt Bella and Lily will take you to the community center, and I will meet you there when I return from the synagogue. You can pray there with the others."

We all walked together for two blocks, then he turned off to the synagogue while the three of us continued on.

There it was again, I thought. Aunt Bella. I hadn't brought the subject up the previous night, because I was sure it was insignificant. I thought I understood the situation perfectly. The tragedy of Shloime's death undoubtedly always hung heavy in the air when the three of them were alone together. A guest in the house, especially someone his age such as I, would be like a breath of fresh air, like balm to their aching hearts. The charade that I was Mrs. Gaspar's nephew had been a ruse to get the captain to give me permission to spend the night with them. Nothing more. But now, Mr. Gaspar had referred to his wife as Aunt Bella in the privacy of his own home, and he had said it without a mischievous wink or twinkle in his eye. Apparently, he was serious. Did he really think I was a long lost nephew of the Gaspar family? What did it mean?

We arrived at the community center just as the dawn tinged the horizon with a faint gray light. The lieutenant and the men were still fast asleep, and we did not disturb them. I went off to pray in a small room near the clothing warehouse. By the time I finished, Mr. Gaspar was back from the synagogue. The women had prepared a light breakfast, and we ate together with ease and intimacy of old friends. I could not have been more comfortable if she had indeed been my Aunt Bella and he my Uncle Miklos.

We lingered over breakfast talking animatedly and telling jokes and funny stories, a far cry from the tense emotions of the previous night. We could have sat there for hours, but we were interrupted by the lieutenant who wanted to know when the shipment was scheduled to arrive. Mr. Gaspar promised to make a few calls, and he excused himself.

The lieutenant went back to the clothing warehouse where the men were assembled. I accompanied him, of course. After all, I was still only a labor conscript, not a man of leisure who could linger over breakfast with his alleged aunt and cousin. Mrs. Gaspar and Lily came along to help with the shipment when it arrived.

Twenty minutes later, Mr. Gaspar returned to report that the truck would be arriving within the next two hours. The lieutenant grumbled and cursed, but there was nothing he could do but wait. I saw Mr. Gaspar catch his wife's eye and nod imperceptibly, and I immediately understood who had engineered the delay in the delivery. It was obvious, at least to me, that the Gaspars were stalling.

Two hours later, the truck had still not arrived. Mr. Gaspar went off to make some more calls and returned with a new scheduled time of arrival. This happened several times, and it was not until three in the afternoon that the truck finally appeared. By then, the lieutenant was fuming, but the quality of the clothing in the shipment and the promise of a delicious supper appeased him quickly.

Even with the help of the Gaspars, the task of unloading the truck, unpacking the bundles and sorting the clothes took quite a few hours, and by the time we were finished, it was well past dark. The lieutenant called the captain and arranged for us to stay over for a second night. He also got permission for me to spend this second night as well with my uncle and aunt, which was clearly their intention all along.

Relationships formed under trying circumstances always cement quickly, and our case was no exception. Dinner the second night was even more delightful than the first. We were already such good friends, and the last two days had even given us a few shared memories. The conversation was warm and sparkling but, after a while, I sensed an undercurrent of tension. There were unspoken thoughts in that room, important ones, but in spite of my curiosity, I was not going to pry.

After dinner, we drank coffee.

"We are having such a good time, Maier," said Lily. "It really was such a stroke of good luck that you could be with us for a second night."

I smiled. "A stroke of good luck with an assist from your father, Lily. He made sure that truck didn't come until three o'clock in the afternoon."

They all laughed.

"You see, Bella?" said Mr. Gaspar. "I told you Maier was on to our tricks. He is a clever fellow. I saw that right from the beginning."

Mrs. Gaspar giggled nervously and gave me a sidelong glance. I looked at Lily and saw she was also fidgeting. What was going on?

Mr. Gaspar cleared his throat. The unspoken was about to become spoken. "Maier, listen carefully to what I am about to say. From the first time we saw you in the community center yesterday, all three of us took an immediate liking to you, and as we got to know you better, we liked you even more. There was also something else. When I first saw you, I thought for a split second that Shloime had returned. There is a certain resemblance of the face and the mannerisms. Bella and Lily had the same reaction. We felt we had to meet you, to talk with you, to get to know you."

He paused to give me a chance to say something. I felt a crawling sensation in my stomach, but I said nothing. He plunged ahead.

"You must think us strange, and you're probably right. But we couldn't help it. We just had to. I told the lieutenant about the next day's shipment of clothes, and then I maneuvered and maneuvered until I got you to come to us for the night. What can I tell you, Maier? I plead guilty. I asked you to sit under the painting, and we kept comparing. The truth is, the more we got to know you the less you resembled Shloime. It was only a superficial resemblance anyway. But in the course of the night, we got to know you for who you are yourself, Maier, and we think you are just wonderful."

He took a deep breath and screwed his courage to the sticking point.

"Maier, we want to ask you . . . to be our son!"

In all my speculations, this offer had never occurred to me. Mr. Gaspar appeared simultaneously hopeful and embarrassed. Mrs. Gaspar and Lily were looking at me anxiously. I had nothing to say. I was shocked.

"Please don't get us wrong, Maier," he continued hurriedly, interpreting my silence as disapproval. "We know how devoted you are to your parents, how much you love them and care about them. And we hope with all our hearts that they have somehow survived in Germany and that they will return when this terrible war is over. We do not want to take away even the tiniest bit of love that you have for your family. But we want you to belong to us, as well. We are not asking you to call us Father or Mother. Call us Uncle Moshe and Aunt Bella, but be our son. There is a lot of unclaimed love in our hearts, and we want to give it to you. What do you say, Maier? Is it such a crazy thing?"

There was a lot of unclaimed love in my heart as well, but was I prepared to give it to the Gaspars? Was I prepared to accept them as my parents in a manner of speaking, or at least as my Uncle Moshe and Aunt Bella? This whole thing seemed so bizarre. And yet, what harm was there in seeking a little love to counteract the pain and the sorrow of our unspeakable losses?

But then I thought about my family. How would they have felt about this? Would there be an element of betrayal in accepting the Gaspars' offer? Perhaps I should consider it like an adoption. My relationship with my stepmother had not infringed on my filial devotion to my mother, nor would my relationship with the Gaspars infringe on my filial obligations to my parents. But what about the Gaspars themselves? Would my parents approve of my adoption by a modern family with values so different from ours? But then, I thought, these were such unusual times, and under the circumstances, they might very well give their blessing.

It occurred to me that if the Gaspars were so eager to shower me with love it would actually be an act of kindness to accept their offer. And I was sure I would be able to return their love in equal measure. It also occurred to me with a sudden jolt that, for all intents and purposes, I was alone in the world. How could I not embrace this wonderful family? But what was the nature of this commitment?

"I don't know what to say," I said, trying to remain somewhat noncommittal. "I think you are among the finest people I've ever met, and I am touched by your offer. It would certainly be a great honor to be accepted into this splendid family."

Mrs. Gaspar leaped from the couch with an ecstatic shriek. "Does that mean you accept, Maier? I can't believe it!"

I couldn't believe it either, because that was not quite what I had meant to imply. She had misunderstood me, and now there seemed to be no backing up. And to be perfectly honest with myself, the idea was growing on me fast. My past was destroyed, my future uncertain at best. The Gaspars were offering me a chance for love and happiness in the here and now, regardless of what fate held in store for us. For all its strangeness, it was a good offer.

"Of course, I accept," I said. "Aunt Bella."

Chapter 9

We talked all night, there being so much more to talk about with an adopted son than with the most honored guest. We talked about the past, and we even dared speak a little about the future. We also talked a lot about Shloime. I fully expected it and was afraid it would be strange and uncomfortable, but it wasn't. It became clear to me that the Gaspars really did not view me as a surrogate Shloime, and I was relieved. As for me, I actually formed a bond of sorts with him. Lily was my sister, and Shloime was the heroic brother I had never known and lost.

The next morning, we once again left at the crack of dawn, Uncle Moshe to the synagogue and the rest of us to the community center, where we arrived while the city still slept. We discovered that the captain had called the night before and ordered the lieutenant and the men to return immediately to the camp without the bundles of clothing. They left me a message that a vehicle would come at ten o'clock in the morning for the clothing and me. While we waited, Aunt Bella insisted that I have my photograph taken, to be kept on file in the Budapest community center.

When Uncle Moshe returned from the synagogue, we had an enjoyable, leisurely breakfast, but I could see he had a lot on his mind. It did not take long for him to reveal it.

"Listen, Maier," he said. "In general, you are better off not knowing about some of the things we do for people. It's not so easy to secure good documents, and the truth is that some of the documents we provide would not stand up to scrutiny. We try to stay above suspicion, but there is always some danger."

A chill passed through my body. I didn't know what to say.

"Believe me, Maier," he said, responding to my obvious concern, "we are as careful as can be, but it is impossible to avoid risk completely. It just can't be done. Someone talks. A piece of evidence is left behind. Who knows? We are in the hands of the Almighty. Next week, we are going to change apartments, because we are afraid some of our Hungarian neighbors are becoming suspicious. For your own protection, I won't give you the new address. From now until this war is over, you won't come to us at home. Instead, we'll visit you at the camp. It'll be safer that way."

"You're frightening me," I said. "Not for myself, but for you."

"Don't be frightened," said Aunt Bella. "We are just trying to be extra cautious. Uncle Moshe will visit you every other week. Lily and I will come more often."

"How will we meet?" I asked.

"I have the perfect meeting place," said Uncle Moshe. "There is a small kiosk right near the camp that sells cigarettes. There are always crowds of people coming and going, and we will be inconspicuous. In the afternoons, when you return from work, just stop by there as if to buy cigarettes. I will try to be there every other Wednesday. Aunt Bella and Lily will come as often as they can."

There was a knock on the door, and the secretary came in to announce that a military truck had arrived to take me back to the camp along with all the bundled clothes. It was five minutes to ten.

I stood up. "Time to go. Hopefully, this war will soon be over, and our time will be our own again."

Aunt Bella gave me a warm smile. "From your mouth to His ears."

"Wait a minute, Maier," said Lily. She opened her bag and pulled out a few neatly wrapped packages. "Here is food for you. We even found you a salami with the Mehadrin kosher seal. It will keep up your strength. And when you eat the cookies, think of me. I made them myself."

I grinned at my new sister, and my thoughts immediately flew to my beloved Chaya. What had happened to her and the baby? Had she received the money I left for her in Satmar? Had she managed to escape to Romania? I felt a terrible sadness in my heart, but I banished it quickly. I wanted this moment of parting to be a happy occasion, a time of hope, not sorrow.

With the help of Uncle Moshe, it took me about an hour to load the clothing onto the truck while the driver went inside to eat. Then I bid farewell to Aunt Bella and Lily, and we pledged fealty to each other once again. Uncle Moshe accompanied me back to the camp in the military truck.

Before we parted at the gate, Uncle Moshe handed me a wad of bills. "This is your test, Maier," he said with a twinkle in his eye. "Let's see if you handle this like a true son."

What was I supposed to do? I didn't want to take the money, especially since I knew nothing about their financial situation. But I didn't want to offend him by refusing it.

I shrugged and put the money in my pocket. "Thanks a lot," I said. "This should last me for at least three months. If not more."

Uncle Moshe threw back his head and laughed. "I really enjoy your clever touch, Maier. Promise that you'll ask for more when you need it."

"Do you even have a question?" I replied. This time the twinkle was in my eye.

Uncle Moshe laughed again and embraced me. "I'll miss you, Maier."

"And I'll miss you, Uncle Moshe. I already do."

"Good bye. I'll see you in two weeks."

As I watched him walk away, I realized I was alone again for the first time in two very long days. I had left the camp the day before, never having heard of the Gaspars and, now, I was returning as an intimate member of the Gaspar family, a son, no less. Was it real? Or was it only a dreamlike madness spawned by the fearsome, figurative night that held us in its grip? Would the Gaspars continue to occupy a solid place in my thoughts? Or would they fade into the remnants of a pleasant, half-forgotten dream? Did I care about them? Really care? Did I love them?

The disloyalty of my thoughts perturbed me deeply. Here I was, back on my own for only a few minutes, and already I was questioning the relationship to which I had pledged my fealty with such vehement sincerity. Was I such a fickle person? Or had I been in a trance for two days?

I watched the receding back of my newly acquired Uncle Moshe. A bus was coming around the corner, and he quickened his steps to catch it. At the last moment, he turned around and waved to me from the distance, and I felt a surge of emotion. He was such a good man, so devoted, so loyal. My heart went out to him, and I resolved to accept without further question my new relationship with the

Gaspars for all its strangeness. They had given me their love, and they were entitled to mine in return.

On Friday, Aunt Bella and Lily came to visit me. I saw them when we were returning from work. They were standing near the kiosk, their arms laden with packages. I mumbled something to the sergeant about buying cigarettes and stepped out of the line.

In retrospect, I think this meeting cemented our relationship. Absence had indeed made the heart grow fonder on both sides; the joy I felt when I saw them was mirrored in their eyes. We talked and laughed, forgetting for a while that we were sitting beside a slave labor camp in which I was interred. As was to be expected, they brought me plenty of food, including *challos* for Shabbos, and I could only accept everything graciously.

The women came twice the following week and on Monday the week after. Uncle Moshe came on Wednesday as scheduled. We embraced and sat down to talk in the shadow of the kiosk. He told me that, according to all indications, Horthy was soon going to surrender to the Allied powers, thus bringing the war to an end for Hungary. He also brought me up to date on the war news from the fronts. The Russians were advancing inexorably from the east, and the Americans and British were rolling across France. They would probably cross the German border within a month or two. The Germans were losing the war on all sides, and it was only a matter of time before it ended. All we had to do was hold on just a little bit longer.

During the next two weeks, Aunt Bella and Lily came to visit me a number of times, and each was a pure delight. My new life was taking on a familiar rhythm, and I liked it. Uncle Moshe was scheduled to come again on the second Wednesday. I couldn't wait to see him.

There was a light drizzle when I came back from work that Wednesday. Uncle Moshe was nowhere in sight, but I was not alarmed. I was sure he was waiting in the kiosk. But he was not. I stood in the kiosk for an entire hour, looking out every few minutes to see if he was coming. There was no sign of him. I was beside myself with worry and a terrible foreboding. But what could I do? I couldn't go off to look for him or even make a telephone call, and besides, I didn't even know their new address or how to reach them by telephone. Something unexpected must have come up, I reassured myself. There would surely be news the next day. And indeed, there was.

Thursday morning, we lined up outside the camp to go to the antiaircraft installation. The din of honking horns and the hustle and bustle of scampering pedestrians were all around us.

Suddenly, I felt a sharp bump on my right side and saw that a letter had been shoved into my hand. I looked up and saw a woman pushing through the crowd to get away as quickly as possible. From the brief glimpse I got of her, it seemed to me that it was Lily, but she was gone before I could get a better look.

I had to fight down the urge to open the letter right then and there, because I knew it would be confiscated. Instead, I shoved it into my pocket with a trembling hand. The letter felt hot against my leg. I could only speculate about what it contained, but I knew it was not good. I couldn't wait to read it in the latrine as soon as we arrived at the installation.

The air raid siren sounded just as we arrived, and I had no opportunity to slip away to the latrine. For the next two hours, I lugged ammunition boxes from the bunkers to the gun emplacements through the usual barrage of fire and death raining down from the skies. The roar of exploding bombs and the answering fire nearly tore my eardrums apart.

When the raid was over, we were given an hour to rest, and we all collapsed on the ground right where we stood. I pulled the letter from my pocket. It was from Lily, as I had suspected, and it was dated Wednesday. My face and forehead were aflame as I read what she had written:

Dearest brother,

It hurts me to write this to you, but I know that the agony of not knowing would probably be even worse.

Last night, at 2:30 in the morning, four policemen and two gendarmes showed up at our apartment. They searched it from top to bottom, but they found nothing. So they left. But they took Father along with them.

Mother and I have called on every connection we have, and nothing has helped. We don't know where he has been taken or what has happened to him. We are beside ourselves.

We are continuing our efforts, but in the meantime, Maier, we don't want them to find out about our connection with you. It will only make things worse for all of us.

Maier, this is not the first time Father has been in trouble, and he has always found a way of coming through safely. We have not given up hope, and we don't want you to give up hope either.

We will contact you as soon as we hear any news. In any case, one of my friends will come to the cigarette kiosk next Wednesday evening at seven. Her name is Irina, and she will be wearing a red hat. She will be our only contact for the time being.

Your devoted sister,

Lily

I folded the letter carefully and put it in my pocket. I felt totally helpless, which indeed I was. All I could do was wait.

The next week passed with excruciating slowness. Day and night, I could think of nothing but my Uncle Moshe imprisoned and Aunt Bella and Lily running from door to door in desperate futility.

Finally, Wednesday arrived, and with it, Irina in her red hat. She was waiting for me beside the kiosk, as arranged, smoking a cigarette. She gave me a speculative look, as if wondering, so this is the new brother?

"Irina, I assume," I said.

She nodded.

"What is happening with the Gaspars?"

She released a stream of smoke. "The news is not good."

"Tell me!"

"Miklos is in serious trouble. It involves a family from Hust who somehow managed to relocate to Budapest before the Jews were confined to the ghetto. It turns out they had forged documents . . . and the authorities suspect that those documents were supplied by our own Miklos."

"How do they know?"

Irina shrugged. "They suspect. That's as good as knowing, isn't it?"

"How are Mrs. Gaspar and Lily holding up?"

"It's hard to say. Lily is still free to come and go as she pleases."

"Oh?" I said, alarmed at the implication. "And Mrs. Gaspar is not?"

Irina looked away. "Bella Gaspar has been arrested."

"Mrs. Gaspar was arrested?" I said, stunned. "Lily is all alone? I can't believe it."

"Lily will be fine," said Irina. "She is a capable girl. Here." She handed me a package. "That's for you. From Lily."

I took the package reluctantly. "Listen to me, Irina," I said. "Tell Lily that this is the last time I am accepting a package from her. She has to take care of herself. I have everything I need here. Let her worry about herself, not me." I had one hundred and twenty-three pengos stashed away in my pocket, my entire fortune. I pulled out a one-hundred-pengo note and gave it to her. "Give this money to Lily from me. I insist that she take it. Tell her to be strong. Tell her not to give up hope."

Irina took the money and nodded. "I'll tell her."

"Irina."

"Yes?"

"Thank you very much for coming here today. I know it couldn't have been an easy thing for you to do."

Her eyes softened. "You're very welcome, Maier. These are hard times for everyone. I'll see you again in a week."

But Irina did not come the next week, nor the following week either. Nor did anyone else come with word from Lily about her parents. There could only be one explanation. Lily herself had been arrested. I knew it without a doubt, and I wept tears of frustration. How could I help them? What could I do for them?

There was only one answer. I could pray for them. But when I started to pray, I found myself complaining to the Almighty. How could He allow such a thing to happen? Didn't our Sages tell us that "the Holy Blessed One rewards all those who work faithfully for the public good"? So where was the reward for the Gaspars? Who was more dedicated to the public good than the Gaspars?

My complaints, of course, did not do me much good. They only helped to disturb me more. As always, I made my peace with the Almighty, granting Him the privilege of acting without consulting with me or justifying Himself to me. Then I prayed for the Gaspars. I don't know how much my prayers helped them, but they definitely helped me get through those days of uncertainty.

One Sunday morning, I was standing on the assembly field of the camp, thinking about the Gaspars, which I did during all my spare time. Sundays were generally special, because we did not work. In my present situation, however, idleness was driving me to distraction. As long as I was busy building earthworks, lugging ammunition or dodging bombs, I didn't have time to think much. But on Sundays, the torture was almost unbearable.

I heard a low whistle behind me and turned around. It seemed to be coming from a woman on the other side of the fence. Although I caught just a glimpse of her between the fence posts, I was almost sure it was Irina. My intestines cringed. Much as I had wanted her to come, her actual arrival filled me with dread. What would she tell me? I hurried through the gate, half-hoping I was mistaken, but I was right. It was Irina. I recognized her even without her red hat. She turned and walked away until a small shed obscured her. I waited a minute or two and followed.

"Hello, Maier," she said as soon as I stepped behind the shed. "I can only stay for a minute. As you probably guessed, Lily was arrested two weeks ago. But she is all right. Last Thursday, she and her mother were released from jail. I have a letter for you."

She handed me an envelope, which I slipped into my pocket.

"How are they?" I asked. "How about Mr. Gaspar? Any word? Why didn't they come themselves?"

"They may come on Friday. Read the letter. Good bye, Maier."

She glanced around the corner of the shed and then walked away with a deliberately leisurely gait.

I tore open the letter. It was in Lily's handwriting.

Dearest brother,

As you can well imagine, these last two weeks have been a harrowing experience. Knowing that you were so worried just made matters worse. They accused us of forging documents, but they really had no evidence, and so they released us. We are hoping they will release Father as well. We've made some investments in that direction, and we hope they will soon pay off.

We would have come to visit you today instead of sending Irina, but we are still too weak to travel. We also didn't want you to see us all bruised and beaten. Perhaps in a few days, we will be able to cover the marks of our imprisonment with make-up.

Your devoted sister,

Lily

When they came to visit me on Friday, I breathed a long sigh of relief to see them at last. They were more battered than

I could have imagined, and even the heavy make-up did not help much to conceal the welts and the bruises. They walked as if every step were painful.

I listened to their story with a mixture of dismay and admiration. For a long time, the Gaspars had been working tirelessly to secure Budapest residence permits for refugees from other parts of Hungary and abroad. If they could not secure residence permits, they tried to get Swedish passports instead. They also helped refugees with travel arrangements as well as food and lodging. All these fairly aboveboard activities, which produced only limited results, camouflaged their deeper involvement in the large-scale production of forged documents. It was an extremely dangerous enterprise, real cloak-and-dagger, and as I listened to some of their stories, I felt the hairs bristle on the back of my neck.

Several months before, they had procured forged documents for a family in Hust and brought them over to Budapest just before the Jews had been confined to the ghetto. The family had a number of small children, and Uncle Moshe found them a small but decent apartment. Aunt Bella and Lily brought them food for weeks.

Everything was going well, until one day the family was arrested and deported to Germany. Someone had apparently informed the authorities that their papers were forged. Suspicion fell on the Gaspars because of their close association with the family, and they were arrested and tortured. Aunt Bella and Lily spared me the gory details of the torture; the story itself was gruesome enough.

The Gaspars denied all knowledge of any forgeries. They claimed they had only offered the family humanitarian assistance, and they held fast to their story despite being imprisoned and tortured. Lacking incriminating evidence, the police released Aunt Bella and Lily, battered and bloody but still breathing.

"You should have come earlier," I said after they finished.

Aunt Bella shook her head. "We really couldn't have come all the way to Budakalasz even if we wanted to. We just didn't have the strength."

I couldn't argue with that. "So at least you had a good rest," I said. "A few quiet days at home would do anyone a world of good."

I saw Aunt Bella and Lily exchange a quick look.

"All right," I said, "what are you hiding from me?"

"Nothing really," said Lily.

"You are making me feel like a child who has to be protected from hearing things that upset him. I want to know. Believe me, I can handle it."

Lily stole a glance at her mother, who shrugged and looked down at her fingernails. "We didn't quite stay at home all the time, Maier," said Lily. "We had several appointments to keep."

"Appointments? What sort of appointments?"

"Well, with our engravers, for one."

My eyes widened in shock. "Engraver? You mean document forger?"

Lily nodded. "I guess that is one way to put it."

"But you've just been released from jail! If they catch you again, even on suspicion, they'll shoot you! What are you doing?"

Aunt Bella ran her hand over her forehead. "What can we do, Maier? Wait until the coast is clear and everything is safe? What about the people that need these documents to avoid deportation? Should we ask them to wait as well? All we can do, Maier, is be as careful as we can, and pray that we don't get caught. We have only two choices, to do something or to sit on our hands. If we choose to do, we must continue as long as there are people who need our help."

"But can't you at least wait until Uncle Moshe gets out?"

"We really can't, Maier," said Aunt Bella. 'The people need the documents right now."

"And what if you were still in jail?"

"Either they would find someone else, or they would be deported, and at least some of them would die. Simple as that."

Lily forced a nervous laugh. "Don't be so somber, Maier. It's not as terrible as it sounds. We've been doing this for a long time, and there is usually no problem. Hey, Maier, you may need papers yourself, one of these days. Wouldn't you want us to get them for you?"

"Not if it means risking your lives."

"It's easy to say that now, Maier," said Aunt Bella. "But should you ever face deportation to Germany, should you ever feel your life threatened, those papers will be worth everything to you. I hope you never find out, Maier. But if you ever need them, we'll get them for you. I promise."

There was no point in further argument. From her perspective, she was right. But it was a very heroic perspective. I felt humbled in their presence.

A week later, Uncle Moshe was released from jail and taken straight to the hospital. On Sunday, our day off from work, I took the risk of leaving camp and going to visit him. I hardly recognized him as he lay there swathed in bandages with every exposed patch of flesh bruised and bloody beyond recognition. He winced and groaned with the slightest movement, as if every bone in his body were broken. Only his spirit was whole.

"Hello, Maier," he said. "You're looking good. I wish the same could be said about me."

I couldn't help but smile. "At least, you're alive. I'd just about given up hope."

"Never give up hope. Especially not now, with the end of the war in sight. We just have to hang on a little while longer. The Russians are no more than a couple of months from

Budapest, according to what I hear. If Horthy surrenders, as expected, it could be over in weeks or even days."

"It is hard to believe," I said.

"Look, Maier, this thing can't go on forever. It has to come to an end sometime, and it looks like that time is coming fast. For Hungary, at least."

Back in the labor camp, similar rumors were flying. One of the officers had confided to a few men that Horthy would soon surrender and bring the war to an end. The rhythm in the camp changed. Work details were shortened or canceled altogether. Everyone waited.

The following Sunday, anticipation of an imminent armistice roiled the camp. Forced labor was about to become an embarrassment, and all of us, officers and men alike, tried to go through the motions of normalcy. The usually lax camp security was practically nonexistent, and I took advantage of the situation to slip away again to visit Uncle Moshe in the hospital.

It was a blustery October morning, and a cold wind was blowing as I nonchalantly strolled away from the camp. I boarded a bus a little more than a kilometer away from the camp, just to be extra cautious. The Sunday commuters sat impassively, some reading newspapers, some staring out the window. There was very little conversation. Change was in the air, and everyone was waiting.

Aunt Bella and Lily were at Uncle Moshe's bedside when I arrived. They had expected that I would come, and they had brought breakfast for all of us. I was pleased to see that they both looked much better; even Uncle Moshe seemed somewhat improved. Were they further along, I wondered, in the healing process? Or had the spirit of impending freedom invigorated them? Probably both.

It is ironic how we measure happiness in different times and under different circumstances. Our reunion was an occasion of transcendent joy on that October morning in Budapest. And where were we? Sitting in a drab hospital room that smelled of pungent disinfectant. Uncle Moshe, bandaged head to foot, was swallowing painkillers to suppress his groans and grimaces, while Aunt Bella and Lily sat with faded bruises on their faces and welts on their wrists and hands. And I was there as well, with haggard cheeks and in scruffy labor camp garb. Yet we were exhilarated. We were so intensely alive.

The radio at the nurses' station right outside Uncle Moshe's door was playing lovely classical music. About noontime, the regular programming was interrupted by a report that Regent Horthy would be making an important radio announcement to the entire nation at midnight. Whoever could walk or even crawl, immediately gathered around the radio, but no further details were given. We sought out the announcement again and again on other stations, hoping irrationally to glean some additional bit of information from the variations in the phrasing of the report. But we all knew what it meant. At midnight, peace would return to Hungary.

Before I left, I embraced Uncle Moshe, very gingerly, and wished him a speedy recovery and a good night. He held onto my hand tightly and advised me not to return to the camp, but to spend the night in the Jewish ghetto. I promised him I would.

The Pollack brothers from Lower Vishiva lived on Dob Street in Budapest. They had been very kind to me when I first arrived in Budakalasz several months earlier, and I decided to ask them to put me up for the night. It was already dark when I knocked on their door. There was no response. I knocked again, more loudly this time.

"Who is it?" a voice inquired from the stillness behind the door.

"Maier Cahan," I replied.

I heard a chain slip into place, and then the door opened a crack. Berel Pollack's nose and one of his eyes appeared. The eye widened with recognition. The door slammed shut, the chain came off, and the door flew wide open.

"Maier!" he cried out and grabbed me in a bear hug.

"It's good to see you, too, Berel," I said. "Could you put me up for the night? There's going to be an announcement at midnight, as I'm sure you already know."

Berel laughed. "You can have my bed. I'm staying up all night to celebrate. Come, let's join the others."

He led me into the dark salon and switched on the lights. There were some thirty people in the room, mostly young men and women. A few of them blinked in the sudden glare.

"Hey, Maier," Berel explained, "you could've been the police for all we knew. We couldn't exactly tell them we were having a pre-liberation party, could we? Come, Maier, grab a chair, and I'll introduce you to my friends."

We partied the hours away as we awaited Horthy's announcement. We ate, drank, talked, laughed, played parlor games and counted the hours and the minutes until midnight.

At exactly the stroke of midnight on October 15, 1944, Regent Horthy addressed the Hungarian people. The speech was short and fully expected but nonetheless explosive. Hungary had severed relations with Nazi Germany and signed an armistice with the Allies. The war was over. Hungary was at peace.

Berel Pollack's salon erupted with screams, shouts, embraces and kisses even before Horthy was finished. We ran deliriously into the street, where men and women were pouring out of other Jewish houses. The Jewish star emblems nailed to buildings that housed Jewish families were torn down and trampled into the dust. We danced and sang until we were exhausted, later returning to the apartment to bask in the afterglow.

The impossible dream had come true. We were free to pick up those pieces of our shattered lives that we might still find intact. We were free to make our peace with our past and consider our future. The war was over. It was time to wake up from the nightmare. We soared on the wings of eagles.

Back in Berel Pollack's apartment, we switched on the radio for further details. At three o'clock in the morning, an urgent bulletin interrupted the programming: "The following is an urgent bulletin from the Prime Minister's office. Less than one hour ago, Ferenc Szalasi, leader of the Arrow Cross Party, with the support of armored units of the Wehrmacht stationed in Budapest, has assumed the office of Prime Minister. He has relieved Regent Horthy of all duties, cancelled his illegal armistice and removed his restriction against Jewish deportations from the capital. The Regent and his family have been taken into custody and are already on their way to Germany. Hungary will continue to fight alongside our German allies until we achieve total victory, internally and externally."

It couldn't have been worse.

Chapter 10

Freedom had been within our grasp. We had tasted its sweet juices with the tips of our tongues, and then it had been snatched away. In those three heady hours after midnight, we had undergone a complete transformation; we had regained our dignity as human beings. And now, were plunged from the pinnacle of joy into the abyss of the profoundest despair; we were meat for the Nazi grinder once again.

By the next day, it was apparent that Szalasi was every bit as evil as he had claimed to be, and then some. Arrow Cross bands roamed the streets, brutalizing and arresting Jews at will. The resources of the government were mobilized for the immediate deportation of the tens of thousands of Jews crowded into Budapest. The war was grinding to an inexorable conclusion, but Szalasi and the Arrow Cross were prepared to fight for every additional day in which to kill more Jews. Although the Russians were closing in from the east and the Allies from the west, imminent annihilation was staring us in the face.

Even if I had wanted to risk the deportations, I couldn't risk staying in Budapest without papers. On the other hand, I could not venture going out into the street, because if I was arrested or even stopped, I would be shot as a deserter. I had to return to the labor camp as soon as possible, but how? I was stranded in Berel Pollack's apartment, unable to contact the Gaspars, unable to get back to my unit. Berel Pollack brought me news that scattered laborers were being assembled in the center of the city into a special unit that would be returning to the labor camps. If I could join this special unit, I could get back to Budakalasz, but even this was too dangerous to undertake.

Fortunately, there was a Jewish man living in the same courtyard as the Pollacks, who had served as an officer in the Austro-Hungarian army during the First World War. As an honored veteran, he enjoyed privileged status with the Arrow Cross. Mrs. Pollack prevailed upon this Jewish officer to escort me to the assembly point, and I arrived there safely.

It did not surprise me to find ten other men from my battalion, all as frightened as I was. We spent two days in a warehouse waiting for the assembly to be complete, then we returned to Budakalasz.

The camp was not the same one we had left only three days earlier. Security was suddenly tighter than a drum. Guards bristling with weapons patrolled the perimeters of the camp. Officers barked harsh orders to broken-spirited, dead-eyed men.

A captain holding a riding crop met the wayward laborers, myself included, at the gate. Altogether, there were about forty of us. He led us to a large field behind the barracks.

"Line up!" he called out.

We took our positions quickly and snapped to attention. The captain paced back and forth in front of us, continuously whipping the riding crop against his open left hand.

He stopped and turned his glowering face upon us. "So! You Jews were having a party in Budapest, were you? Celebrating the surrender of Hungary to her enemies, were you? Who gave you permission to leave camps?"

He paused and cocked his ear, as if expecting an answer.

"I see no one has anything to say. Well, I have something to say. Hungary will not surrender! We will fight until we achieve victory or die gallantly in the effort. As for all you miserable Jews, you will work your hides off to make sure it happens. And now, to help you get into shape after all your lazy good living, we will begin with some exercise. You will run back and forth across the field. Anyone who runs below full speed will be whipped until there is not a centimeter of skin left on his back. Very well, start running! Now!"

Terrified, I ran as if chased by the devil, which was not far from the case. I ran until my breath came in short gasps and a sharp pain pierced my side, but I did not dare slacken my pace.

After a while, our lieutenant appeared with the rest of the battalion. The captain spoke to him in a low voice and walked away.

"Continue running, you sniveling traitors," the lieutenant shouted at us after the captain left. He turned to the new arrivals. "All of you start running, too. Right now!"

"But, sir," one of the men protested, "we never left the camp. Why should we be punished? We're innocent."

"Innocent? Hah!" he spat out the words. I could not believe this was the same amiable fellow who had taken us to the Jewish community center to collect the clothing. "First of all, there is no such thing as an innocent Jew. Second, from now on you will learn to keep a watchful eye on each other, because if one of you steps put of line, all of you will suffer. Now, enough debates. Start running!"

We ran until we fell to the ground exhausted, and then the lieutenant ordered us to stand up and run some more.

After those dreadful first days, the situation deteriorated. Developments came quickly. The Szalasi government wasted no time in keeping its diabolic promises. Cattle cars were commandeered from all over the country, and the deportations began. We knew our days were numbered.

One day, the lieutenant called together the entire battalion and announced that we were being transferred to Germany, effective immediately. However, since all available rail transport was needed for the ongoing deportations, we would have to walk to Germany. We would be leaving in a matter of days.

I could not believe it. Walking to Germany in the late autumn and early winter was a virtual death sentence, which was undoubtedly how it was intended. What could I do? Escape from the camp was virtually impossible because of the increased security and the constant surveillance by my campmates. And even if I could somehow manage to escape, what would I do without documents? At worst, I would be caught and shot as a deserter. At best, I would be deported.

The next day, we went out to the antiaircraft installation as usual. I looked at those gun emplacement with a perverse nostalgia, thinking I would much rather remain in Budakalasz with the heavy ammunition boxes and the falling bombs than walk to Germany in the freezing rain.

When we came back to the camp in the late afternoon, there were many people, most of them women, waiting near the gates. Somehow, they had learned we were being sent off to Germany, and they had come to bid farewell to their loved ones and give them some provisions for the journey.

It happened so quickly that I hardly had time to think. Lily suddenly emerged from the crowd. She hurried to me, shoved an envelope into my hand and melted into the crowd. I looked up and saw that the lieutenant had noticed that something unusual had transpired. He shouted for Lily to stop, but she was long gone. Instinctively, I handed the letter to a friend in the row behind me. A moment later, the lieutenant was at my side.

"Out of the line, Cahan," he said.

I stepped out and stood at attention, but inwardly, I was quaking. I knew without a doubt what that envelope contained. Aunt Bella and Lily had promised that if I ever faced deportation they would provide me with Swedish identity papers. I was sure Lily had now made good on that promise, using the photograph of me that was on file in the Jewish community center. But if I were caught here in the camp with those papers, it would be a total disaster. I would probably be shot, but not before being questioned under torture about everyone else involved in the fabrication of those papers. I had to prevent the lieutenant from finding those papers.

"What did that girl give you?" he asked. "Show it to me!"

"Girl? What girl? No girl gave me anything."

"Don't lie to me, Cahan." He put his face right up against mine until I could smell the onions on his breath. "I saw the girl come out of the crowd and hand you something. It looked like a letter. Give it to me."

"I'm sorry, sir," I said. "A girl did come over to me a minute ago, but all she did was pat me on the shoulder and wish me luck on my journey. She didn't give me anything."

I saw the lieutenant waver for a moment, and I felt a surge of relief and hope. Obviously, he had not really seen anything change hands. He wasn't sure, only surmising. There was still a chance.

"Empty your pockets," the lieutenant ordered.

A crowd had gathered to watch the unfolding drama. I emptied my pockets and laid the contents neatly on the ground. Then I turned my pockets inside out. "You see? There is no letter."

"All right, you passed it to someone else," said the lieutenant. "To whom did you give it?"

"I assure you, sir. There is nothing. She just wished me good luck, and the next moment you were here."

"I don't believe you, Cahan. I'm going to find that letter, then both you and the worm who is holding it for you are going to regret it for the rest of your very short lives."

I did not dare look at the man to whom I had given the letter, but I tried to catch a glimpse of him from the corner of my eye. During the commotion he had slipped back about two places in the column. He was standing perfectly still, his face drained of color. I could practically hear the thump-thump of his heart.

The lieutenant began his search with the five rows immediately in front of me, and I offered up a silent prayer of thanks to the Almighty. Row by row, he had the men step out of the line and empty their pockets. Meanwhile, I caught the eye of the man holding the letter and signaled to him with a slight inclination of my head. Fortunately, he understood. He moved a little closer to me and, at an opportune moment, slipped the envelope back to me.

After the rows in front of me were searched, the lieutenant turned his attention to the five rows behind me. Altogether he searched thirty men but found nothing. He gave me a nasty look and walked away grumbling. I was reprieved.

As soon as we were back in the barracks, I checked the envelope. It was as I had suspected. Swedish identity papers, showing my picture officially impressed with the seal of the Swedish embassy, my passport to safety and freedom. I returned the papers to the envelope and sewed it onto the inside of my trouser leg.

Late in the evening, a man named Schwartz from Debrecen approached me. "What was in the envelope, Cahan?"

"Nothing," I said.

"Where is it?"

"I read it and threw it away."

"It wasn't papers or something like that, was it?"

"Believe me, Schwartz, it was nothing important."

"For some strange reason, I don't believe you."

I shrugged. "What do you want?"

"Listen to me, Cahan. I'm not just speaking for myself but many others as well. We remember how your aunt and her daughter were so connected in the community center, and we see them come visit you all the time. We think they slipped you some papers to help you escape, but you're not going to use them."

"Why not?"

"Aha!" said Schwartz. "So you admit they gave you papers?"

"I don't admit anything, but what business is it of yours?"

"What business of ours? What a ridiculous question! Because we don't want you to get us into trouble. You try to get away and we'll suffer for it, regardless of whether you make it or not. We'll be watching you like hawks. If we even suspect you're planning to leave, we'll tie you down and report you to the lieutenant. You have no right to endanger all of us."

"So the lieutenant was right, Schwartz," I said bitterly. "He's made all of us into his guards and informers."

It was Schwartz's turn to shrug. "Take it any way you like. We don't want to be punished for what you do."

I gave Schwartz a long, speculative look. "Let's say, for argument's sake, that I have papers. And let's say, for argument's sake, that those papers would help me escape. Shouldn't you let me go? Doesn't the Torah tell us that whoever saves one Jewish life is considered to have saved an entire world? Don't I qualify as 'one Jewish life'? True, you'll be punished if I run away. But you won't be killed. Is it right to deprive me of my chance to survive because you might be threatened with punishment?"

"We all want to survive, Cahan. Do you understand? We all want to survive. Not only you. We're all in this together. All of us. If the Almighty saves us all, you'll be saved, too. Otherwise, you'll go down with us."

There was no arguing with him, and I can't really say that I blamed him. Nonetheless, I was trapped in the camp with my passport to freedom strapped uselessly to my leg.

Despite my fatigue, sleep came late to me that night. I tossed and turned for hours, devising and discarding plans of escape. The kind images of the Gaspars floated before my eyes, and I felt sorry that they had wasted so much effort and expense on procuring those papers for me. There were thousands of people in Budapest who would have given their right arms for such papers but couldn't get them, and here I had them but couldn't use them. What irony!

The next afternoon, there were once again many people, mostly women, gathered outside the gates when we returned to the camp. I saw Aunt Bella and Lily among them. Uncle Moshe had not come.

Aunt Bella came over and handed me a package of food and five hundred *pengos*. Lily stayed back, afraid the lieutenant would recognize her from the day before, but we exchanged smiles. I explained to Aunt Bella that the prospects of my slipping away from the battalion before we set out for Germany were very slim, and she burst into tears. Seeing her mother crying, Lily understood that I would not be remaining in Budapest. Her eyes brimmed with tears, and she bit her lip to keep from crying, too.

Aunt Bella regained a little of her composure. "Maier, there must be a way. We have to come up with a plan."

"There is nothing we can do, Aunt Bella," I said. "We'll be leaving for Germany in a day or two, and I will be watched every second until then. My only hope is that I'll have an opportunity to escape along the way. Maybe I'll be able to slip into a forest and hide. Or something like that. We'll see what comes up. Once I get away, I'll make my way back to Budapest."

Aunt Bella thought about that for a minute, then she nodded her head and smiled. "Yes, you're a resourceful young man, Maier. I'm sure you'll find your opening and grab it. We'll be waiting for you."

"Send my love to Uncle Moshe," I said. "Tell him I think about him, about all of you, all the time. All we have to do is stay alive for a few more months, and it will be over. Just a few more months."

"A few more months," she said pensively. "Just a few more months. In times like these, that is almost like forever."

"Almost but not quite. Good bye, Aunt Bella. I don't know how to thank you for everything you've done for me."

She sighed. "Thank us by coming back safely. We're waiting for you. Good bye, Maier. May G-d watch over you and bring you back to us."

The next day, we set out on our long march to Germany.

Chapter 11

The elements mocked us as we marched four abreast through the suburbs of Budapest and out into the countryside. The clear November sky was a brilliant blue. The air was cool and dry, and the sun felt warm on our backs, even as our hearts shivered within.

By midmorning, we were no longer marching in formation but trudging along in a ragtag column that clogged the roads. Each of us carried on his shoulder a heavy duffel bag that contained food, clothing and all his other worldly possessions, which seemed to increase in weight as the days wore on. We walked and walked, stopping only to eat and to take a brief rest. From time to time, we had to stop to allow local traffic to cross, which gave us a few extra minutes of respite. In the evenings, we slept in warehouses and stables in villages along the way. Thoughts of escape were never far from my mind, but there was nowhere to run. Officers on foot and in slow moving military vehicles maintained a tight security on all sides of the column during the day, and a heavy guard was posted around the perimeter of our nightly quarters.

A few days after we left Budapest, the weather changed abruptly. Smoky clouds obscured the sky, and a cold wind chilled our bones. In the late afternoon, the rains came down in such a torrential deluge, that it seemed as if we were walking underwater. We were caught out in the open countryside, the closest village being several kilometers away, too far to walk in such a rainstorm. We sought shelter under some trees, which was only a marginal improvement, while two officers went off to investigate the options available to us in the immediate vicinity.

Thirty minutes later, they returned with news. A peasant living just down the road had told them about a farm not more than a kilometer down a nearby country lane. The farm had a large main house and many spacious outbuildings, stables and barns. It belonged to a rich lady who lived in the main house with her young daughter. The outbuildings were occupied by farmhands and servants. According to the peasant, there was plenty of room for us to stay until the rains let up. Best of all, we could be there in fifteen minutes.

We arrived at the farm, mud-splattered and thoroughly soaked. The lady who owned the farm welcomed the platoon graciously and had her farmhands clear space for us in two barns. The pungent smell of the cows assailed our nostrils as we came into the barn, but the place was warm, clean and dry. We took off our wet garments and hung them up to dry.

The farmhands brought us fresh straw and thick blankets for bedding. I took the thickest horse blanket I could find and found myself a place in the corner of a stall. I piled the straw in a neat little mound and covered it with the blanket. Then I recovered my wet clothing and hung it on the wall near my makeshift bed. I rubbed myself with the blanket until I was dry, then I wrapped myself in it and lay down.

I burrowed into the fragrant straw, luxuriating in its springy embrace and the rough feel of the blanket against my skin. In my thoughts, I was transported to another night many years earlier when I had also luxuriated in a bed of straw, and I relived all the experiences leading up to that night in loving detail.

I was nine years old when my father decided it was time for me to become serious about my studies. He arranged for his cousin in Sighet, Reb Yosef Leib Cahan, to take me under his wing. I returned home only for the holidays and special occasions. There was no dormitory in Reb Yosef Leib's school, not even a schoolroom, just a group of boys gathered around a table in the Vizhnitzer synagogue. Most of the boys lived in Sighet, but a few like me came from afar and had to make arrangements for room and board. This was not Reb Yosef Leib's responsibility. Each family made the arrangements according to a system called *teg*, the Yiddish word for days. The boy would be lodged with one family but he would eat in the homes of other families, depending on which day of the week it was.

The prospect of leaving Lower Vishiva did not appeal to me at all, but I never would have dared say anything to my father. If he decided this was best for me, then undoubtedly it was. One side of me actually looked forward to living in a big city such as Sighet after spending my whole life in our small village; it appealed to my sense of adventure. Also, being accepted as a pupil of the renowned Reb Yosef Leib Cahan was a high honor that I duly appreciated. But I was still a child, and I wanted to play with my sisters, my friends and the little lamb that always followed me around.

We all stayed up late the night before I left. My stepmother was busy preparing my things and packing them in my little wooden trunk. She also packed a needle and thread for me and showed me how to use them. My younger sisters refused to go to sleep, trying to capture a few more minutes with me. As for my sister Chaya, she solemnly gave me, as a going away present, her hoard of dried carob pits, painstakingly collected over many months and two handkerchiefs she had embroidered herself. I accepted the gifts with equal solemnity, since I appreciated their value.

We got up before dawn the next morning and went to the synagogue. It was still very early when we returned, but the entire family was already gathered around the breakfast table. Fifteen minutes later, my father and I were on our way to the train station.

Sighet was a revelation. Upper Vishiva had always been my idea of a great metropolis, but it was nothing compared to Sighet. Our destination was three kilometers from the train station. Three kilometers in one city! It boggled my imagination. As we walked along avenues far broader than any I had ever seen, I stared at the tall buildings, the factories, and the large stores selling food, clothing and electrical appliances. I saw grand hotels, and I dreamed that my father had arranged for me to stay in one of them. But the dream did not last long. We turned into a narrow street and stopped in front of a fairly large building. A small sign identified it as the synagogue of the Vizhnitzer Chassidim.

My father continued on to a modest house about a hundred meters past the synagogue and knocked on the door. The old lady who lived there greeted my father with cordial formality, then she compressed her lips and gave me a beady-eyed look.

"So this is the boy?" she asked.

"That's him," said my father.

"Well, come on in." She led us into a dim parlor. "Here, sit down. I'll bring you something to eat."

"That's very kind of you," said my father, "but we really don't have time. I must take Maier around to all the places where he'll be taking his meals, and I still have to get back to Vishiva this evening."

She didn't seem very upset that we weren't staying. She led me to a small alcove. "This is where you will sleep."

I surveyed the alcove slowly and carefully, but I could not find any sign of a bed, nor of anything else for that matter.

"Just put your things here," she said. "I'm getting a sack filled with straw. You will use that as your bed. But it won't be ready for tonight. You came a little bit too early."

"That will be no problem," said my father. "Maier can sleep at my sister Esther's house tonight. They'll squeeze him in. He'll be eating there anyway every week."

"Very good," she said. "Come back tomorrow. We'll see what to do."

My Aunt Esther and her husband, Pinchas Halpert, were nice people, but I didn't know them well. Lower Vishiva and Sighet, although just hours from each other by train, might as well have been on different continents for all the contact there was between us. We met only at large celebrations, such as weddings, which did not give me much opportunity, at nine years of age, to bond with close family from distant places.

Aunt Esther received us warmly. The table had been laid out for us, and the food smelled delicious. Sitting next to my father, I relished the exotic experience of dining in the big city in a strange but friendly home. I did not allow myself to think that my father's imminent departure would leave me here all alone to fend for myself. It would have spoiled the moment.

After dinner, my father bid farewell to his sister and her family, and we went out into the street. It was already late afternoon, and I knew he would have to hurry to catch the train back to Vishiva. An old man was selling holy books from a pushcart. My father bought me a new Siddur, and he told me to open it to the flyleaf and write the names and addresses of all the people at whose houses I would be eating during the week and on Shabbos.

"Remember, Maier," he said, "if you can't find an address or if you get lost, ask directions from the nearest adult."

My first day in Sighet was one ordeal after the other. The boys in school poked fun at me mercilessly, calling me a hayseed from the country, which indeed I was. When I finally got away from them at breakfast, I forgot where I would be eating that day. The flyleaf of my Siddur reminded me that on Tuesdays I was to go to my father's niece Leichu Perl at Szinhaz Street 12.

I stood outside the door for fully ten minutes before I worked up the courage to knock on the door. My cousin Leichu welcomed me warmly and showed me to my seat at the table, but I was too overcome with embarrassment to eat anything. I only nibbled at the food she placed in front of me, although I was so hungry I wanted to devour it. I was so nervous that I dropped my fork on the floor several times, but my cousin Leichu very wisely did not comment. She did ask me, however, if I was feeling ill, because my face was flushed bright red.

I returned to class, hungry and dejected, and somehow got through the rest of the day. I couldn't wait to get into my bed, even if it was only a sack of straw, and go to sleep. But it was not to be. The old lady informed me that I could not sleep in her house yet because she still hadn't managed to arrange a bed for me.

What was I to do? I considered asking my Aunt Esther or one of my other relatives to put me up for the night, but I was too embarrassed. Besides, my father had told me many times never to be a burden on anyone. Moreover, how did I know it would be only for one night? What guarantee did I have that the old lady would have a bed for me tomorrow?

Having nowhere else to go, I returned to the synagogue and prepared to spend the night. I spread my coat on the cold floor and curled up on it, but I could not fall asleep. The synagogue was empty and completely dark. The wind penetrated through cracks in the walls and around the poorly sealed windows with a soft moaning sound, and the building creaked with age and cold.

As I lay there listening to the eerie sounds of the night, I recalled hearing the old men of Lower Vishiva say that departed souls return to the synagogue in the dead of night to read from the Torah. They also added, in lowered voices, that if the departed souls find a living person in the synagogue they invite him to come forward and read from the Torah, but that person is doomed to die within the year. Would the spirits come to the synagogue tonight while I was there? Would they ask me to read from the Torah, despite my very young age, and thereby condemn me to death?

For most of the night, the cold and the terror kept me wide awake. I may have dozed off for a short while now and then, but my anxiety did not let me sink into the sweet oblivion of sound sleep. I tossed and turned until I heard the chimes of the city clock strike the hour of three in the morning. Abandoning any hope of falling asleep, I decided to go to the *mikveh*, the ritual bathhouse, that was right next door to the synagogue.

The attendant, a gaunt man with a red beard and a long nose, was just opening the door when I got there.

He gave me a strange look. "And what, might I ask, is a boy your age doing at the *mikveh* at three in the morning?"

"It's a long story," I said.

"At three in the morning, I have time to listen to long stories."

"Well, I live in Lower Vishiva, and I've come here to Sighet to study with Reb Yosef Leib Cahan. The place where I'm supposed to sleep isn't ready for me, so I slept in the synagogue. But it was so cold, I thought I might come down here and warm up in the *mikveh*."

"Do you have parents?"

"Sure. I also have three sisters. My father brought me here yesterday."

"All right," he said gruffly. "Come in and warm up. I won't even charge you anything."

He threw a pile of wood onto the fire and left. A few minutes later, I heard the pitter patter of footsteps, and I felt a new surge of fright. I undressed hurriedly, tossing my clothing neatly onto the bench, and plunged into the *mikveh*. The water was very hot, but at least it offered me a measure of concealment.

I heard the door open and people come in. I heard them conversing about ordinary things, and I was relieved to discover that they were just early risers, not the spirits of the dead.

With my mind set at ease about the source of the footsteps, I became aware of the intense heat of the water, which was more suited to thin-blooded old men than to a warm-blooded young boy. My head suddenly felt as if it would float away. Everything began to spin before my eyes, and I fainted right in the water.

Fortunately, the newcomers saw me and pulled me out right away. They poured cold water over me to bring me back to my senses. When I opened my eyes, I saw the red-bearded attendant looking down at me with concern. He lifted me up and carried me to a bed of towels he had arranged on a bench. Warm, safe and exhausted, I instantly fell into a deep sleep.

When I awoke, it was fully light outside but still very early. I dressed quickly and went to the synagogue for morning prayers. The old beadle was carrying a bundle of firewood when I got there, and I ran to help him.

"Thank you, little boy," he said. "Who are you? What's your name?"

"My name is Maier Cahan from Lower Vishiva."

"Really? From Lower Vishiva no less? You are a long way from home, Maier Cahan. One thing is for sure, I won't have any trouble remembering your name, because my name is also Maier. Are you hungry?"

I nodded.

"Come with me, Maier from Lower Vishiva," he said. "I'll give you a piece of cake and a glass of milk."

From then on, the old beadle and I were fast friends. He took care of me like an uncle, looking after my welfare and feeding me cake and other delicacies. He also let me look into the mystical books he carried with him all the time, although he claimed not to understand a word of it.

After prayers, I consulted the list on the flyleaf of my Siddur and went to another uncle's house for breakfast. I found eating at strange tables just as embarrassing as I had the day before, only this time I forced myself to eat a full meal. If my embarrassment had not diminished, at least my ability to deal with it had improved.

That evening after dinner, I went to the old lady's house to see if I could move in already. For some reason, I cannot say that it surprised me to find the alcove as bare as it had been the day before. The old lady dismissed me impatiently and told me she would have it all arranged the next day. I had no choice but to spend another night on the floor of the synagogue.

I took the old lady at her word and came back the next evening fully expecting to find a bed of fresh straw and a warm blanket near my trunk, but I was sorely disappointed. Nothing had changed.

"Where's the bed?" I asked plaintively.

"Little boy," she said, "do you think straw falls from the sky? It's too heavy for me to carry on my back, and it doesn't fly in all by itself."

"But you promised!"

She arched her eyebrows and looked down her nose at me. "So what have we here? A rude and disrespectful little upstart.

Why would I want to take such a troublemaker into my home?" She pulled a wad of Romanian currency from her apron pocket, peeled off a few bills and handed them to me. "Here, take back the twenty *lei* your father gave me for your upkeep, and go find yourself another place."

She obviously didn't want me there, and I wondered why she had ever agreed to let me into her house in the first place. Probably, I thought, out of a sense of family obligation, because my father was a fairly close relative of hers. But now she had contrived a good excuse for breaking the agreement, and I was out on the street. What could I do?

With a sigh, I retrieved my father's money and put in into my pocket. Dragging my trunk behind me, I returned to the synagogue for yet another night on the hard floor. It seemed I would be making this my permanent place for the night. I was too embarrassed to go to my relatives, and I certainly did not want to inform my father of my predicament. I was supposed to be able to take care of myself. But still, something had to be done. I couldn't continue to sleep on that cold hard floor. I do not remember if I cried myself to sleep that night, but I do remember that my misery knew no bounds. I had nowhere to go. All I could do was arrange a bed for myself right in the synagogue and try to survive for a few months until I went home for the holidays.

Friday morning, I went to the marketplace and bought burlap, a large darning needle and heavy thread. The cost of these materials was twelve *lei*, leaving me just eight *lei* in my pocket with which to buy straw to fill the sacks. I had no idea how much straw cost, but I hoped it would be enough.

The stall in which straw was sold was piled high with tightly wrapped bundles. Seated in front of the stall, a bald little man was reading a newspaper and glancing up every few minutes to see if customers were approaching. He gave me a quick glance and returned to his newspaper.

"Excuse me," I said, "I would like to buy some straw."

The straw merchant lowered his newspaper and gave me second look. "How much do you want?"

"I think one bundle should be enough," I said.

"Help yourself."

"How much is a bundle?"

"Ten *lei*."

"I only have eight *lei*," I said miserably. "Can you open a bundle and take out some straw? I don't have enough money for a full bundle."

The straw merchant smiled at me. "Don't be so upset, little boy. I'll tell you what I'll do. You can have the whole bundle for eight *lei*."

My father had warned me never to spend my last *lei*, but under the circumstances, there was nothing else to do. On the contrary, I considered myself fortunate that the straw merchant was willing to accept eight *lei* for a full bundle. I thanked him profusely and gave him the money. Then I grabbed hold of one of the bundles and yanked it. It only moved a few centimeters. How was I going to drag that heavy bundle back to the synagogue all by myself? As I pondered this difficult question, another customer appeared.

"I need a bundle of straw," he said. "How much is it?"

"Ten *lei*," said the bald little straw merchant.

"Much too expensive," said the new customer. "I can get it for six *lei* on the other side of town."

"Then by all means, you should buy it there. And while you're there, get me a few as well for that price. But in the meantime, if you want, I'll sell you a bundle for eight *lei*."

"Eight *lei*? You must be joking. It's not worth more than six *lei*. But I'll tell you what, to save myself the bother of going to the other side of town right now, I'll give you seven *lei* for a bundle."

"Done."

The customer paid his seven *lei* and dragged off his bundle of straw. I stood there looking at the straw merchant, eyes brimming with tears.

The straw merchant shrugged sheepishly. "That fellow really knows how to drive a hard bargain, doesn't he?" he said. "If it hadn't been such a slow day, I never would have accepted his offer. But now that I did, I think it's only fair that I do the same for you. Here, I am giving you back one *lei*."

I took the money and put it in my pocket. "Thank you kindly," I said. "But I also have another problem. The bundle is too heavy for me. Can you divide it into two bundles? I'll take one with me, and then I'll come back for the other one."

"Sure, I will," said the straw merchant. "And I'll do even better for you. I'll send my son to help you take home the straw. You take one of the bundles, and he'll take the other."

As we walked through the streets, I kept worrying that I would have to give the straw merchant's son something for his efforts, and that would take my last *lei*. But the boy didn't ask for anything, and I didn't offer. I thanked him, and he ran off. I breathed a sigh of relief. I stuffed the straw under a bench and went off to my studies.

After we were dismissed, I spent the better part of the day sewing and stuffing and sewing again until a real bed materialized in front of my eyes. I stretched it out on the ground and lay down, letting its springy softness enfold me. I savored the luxury of the moment, but I did not allow myself to linger in it. It was almost Shabbos, and there was much to do.

That night, I returned to the synagogue from the home in which I had eaten the Shabbos meal. I lay down on the bed I had made with my own hands, and for the first time that week, I fell into a deep, untroubled sleep. Somehow, I knew that the worst was over and that I would make it through my ordeal.

These memories passed through my mind as I lay on the fragrant straw in the barn with the rain battering the roof overhead. I remembered how miserable and forlorn I had felt and how that simple bed of straw had invigorated me. I smiled inwardly at the awful fears that had occupied my young mind at the time and how inconsequential they seemed now. I tried to draw some message of hope from the parallels. I tried to tell myself that no matter how bleak my prospects seemed, no matter how depressing my life had become, tomorrow could bring a complete turnaround. But I didn't believe it. I was marching toward my own death, and I could think of nothing that would save me.

Chapter 12

My eyes flew open, and I sat bolt upright. I had fallen asleep on my bed of straw, but something had awakened me. Most of the other men were napping or just resting quietly. Nothing seemed amiss, and then I realized what it was. The relentless pounding of the rain on the roof had stopped, and the stillness was deafening. It had woken me from my sleep.

The door flew open, and all the lights came on. The lady farmer, her daughter and a group of farmhands came in.

"We're sorry to disturb you, gentlemen," the lady announced. "We've fallen a little behind in our work because of the rain, and we have to catch up. We'll try to stay out of your way as much as possible. Just don't you pay us any attention."

It was, of course, impossible not to pay any attention to them. In a few minutes, the entire place was bustling with activity. Animals were being fed and brushed down, cows were being milked, and all sorts of other farmyard activities were going on. It was impossible to go to sleep, so I sat back against the wall of the stall and tried to think about happier days.

A few minutes later, the farmer's daughter returned and stopped a few meters away. She leaned against the stall and gave me a speculative look.

"What are you thinking?" she asked. "You seem to be off someplace a million kilometers away."

I looked up and gave her a rueful smile. "I wish I were. I was thinking about my parents and my sisters and my little brothers. I don't know who is still alive and who isn't."

"That's so sad. War is a terrible thing, isn't it? People always get hurt in wars. A cousin of mine was in the Army. He was killed in the Ukraine."

Her comparison was ridiculous, but I didn't say anything. What does a soldier dying in battle have in common with children thrown out of their home, packed into a cattle car and sent off to their deaths?

"Can I get you anything?" she asked me. "Do you want something to eat or drink?"

"No, thank you," I said. "I have food in my knapsack. But it's very nice of you to offer."

"How about an extra blanket? It gets a little chilly late at night. Would you like me to bring you another blanket?"

"This blanket here is more than enough," I said. "You're too kind."

I really wouldn't have minded a fresh slice of bread and another blanket, but I had a feeling that this girl spelled trouble, of which I already had more than enough of my own.

"Suit yourself," she said. She gave me a warm smile and walked away.

A little while later, she was back again. This time she brought me a bowl of fresh milk.

"Now, don't tell me you're going to turn down some fresh milk." She laughed and tossed her head so that her hair fell away from her face. "I can almost see you salivating for it."

I ached for that milk, but I said nothing.

"Do you want it or should I take it back?" she teased.

"I want it. But I want to pay you for it."

"Oh, come now," she said. Her eyes twinkled with laughter. She was enjoying herself. "Is that a nice thing to say? Offering me money? Here I go out of my way to do the hospitable thing, and you offer me money?"

"Don't be offended," I said. "It's just the way I've been brought up. My parents taught me not to accept gifts from people I don't really know."

"Well, I wouldn't want you to go against your parents. I'm not that kind of a girl. So, I'll tell you what. Give me ten *filer* for the milk, all right?"

Ten *filer* was one tenth of one *pengo*, a minuscule sum.

I reached into my pocket for some change. "You have a deal."

That was the beginning.

Unfortunately, I was right. The young woman, Marishka, kept trying to become to familiar, and I realized that – dangerous though it would be – I had to escape from this safe haven that was no longer so safe.

My first impulse was to wait for the right opportunity to leave without turning her against me.

I had to be careful and measure every word I said to her. I knew that if I really offended her, she could get me into big trouble. Then my thoughts turned in a different direction. Ever since we had left Budapest, I had been looking for a chance to escape and return to the Gaspars, but nothing had materialized. Perhaps this was my golden chance.

Perhaps I could enlist Marishka as an accomplice in my escape plans. In another few days, we would cross into Germany, and all hope of escape would be lost. This was my chance. Or was it?

"Listen to me, Marius," she said, her voice suddenly serious. "A few hours ago, neither one of us knew that the other existed. But now, my heart tells me that I have to save you from certain death in Germany."

"I appreciate your concern, Marishka, but what can you do for me?"

"I have a plan, Marius." She leaned forward and handed me a key.

I looked at it, then at her. "What is this key?"

"It is the key to your future, Marius. It is the key to life."

"I see." But of course, I didn't.

"There is a tool shed a short distance behind this barn. It is locked with a padlock, and it stays locked until after the winter. There is running water in there and a toilet and an old mattress up against the wall. I've stocked the shed with food and blankets for you, and you can stay there without anyone knowing where you are. I won't even tell my mother."

She paused, waiting for me to say something.

"I don't know what to say," I said. I really didn't.

She smiled. "You don't have to say anything, Marius. Just listen. Later tonight, you will go to the shed and use the key to open the padlock. The third board to the left of the door is loose. Once you are inside the shed, you will move the board aside and reach through to lock the padlock again. Then you will replace the board. Whoever passes and sees the padlock on the outside will never suspect that someone might be hiding inside. That's my plan. Simple but brilliant. What do you say?"

"I agree. Simple but brilliant. How can I ever thank you, Marishka?"

"We'll figure something out, Marius. Right now, we have to save your life.Come outside with me now for a minute, and I'll show you where the shed is."

We went out through an unguarded back door. A dirt path led us to a clearing. Marishka pointed to a small structure nestled among the trees on the other side of the clearing.

"There it is," she said. "Your new home. At least for a while. Do you have the key?"

I touched my shirt pocket. "I've got it. Thank you, Marishka."

She slipped away into the night.

I returned to the back door of the barn and sat down to smoke a cigarette. I had a lot to think about.

My first reaction was exhilaration. At last, here was my opportunity to escape and save my life. In a few days, I could be on my way back to Budapest. But then I realized that it was not so simple. Marishka wouldn't let me go so easily and, if I went without her knowledge, she would turn against me. She could report me and level such accusations at me that no Swedish papers would do me any good. No, clearly I would have to remain on her good side. But if so, would I become her prisoner? Perhaps I could just tell her that I needed to take care of some business in Budapest for a day or two and then I would return. Would she accept that? I doubted it. Clearly, I would have to turn down her offer.

"I'm surprised at you, Maier," I heard an inner voice say to me. "Have you forgotten everything you learned about Jewish law? Don't you know that saving your life overrides just about everything in the Torah? Don't you know that you may even violate the laws of the Sabbath in order to save your life?"

The inner voice was persuasive, but I was still suspicious. Were these arguments inspired by pure motives or perhaps by my base instincts?

After much thought and conflict I finally recognized the identity of the inner voice. It was my evil inclination, or as he is called in the Talmud, the Old Fool. This gave me pause. If staying here was really the right thing to do, why would the Old Fool encourage me to do it?

I remembered that, on that last day in Lower Vishiva, my father had cautioned us always to remember who we were and where we were brought up. I knew I had to resist the Old Fool. The Talmud describes him as a very clever fellow. One day he tells you to do this and the next day he tells you to do that, until little by little he has you completely in his clutches. As long as you live, our Sages warned, don't be sure of yourself. Staying here would be taking a terrible risk. I could see the gaping Abyss opening before me.

I walked back toward the shed, fingering the key in my pocket to make sure it was still there. The farm was silent in the cool night air. I heard the scrunch of my footsteps as they brought me closer to the crossroads of my life. I thought I heard voices calling out to me. "Go back! Don't do it!" I turned around, but no one was there. I was all alone in the darkness. I shook my head to clear it of the voices, and quickened my pace.

Presently, I found myself standing in front of the shed. Although I was standing right in front of it, I could barely make out its shape in the shadows of the trees that surrounded it. I groped for the front door and found it. I groped a little more and found the padlock. I gripped it with my left hand, and with my right, I fumbled in my shirt pocket for the key.

Until that moment, I had been speculating and fantasizing, but now, it was actually happening. The reality of what I was about to do hit me like a sharp blow, and I began to tremble. With great difficulty, I managed to get the key out of my pocket without dropping it. I tried to insert it into the padlock, but I couldn't find the keyhole. Again and again, I traced it with my finger and found the keyhole. Each time, my hand trembled so hard that I could not insert the key. I took a deep breath and waited a few minutes to relax myself. It didn't help. I could not get the key into the lock.

There was no point in standing there any longer. Someone was likely to come by and wonder what I was doing there. I decided to go back to the barn and try again a little later.

As I walked back to the barn, I thanked the Almighty for stopping me at the last moment. I would not come back later, I told Him, but He had to protect me in Germany and get me out of this thing alive. After making this promise, I felt at peace. But I still did not trust myself to stand up against the Old Fool. I closed my eyes and hurled the key into the darkness with all the strength I could muster. Then I breathed a sigh of relief. It was over.

When I slipped back into the barn, everyone was asleep. Only the sounds of snoring punctuated the silence. I lay down on my straw bed and pulled the blanket about my shoulders, but sleep eluded me that night.

Chapter 13

We left the farm just after dawn in order to make up for lost time. I was first on line, eager to be gone before Marishka awoke. Although it didn't make a difference any more, I just didn't want to come face to face with her. We set off at a brisk march, which suited me fine even though I hadn't slept all night, and we didn't stop for breakfast until we reached the village in which we were supposed to have spent the previous night.

How much heartache could have been avoided, I thought, if it hadn't rained yesterday. But then again, perhaps this painful detour would prove my salvation. Although I had come close to succumbing, in the end I had tossed away the key. Surely, I thought, the Almighty would take note of my courageous act and send me a more appropriate opportunity to escape.

The weather steadily deteriorated as we drew closer to winter and to Germany. We shivered in the bitter cold and sloshed through the rain and the mud, but relentlessly we marched on, our dedicated officers intent on delivering their battalion of Jewish slave laborers to Germany on schedule in the waning days of a lost war.

One day, we stopped to spend the night in a tiny village whose name I do not recall. The officers advised us to bid our last farewells to Hungary. Tomorrow, we would be crossing into Germany. Since there was no single place in the village large enough to accommodate the entire battalion, our quarters were divided among three peasants who lived some distance apart. We stopped at the first and a number of men were led off to the loft of the stable. When it was filled to capacity, we moved on to the second, and then to the third. I found myself in the third group.

Once again, security was rather lax. After all, if one of us were to escape, where could we go? He was likely to be picked up within hours and either shot or returned to the battalion and punished. But I was different. I had Swedish papers sewn into my trouser leg, and I was desperate to escape. I knew that it was now or never. Once we crossed into Germany, I was doomed, with or without the Swedish papers. But how was I to escape? I was no longer concerned that the others in the battalion would try to prevent me from escaping. They had watched me carefully for the first week after we left Budapest, and then they forgot about me. But even if I could get away from the stable, where could I go without arousing suspicion? I couldn't just wander around the countryside looking for an opportunity to get back to Budapest. And yet, I had to do something quickly. This was my last chance.

As the men busied themselves settling in to the loft for the night, I dropped my backpack in a corner and went down to sniff around. The days were getting shorter, and although it was still early, the sun had long since gone. I watched the peasants doing their evening chores in the stable yard, and I wondered if I could enlist one of them as an accomplice in an escape attempt. I had the money to pay an accomplice, but how could I trust him not to turn me in after he took my money? The sullen and boorish expressions on their faces were not very encouraging.

Presently, an old peasant staggered into the yard with a heavy bundle of firewood on his shoulder. The other peasants paid him no heed, but I was instantly at his side.

"Let me help you, uncle," I said and grabbed one end of the bundle.

The peasant gave me a gap-toothed grin. "Thanks, young fellow. These old bones of mine aren't what they used to be. Just help me set it down right there up against the wall."

We lowered the bundle to the ground right about five meters from the front door of the stable. A solitary soldier stood in the doorway and watched us. The peasant sat down on the firewood and motioned to me to sit down beside him, which I did. The soldier gave us a quizzical look, then ignored us completely.

"What's your name, young fellow?"

"Maier Cahan."

He shook my hand. "My name is Peter. I own this stable. You'd think that one of these roughnecks who work for me would lift a finger to help me, but they wouldn't even think. Bah, what's the world coming to?"

"I wonder about the same thing."

"They're taking you to Germany, right?"

"Right."

"Tough luck."

"Yeah, pretty tough," I said.

"It's not right to send off a nice young fellow like you."

I shrugged. "Not much I can do about it, is there?"

"Yeah, it sure seems like it. When those government fellows want to do something, little folks like us just get trampled. Take the village council right here. They take away just about everything I produce and give it to the war effort. Why should I give so much to the war effort? Who needs this war anyway? And besides, I have three sons fighting on the front. Shouldn't that be considered giving enough to the war effort? Why should I give more?"

"I hope your sons all come back well," I said. Inwardly, my heart skipped a beat. Old Peter here might just be the answer to my prayers. "Can I offer you a cigarette?"

"Very nice of you," he said. "Don't mind if I do."

We sat together, smoking companionably for a few minutes. In my mind, I was making plans.

He stubbed out the cigarette when it was only two thirds of the way down and put the butt in his pocket. "Did I tell you, Maier, that I also had a son-in-law at the front?"

"No, you didn't."

"Well, I did. He got shot up and came back without both feet and part of one hand. Awful mess, and what good is he now? So didn't I do enough for the war effort? How much more do they expect from me?"

"Take heart," I told him. "The war will soon be over. In the meantime, can I interest you in another cigarette?"

His face broke out in a big smile. He must have been thinking about the large butt he had squirreled away in his pocket, and now he was getting another whole cigarette. He took the cigarette and sniffed it. "Another cigarette," he said. "That's real nice. But you wait here. I'll be right back."

In no time at all, he came back with a cup of fresh milk and gave it to me. "Here, Maier. Drink this. It'll do you good."

I took the cup and handed him a few coins. "Don't be offended, Peter. You and I are both gentlemen, and a gentleman always pays for his drinks."

He mulled over the wisdom of my words and decided to accept them. I drank the milk, then I lit up for both of us and we sat back to enjoy the smoke and talk. Ten minutes later, we were fast friends.

"Peter," I said, "I want you to help me escape."

He sat bolt upright and glanced quickly over both shoulders. "Are you out of your mind?"

"I'll pay you two hundred *pengo*."

"Two hundred *pengo!*" he gasped. The size of the sum literally took his breath away.

"That's right," I said. "And you really have to do very little for it."

He took a deep breath and released it slowly. "Go ahead. I'm listening."

"Listen to me, Peter. I have Swedish papers. All I need to do is get away from here and get to a train. Once I'm on the train, I'll be fine. Does the train pass anywhere close by?"

"There's a station in the next village. A train departs at 12:45 tonight."

"Excellent. And how far is the station?"

"Four and a half kilometers."

"Wonderful. All I need you to do is guide me to the station. Nothing else. For that, I'll give you two hundred pengo."

He squinted his eyes and chewed his knuckles. "And how are you going to get out?"

"I'm not sure yet. I'll think of something."

"I'll tell you how. Make you bed near the hatch in the hayloft in the back of the stable. I'll put a ladder up against it. When I see that the coast is clear, I'll whistle twice. Wait till you hear me whistle, and then climb down. After you're down, go to the old branchless tree about fifty meters down the path. You can't miss it. I'll take the ladder away and meet you there."

"Good," I said. "Better than good. Excellent."

"It's almost eight o'clock now. We'll leave at eleven. That should give us plenty of time to get there. Let's just hope for good weather."

"Great. I think this is going to work. Thank you so much, Peter."

"You're very welcome, Maier. Believe me, I'm not just doing this for the money. You're a good boy, and I don't want anything to happen to you."

We parted with a handshake and a promise to meet at eleven. I was ecstatic. I went up to the loft and sought out the hatch. A few men were sitting nearby and talking. I squeezed by and placed my backpack on the ground right near the hatch. Then I lay down and pretended to sleep.

All the men were tired after a long day of marching, and within a half-hour, they were all fast asleep. I sat up and looked around. Essentially, I was all alone.

First, I retrieved my Swedish papers and three hundred *pengo*. I sewed the papers into my cap and put the money in my back pocket. Then I opened my backpack and took stock. I kept my *tefillin* hidden in a hollowed out loaf of bread, and I made sure it was still there. I also had shaving powder so that I wouldn't have to use a razor on my face hair, under-shirts, socks, a few simple toiletry items and some food. I closed the backpack and leaned back to wait. It was a long time till eleven, and I couldn't afford to fall asleep.

Maybe twenty minutes later, I heard the ladder scrape against the outside wall and the pitter-patter of feet climbing up. I opened the hatch a crack and looked out. It was Peter clambering up barefoot.

"Maier!" he said to me in a hoarse whisper. "I can't do it!"

"Why not?" I whispered back.

"The officers just came into the house and warned me and the wife that anyone helping one of you boys escape will be shot on the spot. It's too risky, Maier. I like you, but not enough to risk my life for you."

"What if I add fifty *pengo*? Two hundred and fifty *pengo*!"

He shook his head. "I wouldn't do it for five hundred. Not even for a thousand. I won't risk my life."

"But listen, Peter, I'll be so careful," I pleaded desperately. "There's really no risk. You don't even have to walk with me. Just walk far behind and watch me to make sure I don't get lost. If I get stopped, you can just disappear. And I give you my solemn word, if I'm questioned I will not say a single word about you. So you really have no risk, you see?"

"No, Maier, I don't see. All I see is risk. I'm sorry. I would love to help you, but I can't."

He started back down the ladder, but I grabbed his hand.

"Wait a minute, Peter. All right, all right. I understand. I really do. But help me out just a little bit. Draw me a map and watch me for a half-kilometer or so. Leave the ladder here, and give me the all clear whistle. Will you do that? I'll give you one hundred *pengo* for doing it."

He scratched his chin and considered my offer. "All right, Maier. I'll do it. I'll leave the map for you in the old branchless tree a few minutes before you come. I'll leave it right in the notch. You'll find it right away."

I wanted to hug him. "Peter, you're a prince," I said. "One more thing. Since I'll be going myself, let's move the departure time up one hour. I think I should leave by ten o'clock. That will give me some extra time in case I get a little lost."

I gave him the hundred *pengo*, and he left. I looked around. Everyone was still snoring peacefully. No one had seen Peter or heard us speak. My nerves jangled with tension. One hour. I had to wait one more hour, and then the ordeal would begin. I closed my eyes and prayed to the Almighty.

I became so absorbed in my thoughts and prayers that the sound of Peter's two sharp whistles startled me. With bated breath, I waited a few minutes to ascertain if the whistles had aroused any suspicions, but apparently, they hadn't. The silence of the night remained undisturbed. I crept to the hatch and nudged it open. The ladder was in place. I looked up at the sky. A thin cloud cover shrouded the moon, but there was enough light left to guide me to my destination.

With my backpack firmly in place, I descended the ladder ever so slowly, terrified that a loose or squeaky rung would give me away. Once my feet were planted firmly on the ground, I adjusted my backpack and looked around. I saw a man standing back among the trees, and I felt my stomach turn to ice. Then he raised his hand and waved, and with a sigh of relief, I realized it was Peter. I waved back and set off down the path.

The old branchless tree was exactly where Peter had said it was. It was an ancient remnant of jagged oak, a large piece of driftwood jutting from the bare ground, twisted and tortured by time and the elements. There was a sharp notch right down the middle, as if it had once been struck by lightning, and in this notch, I found my map. It was a surprisingly good map, clearly made without haste. Roads and forks were marked clearly, and landmarks all along the way. Silently, I thanked Peter for his kind heart and the Almighty for sending him to me.

For ten minutes, I walked quickly without looking back. Then I turned around. Peter had followed me at a distance of about forty meters. I motioned to him to go back. He waved to me once, then he walked away. I watched him until he disappeared. I was now completely on my own.

I felt a cold wind blow in from the east, and I shivered and pulled my coat more tightly about my shoulders. The wind carried in more clouds, and the sky grew overcast. Still, I could see the road clearly, and my heart was full of hope. I walked ahead in the stillness of the night. All I heard was the howling of distant dogs and the nagging shriek of the wind.

After about a kilometer, the skies suddenly opened and it began to rain heavily. Moments later, the sharp rattle of hail joined the splatter of the falling rain. I had never realized that rain and hail made so much sheer noise, and I was sure the entire neighborhood would wake up. Within two minutes, it actually started to happen. I saw lights come on in farmhouse windows, and I saw people part their curtains and look out. I huddled forward against the rain and hurried even faster, hoping I would be mistaken for a farmer rushing home before the rain soaked him to the bone.

The storm, however, did not abate, and I sought shelter under some trees by the roadside, drawing back deep into the shadows to avoid being seen by any of the peasants who had been awakened.

Suddenly, I heard many shouts and the sounds of barking dogs. I froze in terror. What could have happened? Had Peter informed on me? Had my absence and his complicity been discovered, all in the last half-hour? It couldn't be. Perhaps someone had seen me from the window and informed the police. That was possible. I covered myself with branches, hoping the dogs would not find me if I were off the ground. And I prayed.

The shouts were much closer now, and through the curtains of rain, I could see a large sheep dog bounding toward me on the road. Ahead of him scurried a lamb, bleating in fright. The sheep dog overtook the lamb just as the peasants caught up with them. One of them lifted the lamb and put it under his coat, and they all ran off in the direction from which they had come. Now, I understood the cause of all the commotion. Obviously, some animals had gotten loose because of the storm, and the peasants had gone out with their dogs to retrieve them. For the moment, I was safe.

I waited under the trees until the rains subsided and all was quiet once again. Then I continued on my journey of escape.

Walking through the stillness of the night, I felt strangely safe. It was as if for these few hours I was completely removed from the war, alone with the moon and the trees and the cold wind. But I knew it was only an illusion. I was not really alone. Just a few dozen meters in any direction, slept people who were my mortal enemies, who would turn me in without a second thought, some of whom would even kill me with their own bare hands. And so, I walked along under cover of darkness, my heart vacillating between misery and hope.

Presently, I came to a fork in the road. It had been clearly marked on Peter's map, and I was expecting it. I was to take the fork on the right, which would eventually bring me to a well by the roadside. But to my dismay, the road forked into three roads, not two as Peter had marked. Which was I to take?

I looked closely at Peter's map and decided that the road on the left was clearly not the one. The other two roads, however, were fairly close together and both on the right side. I could not tell which was the road Peter had indicated.

Finally, I chose the middle road, because it seemed better paved. I reassured myself that I had enough time to make a mistake, retrace my steps and still get to the train on time. It was a good thing, I told myself, that I had left an hour earlier and given myself a little extra margin. I was still fine.

It quickly became apparent I had made a poor choice. The better paving that had inclined me in its favor disappeared after two hundred meters, and the road became a dirt track that was now a river of mud. Several times, I had to wade through puddles as large as small ponds. I should have turned back right away, but I couldn't be sure, and so I was drawn deeper and deeper into this detour. I kept looking for the well that would vindicate my choice, but it never appeared.

After twenty long, mud-splattered, nerve-wracking minutes, I retraced my steps and returned to the fork in the road. This time, I took the road on the extreme right, and within a few minutes, I was rewarded by the sight of the well by the roadside, exactly where Peter had marked it. I drew some water from the well and drank some. I used the rest to wash some of the mud off my clothing. I couldn't very well come to the train station covered in mud. I looked at my watch. It was 11:45 already. I had wasted a lot of time, and I was still far away from the station. I had to hurry.

I lit a cigarette and continued walking, wet, cold and miserable. Just then the Old Fool decided to engage me in conversation. "So, Maier, what do you have to say for yourself now?" he asked. "Will you finally admit you were wrong? You could have been lying on a comfortable bed back in that farm, sleeping peacefully under a warm blanket, your stomach full, a roof over your head. And look where you are now! Was it worth it?"

I didn't respond.

"What's the matter, Maier?" he persisted. "Your silence is admission."

I remembered a story I once heard about the sainted Ruzhiner Rebbe. He was once incarcerated in a Czarist prison, and the Old Fool came to him and tried to get him to blaspheme. "I always wondered why you're called the Old Fool," the Rebbe told him. "Old I understand, since you've been around such a long time, but why are you called a fool? You actually seem to be quite a clever fellow. But now I understand. I am here in this wretched prison because I had no choice in the matter, but what are you doing here?"

I was debating with myself about what I should tell the Old Fool when I suddenly heard a loud shout, "Stop!"

This was not the Old Fool's voice. I stopped in my tracks and turned slowly around. A man was running after me, waving his arms and shouting, "Stop! Stop!"

I didn't know if I should stand still or run for my life, but I decided to take my chances. He didn't seem to be from the police. He pulled up huffing and puffing and gave me a friendly smile.

"Hey, buddy," he said. "I saw you smoking a cigarette, and I thought you might be able to help me. My kerosene lamp went out in the wind, and I don't have any matches in the house with which to relight it. I saw you smoking a cigarette, and I thought you might be able to spare a few matches."

"Sure," I said. "No problem at all." I gave him most of my matches. He thanked me profusely and left.

I didn't know how many more crises my nerves could handle, but ten minutes later, thankfully, I could already hear the steam whistles of the trains in the distance. In another fifteen minutes, I arrived at the station. It was 12:35. Ten minutes to spare.

I wanted to buy a ticket to Budapest, but I was afraid to do it. This was a very remote little village, and not many people from there traveled to Budapest. A mud-splattered stranger arriving after midnight to buy a ticket to Budapest would surely have raised eyebrows. Instead, I bought a ticket for Sopron, intending to switch there for Budapest.

On the train, I chose a window seat across from a woman traveling with two small children. I took my Swedish papers from my cap and slipped them into my pocket. Then I hunkered into the corner, pulled my coat over my head and feigned sleep. The woman seemed oblivious to her surroundings. The children looked at me with curiosity, but they were soon asleep on their mother's lap. So far so good.

The train left a few minutes late. It started with a hiss and a jerk, and soon it was rumbling slowly through the countryside. The next stop was in a tiny hamlet of which, of course, I had never heard. It seemed to consist of the train station and four houses. Surprisingly, a fair number of people boarded from the hamlet, all of them farmers. Though half-closed eyes, I watched them come on. Some of them carried baskets of fruits or vegetables, some carried flats of eggs, and some carried live chickens. They were probably going to the market in one of the larger towns. They made a lot of noise, and I was grateful for it. With them around, I was less conspicuous.

I remembered the first time I was on a train, when my father took me to Sighet at nine years of age. I remembered watching everything with fascination, everything was so new, the conductor collecting the tickets, the scenery rushing by outside my window, farmers bearing produce to market, along with groups of men playing cards and drinking beer. One thing was different, though. Almost all the passengers on that train from Lower Vishiva to Sighet had been Jewish. Now, I was the only Jew, and if that fact were discovered, I would be finished.

The next station was much larger, although I did not recognize that name either. More people boarded the train. The seats began to fill up. Then three gendarmes came onto the train and began checking papers. I was frightened out of my wits, but I tried to keep my sentiments off my face. I closed my eyes and pretended to sleep.

After a few minutes, I felt a tap on my shoulder. I opened my eyes and saw a gendarme leaning over me.

"Papers, please," he said.

I yawned and reached into my pocket with a great show of nonchalance. Without saying a word, I handed the papers to the gendarme and closed my eyes again. A moment later, there was another tap on my shoulder.

"Your papers, sir," said the gendarme. He tipped his cap and continued down the car to the next passengers.

I wiped a few beads of sweat from my forehead and leaned back, emotionally exhausted. Things were beginning to look up. I had made it from the stable to the train with much difficulty but without mishap. And my papers had passed their first test. All I had to do now was get off in Sopron and transfer to Budapest. The worst was over.

Or was it? Just as the gendarmes were finishing at the back of the car, two border police came on in the front of the car and started checking papers all over again.

The conductor stood by impatiently as the border police began their inspection, one of them working the right side of the aisle, the other the left. The passengers fidgeted but did not protest. They presented their papers, and the border police checked them more thoroughly than the gendarmes had done. As they came closer to me, I shook with fear. Still, I closed my eyes and feigned sleep.

I smelled the alcohol on the policeman's breath as he leaned over me. He grabbed my arm and shook me awake.

"Let me see your papers," he demanded.

"Of course," I said and handed him the papers.

He examined them carefully, then he looked at me closely and back at the papers. He called his partner over, and they huddled over the papers in close scrutiny.

"What is your name?" the first policeman asked me.

"Markus Karlsborg." That was the name on my papers.

"And where were you born?"

"Uppsala. It's a university town not far from Stockholm. I am a Swedish citizen, but I've lived in Hungary most of my life."

"Are these your papers?"

"Certainly," I replied with a confidence I didn't feel. "Don't you see my picture on it?"

"What are you doing here?"

"I am on my way to Sopron, and then to Budapest. I have business there."

"I'm sure you do. What sort of business?"

"Wholesale produce and logging."

"And what are you doing here in this district?"

"Visiting family."

He pursed his lips and slapped the papers repeatedly against his palm. Then he shoved the papers into his pocket and pointed to me. "Get your bags and come with us."

"But I am a Swedish citizen!" I protested.

He gave me a look of pure disdain.

"Come!"

Chapter 14

They brought me to a room in the rear of the train station. I felt my stomach drop as the door slammed behind us. The room was bare, except for a metal desk, two chairs and a pot-bellied stove that gave off some faint heat. The air was heavy with stale cigarette smoke. There were no windows.

One of the policemen leaned back against the desk, while the other sat down on a chair. I remained standing in the middle of the room, holding my backpack.

The policeman leaning against the desk took out a cigarette and stuck it in his mouth. He gave me a searching look, then he struck a match on the sole of his boot, lit his cigarette and blew a stream of smoke in my direction.

"My name is Lieutenant Korosi," he said. "My colleague here is Sergeant Heves. It is a cold night, and we would like to finish with our business quickly and go home. We know exactly what you are doing here. We know that you are a spy. So why don't you just tell us everything we need to know and save us all a lot of trouble?"

I was stunned. A spy? Me?

"Sir," I said, "there has been some mistake. I am a Swedish citizen, an ordinary businessman trying to make a decent living. You saw my papers. I am no spy."

The lieutenant pulled my papers from his coat pocket and glanced at them. He laughed. "These are papers? These are worthless scraps!"

He walked over to the stove, open the door and tossed my Swedish papers into the flames. I groaned. So much for all the effort the Gaspars had invested into getting me those papers. So much for my chances of escaping. But then I saw the bright side of what had just happened. If I was really going to have to contend with a charge of espionage, I was much better off with the papers destroyed. A little checking would undoubtedly reveal them as forgeries, and that would look terrible for me. But looking at the bright side only goes so far. My world had turned black. There was no way out.

"Empty your pockets," said the lieutenant.

I immediately removed all the contents of my pockets and put them on the desk. The lieutenant immediately focused on the wad of bills I had taken from my back pocket. He snatched it up and counted it.

"Two hundred and seventy *pengo*!" he exclaimed. "Two hundred and seventy *pengo*! Look at this, the man's is walking around with a small fortune. He has to be a spy. Sergeant, check his backpack."

The sergeant emptied my backpack onto the desk. He picked up the bread, sniffed its staleness and tossed it back into the backpack. I breathed a sigh of relief that he had not investigated more closely and discovered my *tefillin* that were hidden inside. The sergeant continued poking through my things. He checked my underwear and toiletries. He pulled out my small canister of shaving powder and tossed it to the lieutenant, then he went to stand behind me.

The lieutenant examined the powder. He stuck his finger into it, stirred it around and lifted it gingerly to his nose. He grimaced at the smell.

"What is this stuff?" he said.

"Shaving powder, sir," I replied.

"Shaving powder? What's that?"

"I have sensitive skin, and I can't use a razor. The powder removes the hair without using a blade."

"A likely story. You have an answer for everything, don't you? A real clever fellow. Well trained, too. But I don't believe you. This powder must be some kind of material used for sabotage or sending secret messages. Look, why do we have to play this cat-and-mouse game? We've caught you. The game is up. Just come clean and tell us what we want to know. Make life easier for all of us?"

"But sir, this is such a terrible mistake. I'm not a spy. I am innocent."

The lieutenant sighed. "What was you name again?"

"Markus Karlsborg, sir."

"No, not that name. Your real name."

"But that is my real name, sir," I insisted.

I didn't feel the blow coming, and it struck me across the back of the neck with a head-snapping force that sent me sprawling to the ground. My head spun, and I felt waves of darkness lapping at my consciousness. As I shook my head to clear it, the sergeant grabbed my shoulders in his two beefy hands and pulled me to my feet. The lieutenant stubbed out his cigarette in an overflowing ashtray, and in one swift motion, he drove his right fist into my abdomen.

Never in my life had I experienced such an explosion of pain. My breath was driven out of me, and I gasped for air like a fish squirming on the sand. I felt as if my heart, my lungs, all my internal organs were about to burst, and I doubled over in agony. But even as the fist in my abdomen bent me forward, the lieutenant's left fist connected with the side of my face and sent me flying back into the sergeant's arms.

The sergeant tossed me to the ground and kicked me repeatedly until I fainted. A splash of cold water on my face brought me back to my senses. Once again, the sergeant grabbed me by the shoulders and pulled me to an upright position.

"So, are you ready to talk, my dear spy?" asked the lieutenant.

"But I'm not a spy!" I protested.

The lieutenant's face clouded with anger, and he punched me full in the face and followed with a barrage of jabs to my face and body that left me bruised and bleeding and numbed with pain. The sergeant grabbed me by one shoulder, spun me around and kicked and pummeled me until I lost consciousness again.

The sounds of their voices penetrated the blackness that enveloped me, and I had the presence of mind to keep my eyes closed and not let them know I was back. This gained me a few additional minutes of rest on the cold floor, each of which was incredibly precious to me. But good things don't last forever. The sergeant poured a bucket of water over my head and pulled me upright again. Instinctively, I contorted my body to protect myself against the blows that were unquestionably on the way. But the lieutenant had other things on his mind.

"Undress!" he commanded. "Take everything off. Right now!"

I removed all my clothing and stood before him.

"Well, well, well," said the lieutenant, "what have we here? Sergeant, do you see what I see? We have ourselves a Jew. A dirty, stinking Jew."

"Yes, sir, lieutenant," said the sergeant. "I believe you're right. It seems we bagged ourselves a Jew.

The sergeant slapped his thighs and laughed uproariously. Then the beatings resumed. Whenever I felt it couldn't get any worse, the beatings reached new levels of sadism that made me wish for the earlier beatings. Blood streamed from gashes all over my face. My eyes were so swollen I could barely see.

I bent over and retched all over the floor. I hadn't eaten in hours, and the sour taste of bile filled my mouth. The lieutenant sprang back in disgust.

"Where do you think you are, Jew?" he said. "In your own home? You can throw up as much as you want and wherever you want in your own home, but not here. Where are your manners, eh, Jew? It's no wonder people call you dirty, stinking Jews. That's exactly what you are!"

"We should have him clean it up, sir," said the sergeant.

"I agree," said the lieutenant. "But with one twist. Are you listening to us, Jew? Clean up the mess you made. With your tongue! Lick it all up!"

There was not much choice. I got down on my hands and knees and started to lick the vomit off the floor. It was thoroughly disgusting, but I consoled my self with the thought that my *tefillin* were still safe inside the stale loaf of bread in my backpack. It was a small triumph, but it gave me the courage to do whatever unpleasant things were demanded of me. I drove all thoughts from my mind and concentrated on my task.

All thoughts except for one. "Maier, it's me again," said the inner voice inside my head. "I won't say anything. I'll just let you speak for yourself. But just tell me one thing, did you make a mistake? Don't you think you should have stayed on the farm when Marishka made you the offer?"

"No, I don't," I replied, furious that he would appear at such a time and pour salt on my wounds.

"Well, it would have saved your life. And that's no small thing. Look at where you are now. Is this how G-d treats you? You give up a chance to be hidden away by a Hungarian girl, and this is your reward?"

I declined to respond to this attempt to lead me into blasphemy, but his words cut me to the quick. Why indeed was I licking my own vomit off the floor when I had made such a supreme sacrifice?

The answer appeared to me in a flash of inspiration. I recalled the famous story of Rabbi Amnon, a man of extraordinary wisdom and Torah scholarship who lived in Mainz, Germany, during the early Middle Ages. One day, the duke summoned him to the palace and offered him a high ministerial post on the condition that he convert to Christianity. Rabbi Amnon, of course, refused. The duke persisted in his offer from time to time, and on each occasion, Rabbi Amnon refused. One time, after the duke had really put a lot of pressure on him, Rabbi Amnon asked for three days to think it over. As soon as he came home, he regretted his request, which implied that he might indeed consider conversion. He let the deadline pass and refused to see the duke until he was brought there forcibly. In anger, the duke ordered that Rabbi Amnon's arms and legs be cut off. Dying of his wounds, Rabbi Amnon asked to be brought to the synagogue, where he confessed his guilt for stalling before he rejected the duke's offer and composed the beautiful Nesaneh Tokef prayer, which has become the highlight of the High Holiday liturgy.

This, I concluded, was where my guilt lay. I should have rejected Marishka's offer right away instead of vacillating and thinking and actually even going to the shed with the key in my hand. Considering what had happened to Rabbi Amnon, licking up my vomit from the floor was getting off easy. I knew I should be grateful, but somehow I wasn't.

When the floor had been polished to the lieutenant's satisfaction, he ordered me to get dressed.

"So, my stinking Jewish spy," he said. "Have you had enough punishment for one day? Are you ready to talk?"

"Please, lieutenant," I pleaded. "Please believe me. I am no spy."

"You're hopeless. You know what we do for spies? A bullet in the head, that's what we give them. And that what I'm going to give you. Right now. Sergeant, tie him up!"

Before I could even respond, the sergeant threw a rope around me and drew it tight, pinning my arms to my sides. Just in time, I tightened my muscles to give me some extra room; otherwise my circulation would have been cut off.

The lieutenant opened the door. "Let's go!"

The sergeant shoved me in the small of the back, and I stumbled forward into the cold night air. It seemed like forever since I had been brought into that windowless, airless room—like an eternity of suffering. But apparently, it couldn't have been more than an hour or two at the most. I had come a long way from Peter's loft, but the sky was still a deep black.

The station was deserted as they led me around to a brick wall behind the ticket office. The lieutenant pulled a large rag from his pocket and tied it around my eyes.

"It's better not to see," he explained as he secured it in place. "You can still save your life, at least for a while, if you agree to talk."

"I wish I had something to tell you," I said, "but I have nothing. Only that I am innocent."

"Have it your way. Sergeant, prepare your weapon!"

I heard the sergeant cock his pistol. He was in point blank range, not more than a few meters away. I knew I had reached the end of my life. I felt a brief moment of the most profound terror, and then a strange calm. Life was such a struggle. From the moment you come into this world, you struggle and strive, struggle and strive, struggle and strive. It takes effort to get through every day, sometimes in a good sense, sometimes in a negative sense, but always an effort. That is life. Tension. But now all my struggles and striving were over. There was nothing else left for me to do. The tension was over, and I felt at peace. I said Shema Yisrael, reaffirming my undying faith in the Almighty. I entrusted my spirit to His safekeeping, and I prepared to receive the bullet that would send me across from this world to the next.

In those few seconds, as I waited for the bullet to strike my skull, my thoughts turned to Chananiah, Mishael and Azariah, who had been willing to be thrown into the Babylonian furnace rather than worship idols at the behest of Nebuchadnezzar. The Talmud tells us that if they had been beaten, they would have given in. I fully sympathized with that feeling. A bullet was more welcome than the beatings I had endured. At least, I consoled myself, there would be no more beatings.

"Ready!" I heard the lieutenant shout. "Aim! Fire!"

I heard the shot ring out, and I heard the bullet strike the wall about a foot from my head, spraying me with tiny pieces of brick. I could not believe I was still standing, and I thanked the Almighty for the reprieve.

The lieutenant removed my blindfold. "The Lord helped you, Jew. Not your G-d but mine. He saved your life."

"Don't talk to me about your g-d," I snapped. "What kind of a g-d is this who teaches his people to be so brutal? If that's your g-d, forget it!"

The lieutenant must have been a religious man, because my remarks struck home. He looked ashamed.

"I'm not brutal," he declared. "I'm a loyal defender of my country, and you're a spy. Am I supposed to be kind and gentle with a spy?"

"I am not a spy."

"Then who are you?" he flung at me. "And what are you doing here? Don't give me any of this nonsense about Markus Karlsborg from Sweden. Who are you really?"

He had me in a corner. If I ever expected to get out of this alive, I had to come clean. "I want to speak to your superior officer," I said. "I will answer all his questions truthfully."

The lieutenant looked at his watch. "It's five o'clock in the morning. I'll have to wake him. But I will. Sergeant, bring the prisoner inside."

The lieutenant strode off ahead of us, and by the time we came into the office, he was already on the telephone. "Yes, sir . . . Korosi . . . at the railroad station . . . I believe we've caught the spy . . . It seems he is a dirty Jew . . . No, sir. I am not joking. He is standing here right in front of me . . . Well, he says he will only talk to you, sir . . . In a half-hour? . . . Yes, sir. Very good, sir. I will . . . No, of course not . . . Thank you, sir."

For the next half-hour, while we waited, the lieutenant wrote his report, and the sergeant smoked one cigarette after the other. I had a little time to think about what was happening with some clarity, and I realized that I had stumbled into an unfortunate situation. The lieutenant had told his superior officer that he had caught "the spy," not "a spy." Obviously, they had been on the lookout for a spy who was operating in the area, and it had been my ill fortune to fall into their dragnet. They had gone hunting for a spy, and instead they had caught a miserable escapee from a forced labor battalion.

At five thirty punctually, a jeep pulled up out front. The door opened, and in marched a stately officer attended by two aides in plainclothes. The officer had two stars on his shoulders and carried a black riding crop in his right hand. A general, no less.

The lieutenant and the sergeant snapped to attention and saluted as soon as the general appeared. The general responded with a perfunctory salute, then he began to pace back and forth, repeatedly slapping his left palm with the riding crop. His face grew redder and redder as he paced. Suddenly, he spun and struck me across the bridge of the nose with his riding crop. I screamed in agony and grabbed at my face. My nose had ballooned to twice the size, and my hands were instantly covered with the blood gushing from my nose.

"Bad Jewish blood," said the general. "We have to rid ourselves of bad Jewish blood. Very well, talk! Who are you? What are you doing here?"

I took a deep breath to steady my nerves. "My name is Maier Cahan, and I am from Lower Vishiva. Last April, I received an order to report for the draft in Banya, where I was assigned to battalion 110/65 under the command of Marik Istvan. Our battalion was sent to Margaretten. After we finished our work in Margaretten, we were sent on to Siklos. Then we were sent to Budakalasz to work on the fortifications for antiaircraft gun emplacements."

"Get to the point," said the general impatiently. "What are you doing here?"

"Yes, sir. About two weeks ago, we were ordered to go to Germany on foot. I admit it to you right now, sir, that I was not happy about this at all. Believe me, I've worked hard and loyally for the motherland. Ask my officers about it, and I'm sure you'll hear only glowing reports. Ever since Hungary took over Transylvania from the Romanians, life has been very good for us. Our wholesale produce and logging business flourished under the Hungarians. We had deals with important Hungarian companies, such as Veti Alyasc, Nashice and others. I love Hungary. But Germany is a different story. I don't want to speak against the Germans, because I know they're allies of our beloved motherland. Still, I would much rather remain here in Hungary, even if I have to sit in a Hungarian prison. Germany is not for me. So last night, I slipped away in middle of the night and caught a train to Sopron at 12:45. Unfortunately, my escape failed.

Not only that, I was accused of espionage and questioned somewhat vigorously. Believe me, sir, I would never, never do anything to hurt Hungary. That is not how I was brought up. My father always taught me not to toss rocks into a well from which I have drunk. I have only gratitude to Hungary, and I beg you, sir, I beg you will all my heart to let me stay here. Please!"

As I finished speaking, I could no longer control my emotions, and I burst into tears. I wept hysterically, giving vent to all the pain and sorrow and frustration and despair that were crammed into my heart. I wept for the past that had been destroyed and the future that was being taken from me even as I felt it in my grasp. I wept because that was all that was left to me.

The general held me in his stony stare for a few long moments. Then he withdrew into the far corner of the room to consult with his two plainclothes aides. The conference took no more than a minute or two. I saw the general glance in my direction and nod. I shivered with anxiety as the general walked back toward me with slow, deliberate steps, slapping his riding crop lightly against his thigh.

"What is your name again, young fellow?" he said to me. His tone and his features had softened, and I risked allowing myself a tiny bit of hope.

"Maier Cahan, sir. From Lower Vishiva."

"Where is your battalion?"

I told him.

"Get your things," he said. "We'll take you there. You did a foolish thing. You may call it escape, but I call it desertion. Come!"

The sky was lightening as we got into the jeep. The general sat up front with the driver, while I sat in the rear with one of his aides. We drove in silence through villages and towns just beginning to stir from a good night's rest, and I thought to myself that I should at least be grateful that the general had not ordered me shot on the spot. It would have been much simpler for him to do so than to drive me back to my battalion. The day grew progressively brighter as we drew closer to our destination, but the gloom in my heart grew progressively darker. Within hours, I would cross the Hungarian border into German-occupied Czechoslovakia. Within hours, I would be in German hands, Heaven help me.

It was still before seven o'clock when we reached my battalion, and most of the men were still asleep. The general turned me over to my commanding officer and said, "You have to keep an eye on a useful dog, even if he is a stinking Jew. He's all yours." Then he drove off.

As soon as the jeep disappeared, the officer slapped me across the face and showered me with insults and invective. "All right, Cahan," he finally said. "I see you've taken a good beating. They didn't seem to leave any undamaged spot for me to contribute, so we'll let it go at that. Let this be a lesson to you. We'll let this little incident remain our own secret, but Heaven help you if you ever try such a thing again. All right, we'll be getting underway at ten o'clock. Go get some rest. I think you'll need it."

I awoke about nine o'clock and made my preparations. A few minutes later, Peter came into the loft to check on things. When he caught sight of me, especially the condition I was in, he blanched.

"Poor Maier," he said. "I feel so sorry for you." He took a fifty-*pengo* note and put it into my hand.

I refused to accept it. "Please take the money, Peter. You earned it."

"I won't hear of it. Fifty *pengo* is more than enough for what I did. You will need the money more than I will. Don't argue."

I smiled. "Peter, you are a ray of sunshine in a dark world. I'm happy to have met you."

"You know," he confided in a lowered voice, "my mother's grandfather was a Jew. She used to talk about him. I'm pleased I could do something for a Jew."

Wonder of wonders, I thought, that a little drop of Jewish blood would still bring out the finer instincts in a human being. But what had become of this Jewish grandfather's lineage? Hungarian peasants. How sad. But this was the fate I had narrowly avoided with Marishka, and I thanked the Almighty for His kindness.

Peter hurried off and brought me a cup of fresh milk.

An hour later, we were marching to the border. I thought about the Gaspars who were waiting for me in Budapest, and I felt so sorry for them, even more than for myself. At least, I knew where I was and where I was headed. Uncertainty was the worst thing.

Chapter 15

Exhaustion and pain are my most vivid memories of my last day in Hungary. I had hardly slept after my harrowing experiences of the night before, and I don't think there was one spot on my body that had escaped being brutally pummeled during the beatings I had endured. I was not really in condition to undertake the long march to the Hungarian border, but I was not given the choice.

Every step I took was a struggle. I did not have the energy to drag my feet from one spot to the next, and when I did, the pain in my bruised legs and ribs was excruciating. I played little psychological games with myself just to keep going. I set small goals in my mind, taking it twenty-five steps at a time. When that became too overwhelming, I cut it down to ten at a time, to five, to one. I couldn't cut it any lower than that. All I could do was bear my agony in silence and pray that I would make it through the day.

After about an hour of this torture, the captain took pity on me. He allowed me to put my backpack on the wagon and walk beside it. Somewhat later, he gave me permission to ride on the wagon for short stretches.

"I am very grateful to you, sir," I said as I climbed into the wagon. "May G-d bless you and your children."

"I couldn't stand seeing you suffer," he said as he strode beside the wagon. "I'm not a career soldier, you know. What do you think I did in real life before this dreadful war?"

"I have no idea, sir."

"Take a guess."

This was a risky business. "I think you were a doctor, sir," I said. I didn't think anyone would be offended by being mistaken for a doctor.

The captain laughed. "Close but not quite. I was a lawyer. Had I been a doctor, I would be an army doctor now. But the army has no need for lawyers, so here I am, attached to a labor battalion. Still, inhumane treatment goes against my grain."

"That's very kind of you, sir. Perhaps you'd like to come along with us to Germany."

The captain shook his head ruefully. "War is a terrible thing, isn't it?" he said, then he walked away.

For him, it was all over. He had expressed his humanity, done his good deed and lamented the evils of the world. He could now go home with a clear conscience. We, however, were headed for Germany. Still, I will always be grateful to him for his kindness.

In the early afternoon, we were joined by a large contingent of forced laborers, among them numerous Jewish prisoners from the city of Bor. These creatures who once were men, presented the most pitiful spectacle, bruised and beaten, dressed in lice-ridden rags, starving and thirsty, hollow-eyed, without spirit. I saw a few of them drink from a roadside puddle, oblivious to the animal droppings that sat like little islets in the water. Compared to them we were human beings.

In the late afternoon, we crossed into German-occupied Czechoslovakia and were met there by SS guards. After the Hungarian officers formally turned over their prisoners to the Germans, they gathered in formation, saluted and recited the traditional Hungarian affirmation in unison, "I believe in the Lord! I believe in Hungary! I believe in the triumph of the Hungarian people!" Then they spun around and returned to Hungary.

We had entered a new phase in our travails. We were in the hands of the beast, and our future was very much in question. Surprisingly, our guards were soft-faced young boys, probably still in their teens, but their sadistic viciousness was fully mature. They snarled at us and struck us at will, a handful of guards strutting fearlessly among thousands of hapless prisoners.

They gave the order, and the march resumed, northwest towards Germany. After a few kilometers, we reached a railroad junction where long strings of cattle cars awaited us in the dim dusk light. With wild shouts and flailing truncheons, the guards drove us into the cattle cars until we were jammed in tightly. Then they padlocked the doors behind us.

"Stay inside the cars," one of the SS officers shouted. "Violators will be shot!"

We were not accustomed to having people summarily shot for disobeying orders, and some of us did not take this warning very seriously. A man standing near me ventured to stick his head out between the boards. A moment later, I heard a burst of machine gun fire. The man was flung back into the car with the right side of his skull blown away. The bullets sprayed into the car, wounding and killing at random. I dropped to the ground, expecting another volley at any moment, but none came. There was only silence and the moans of the wounded.

The train started with a lurch and gathered speed as it carried us toward our doom. Shortly after we were under way, I felt an itch under my clothing. I scratched and scratched, but it only got worse. Then I realized what it was. Some of the prisoners from Bor were crowded into the car with us and had infected us with their lice.

After a few prickly hours, we pulled to a screeching, grinding halt in the middle of the night. The doors on both sides of the train were flung open, and SS men leaped into the cars from one side and started swinging their pistol barrels left and right. "*Los, los! Heraus!*" they shouted at the tops of their lungs. "Hurry up! Get out!"

In order to get away from the blows of the SS men, we all jumped out the other side of the car, but the welcome that awaited us there was even less friendly. We found ourselves running through two rows of SS men who rained a barrage of blows on our heads and bodies. I felt the blood streaming down my face from a gash on my forehead, and a blow to my swollen nose sent a torrent of blood into my mouth.

Guards with large, fearsome dogs herded us into a field illuminated by floodlights, thousands of us, confused and disoriented in the darkness of the night. The dogs strained at their leashes, and their handlers released them whenever they saw one of us lagging behind.

We were told that the camp was a good distance away, that we would have to run all the way and that stragglers would be set upon by the dogs. I could barely stand on my feet, let alone run with a heavy backpack weighing me down. What could I do? If I didn't run, the dogs would tear me apart. There was only one choice. To abandon my backpack. Perhaps then I would be able to run at a pace acceptable to my tormentors. I would lose all my possessions, but at least I would keep my life.

I swung the backpack off one shoulder, and then I remembered the *tefillin* hidden inside the hollowed out loaf of bread. If I abandoned my backpack, I would also be abandoning my *tefillin*. It was unthinkable.

A scene from my childhood flashed before my eyes. It was in the fall of 1936, and I had just come home from the *yeshivah* in Strimtura for the holidays. I was almost thirteen years old, but I was short and thin and didn't look a day over ten years old. My thirteenth birthday fell during the festival of Sukkoth, just days away. Still, I didn't say anything about it. I knew that when my father was ready, he would bring up the subject; it was not for me to speak about it.

In the privacy of my own mind, however, I thought about my *bar-mitzvah* feverishly. I couldn't wait to receive a new pair of *tefillin*, as had all my friends who were already *bar-mitzvah*, even those from the poorest families. I also wondered how my *bar-mitzvah* would be celebrated. I did not expect much, perhaps just a family gathering in our large *sukkah*. Perhaps my stepmother would bake a special cake for the occasion. But no matter what it was, I knew I would accept it happily. It was the way I was brought up. We were not demanding, nor did we allow ourselves high expectations.

On the day before Sukkoth, I was in the synagogue together with my father. We had just finished the morning prayers when a neighbor came over to greet me. He shook my hand warmly and pinched my cheek.

"So, Reb Favish," he remarked, "you have Maier back for the holidays? How nice! Tell me, how old is he? Is he eleven already?"

"Eleven?" said my father. He laughed. "Maier may be a little short for his age. He will be thirteen during Sukkoth."

I was furious with the man for belittling me, but of course, I remained silent. In my own mind, though, I derided him as an ignorant and tactless fool and hurled witty responses at his back as he walked away.

My father stood there in a thoughtful silence for a few minutes. "You know something, Maier," he said at last. "You will be *bar-mitzvah* during the upcoming holiday. But since we don't wear *tefillin* until after the holiday, you should really put on *tefillin* today for the first time. Here, let me show you how."

He took the *tefillin* off his head and arm and gave them to me. He guided me through the proper blessings, then he adjusted the *tefillin* on my head and biceps and helped me wrap the straps around my forearm. I felt my father's warmth against my head and arm, and I relished the intimacy.

For the next fifteen minutes, I felt very mature and important standing there in the synagogue in my father's *tefillin*, and I wondered deliciously when I would receive my own new pair. I couldn't wait.

My father told me a number of the laws that pertained to the wearing of *tefillin*. He helped me take them off, wrap them up and put them away. Then he handed them to me.

"These are my gift to you, Maier," he said. "They are yours. I'll get others. Take care of them. Remember the laws I taught you. You can learn the rest by yourself. After all, you're now a man. From now on, you're responsible for yourself."

I managed to stammer my thanks, but I did not know what to think. Certainly, the *tefillin* my father had worn on his own head were very special, but I had so counted on getting a new pair for myself.

My father told the *shammes* to bring a bottle of plum brandy, clean glasses and a plate of cake. By this time, the synagogue had emptied, and no more than ten or fifteen stragglers remained. We all drank the brandy and tasted the cake.

Everyone drank *lechayim* and toasted me with their best wishes and warm blessings for my future.

"*Mazel tov!*" my father told me.

And that was my *bar-mitzvah*, beginning to end.

My father had really done me a great honor, I told myself, by giving me the *tefillin* off his own head. After all, it was not as if he were some simple water carrier or the like. He was Reb Favish Cahan, the great scholar admired and respected by one and all. The *tefillin* he had worn on his own head would surely become a family heirloom someday, and they were all mine. A new pair of *tefillin* would also have become old eventually, and what would they be then? Maier Cahan's old *tefillin*. Who would care about that? I should consider myself fortunate and grateful to have received my father's *tefillin*.

Just barely. But as time went on, I did value my *tefillin* more highly because they had once been my father's. Especially during these last few months, when I had been separated from my family, when I felt sure my father had perished, the *tefillin* were my only real link to him. Every time I put them on my head I felt his warmth on my head, and I was comforted.

Limping through the field in the middle of the night, agonizing over whether I should abandon my heavy backpack or carry it with me, these were the thoughts that passed through my mind and the feelings that passed through my heart. How could I abandon my father's *tefillin* so that I could run more easily toward the camp of my confinement? What would my father have said about abandoning such sacred articles to be desecrated and discarded?

I emptied as much as I could from the backpack, then I swung it over my shoulder, strapped it on and prepared to run. It was still heavy, but I would do my best.

My best, however, was not quite good enough. I stumbled and fell many times along the way, and after a while, the guards loosed the dogs on me. Fear brought me to my feet, but I did not escape without bloody gashes in my arms and legs.

When the gate of the camp finally came into view, I was more dead than alive. A large sign identified the camp as Flossenberg. I had never heard the name before, but I would never again forget it. It was a combination labor and death camp, and its foremost product was misery.

The scene in the camp as we stumbled in, was surreal. Huge searchlights illuminated the central yard, and SS guards manned the watchtowers all around. Any move that aroused the slightest suspicion of attempted escape or insurrection was greeted by machine gun fire from the watchtowers. People fell mortally wounded right and left.

When all the prisoners were rounded up in the yard, the gates of the camp swung shut behind us with a loud clang. We were lined up four abreast and marched off to the far end of the camp. The way was littered with hundreds of dead bodies, skeletons that once were human, that had once lived, breathed, loved and hoped, that had once known dignity and respect and the value of human life, now scattered like debris on the frozen ground.

The guards rained blows down on our heads as they drove us to a huge pit in the ground with three straight walls and one sloping wall. A spotlight spilled cold light over the ground and onto the bottom of the pit, which was covered with personal belongings of every description. Guards with machine guns looked down from the single watchtower close by. On the ground, an SS officer stood beside the pit, one hand slapping his thigh with a wicked-looking whip, the other holding a flat pistol. Behind him, two guards held slavering dogs on a short leash.

"Toss all your personal belongings into the pit!" the SS officer shouted. "Everything. Backpacks. The contents of your pockets. Everything!"

Ahead of me, prisoners were removing their backpacks with resignation, emptying their pockets and tossing everything into the pit. All worldly possessions, all things of sentimental value, all mementos, all things that gave them identity, all these were tossed down into the pit, leaving their lives stripped down to the barest bones. But at least it was life. At least it was better than a bullet in the head from one of the machine guns on the watchtower. At least there would be a tomorrow.

Then it was my turn. I reached for the backpack, but I could not remove it. I had carried with me, run with it on my battered back, endured unbearable fatigue and savage dog bites, all to hold on to my *tefillin*. How could I just take them off my back and toss them into the pit? I made a great show of emptying my pockets and tossing all their contents into the pit, but the backpack was like a fire to my touch.

I felt a hand grab my shoulder and spin me around. In an instant, the backpack was ripped from me.

"Move!" the officer snarled. "Do you think we have all night?"

He laughed harshly and sent the backpack sailing through the air, end over end, in the garishly lit darkness, before it fell into the pit.

"No!" I screamed. "No! No! No!" But what did my screams matter? Everything I possessed in the world was gone. My last tenuous link to my father was gone. My sacred *tefillin* were gone. I was left without protection, without connection, without anything but the breath in my lungs and the labored beating of my heart.

The officer kicked me in the shin and sent me sprawling, but I instinctively scrambled to my feet. I did not want to take any chances with the machine gunners in the watchtower.

"So look what you've come to, Maier," I heard a familiar voice say. It was the Old Fool.

This was not where I wanted to deal with him. All I wanted to do was survive the next fifteen minutes. I was not exactly in a frame of mind for theological debates. So I simply ignored him.

"Apparently your G-d has no further need for you," the Old Fool persisted. "Look where you are. Look at your condition. He didn't even let you keep your *tefillin*. Why are you still so loyal to Him if He doesn't care about you? Why are you so upset that you don't have your *tefillin* any more? Why do you need *tefillin*? Forget about all those things. Just think about saving your own life. That's all that matters. You should have taken Marishka's offer. I begged you. But you were too stubborn. Well, enough of this foolishness. Who knows if you'll ever have another opportunity like that one, or even any opportunity at all. But one thing you have to admit. No more worrying about kosher food and prayers and the like. Forget about G-d. He has forgotten about you."

My heart filled with a seething anger. How could this creature confront me at a moment when I was so helpless and defenseless? How could I be expected to think clearly about these things? I wanted to respond with a sharp retort. I wanted to devastate the Old Fool with ridicule and sarcasm, but he was gone. He had cleverly faded away after delivering his seditious little speech.

In a daze, I stumbled along with the other prisoners, oblivious to my surroundings, my head filled with a confused jumble of thoughts. Two minutes later, we were at a mammoth bathhouse.

"All clothing on that pile over there," an SS officer commanded. "Then inside and wash, you filthy scum."

Of course, I complied, as did everyone else. Now I was truly without a vestige of my past. My clothing had come from the Jewish community center of Budapest, and it was of good quality. Gone. I recalled that there were still two hundred *pengos* sewn into the pant leg, money I had received from the Gaspars. Also gone.

Nothing was left. Only my life and my soul. At that moment, when all the accumulated layers life had wrapped around me were stripped away, when I was left with only a barely functioning body and the indestructible divine spark of the soul G-d had implanted within me, I finally came to terms with reality. I resolved to accept everything passively, to do what I had to do, never to allow frustration and despair to corrode my insides, and never to help my tormentors destroy me. Most important, I entrusted my fate to the Almighty with absolute humility and acceptance. He owed me nothing, and I had neither claims nor complaints against Him. He could do with me as He pleased. I would accept everything.

At last, I was at peace.

Chapter 16

Dawn was breaking by the time we had all removed our clothes near the bathhouse. I shivered, and my steamy breath mingled with the breath of a thousand other miserable men. In the cold morning air, we watched the sky grow lighter with every passing minute, while within us the darkness grew ever deeper.

After a few minutes that seemed to last for hours, a group of burly guards carrying heavy truncheons appeared.

"Everyone into the baths!" they shouted. "Right now!" So far I had not heard one SS guard speak. They only shouted and screamed.

Cold as it was, we were not too eager to run into the bathhouse. No one knew what kind of hell awaited us inside. The guards, however, did not waste any time on gentle persuasion.

They immediately started swinging their truncheons in all directions, landing blows wherever they might fall.

"That's not a real bathhouse," a man not far from me screamed. "They don't want to wash us. They want to kill us!"

He did not get a chance to say any more than that. A few vicious blows to the head silenced him, and he fell senseless to the ground. I didn't know if he was dead or alive. To this day, I do not know what happened to him.

Was he right? Were we about to be exterminated inside this ostensible bathhouse? I didn't know, nor did anyone else. But what difference did it make? We had no choices. If we resisted we would be gunned down from the watchtowers. If we complied, we would suffer whatever fate was in store for us. Nothing really mattered. We were straw in the wind.

To my immense relief, the bathhouse was genuine. A Jewish barber awaited us inside, and he sheared us of all our hair. Even then, there was an atmosphere of extreme terror until we actually saw water coming out of the showerheads and we were allowed to cleanse our bodies.

We emerged from the bathhouse as naked as the day we were born, and we were issued new sets of clothes. Compared to those we had taken off, they were rags. In fact, compared to anything, they were rags. Each of us was also given a thin blanket. I consoled myself for the loss of my Budapest clothing. I may have lost the garments, I told myself, but the lice that infested them were also gone.

The camp was like a town of large blockhouses arranged in neat, evenly spaced rows. I was assigned to Block 13. I'm sure all the other blocks were identical. There were no furnishings inside. All the walls were lined floor to ceiling with deep and utterly bare shelves. It was obvious that these were to be our beds. No sheets, no pillows, just the blankets we had been issued. The hard wood didn't seem very comfortable, but I didn't think I would have a problem dealing with it.

I hadn't counted, of course, on the sheer number of prisoners that would be crowded into each block. When it was finally time to go to sleep after two days of marching and abuse, I found myself squashed onto the shelves as tightly as the proverbial sardines. Once we had positioned ourselves for the night, none of us could move without the consent of all his neighbors, which was grudgingly given and often refused.

That first night, the overcrowded conditions resulted in numerous altercations. The SS men would not demean themselves to get involved in them and restore order. Instead, in each block a few prisoners were assigned the task of keeping the peace and making sure that the orders of their masters were quickly and fully obeyed. In return, these prisoners, who were called *kapos*, were freed from labor and given other privileges as well. In Flossenberg, all the *kapos* were gentiles. I have no firsthand knowledge of what went on in other camps.

On that very first night in the camp, I saw how the *kapos* excelled at their work. They did not bother to discover who was right and who was wrong. They did not attempt to act with fairness, although they did show a large measure of impartiality. As soon as they sensed an outbreak of discord, they immediately waded in with their sticks flying, delivering blows without prior warning and without regard for the identity or level of involvement of their victims. All who were anywhere near the eruption suffered equally and without preference. Order was restored.

Day in and day out, the *kapos* tormented us with great diligence and no mercy. I suppose they had to show their masters how reliable they were if they wanted to keep their privileged positions, but they clearly enjoyed their work; whenever a *kapo* would strike one of us, I almost invariably saw a glint of pleasure in his eyes. I do not know what our *kapos* were like to begin with, but in their jobs, they all developed strong strains of sadism.

On my second evening in the camp, a terrible fight broke out in the block. The *kapos* were outside smoking, and the fight raged for many minutes in full view of everyone. The combatants were a man in his forties and a young fellow who couldn't have been more than eighteen or nineteen years old.

The older man attacked the younger one with cold fury, slapping at his head and kicking him. The younger one kept shoving the older man away and fending off his blows, but he did not direct any blows of his own at his assailant. Slowly, listening to their shout and accusations, it dawned on me that these two combatants were father and son. The father had hidden away an extra ration of bread, and the son had stolen half of it; apparently, he had not had the heart to steal the whole piece of bread.

The noise and the commotion finally caught the attention of the *kapos*, and they came running in. In their usual efficient manner, they resolved the dispute by beating both of the combatants into bloody senselessness.

Quiet returned to the block, but not to my heart. Oh, how far we have fallen, I lamented. Look what has become of us. Father and son come to physical blows over a crust of bread. I was reminded of the verses from the Book of Lamentations that described Jerusalem under Roman siege just before its destruction, how starving mothers ate the flesh of their children. Had we fallen to this? Were we ready to tear each other apart, parents and children, in the name of survival?

I thought about my own father. What would we have done under the circumstances? I had no doubt that I would have given him my last piece of bread even if I were in the last stages of starvation. I was also sure that he would not have accepted it. I could just imagine the two of us throwing the piece of bread back and forth, each of us insisting that the other take it. Would we ever have descended to the level of these people? I did not believe it, but how could I be sure? Those kindhearted mothers in Jerusalem would also never have dreamed that they would someday eat the soft flesh of their babes. I could not help bursting into tears.

That night was particularly difficult for me. For a long time, I could not stop thinking about the father and son who had fought each other. When I had finally calmed down, I still could not fall asleep. My bruised and battered body found no rest on the hard boards of the shelf. The stench was unbearable, and the crowding made me feel claustrophobic. I was also very hungry, and my rumbling stomach kept me awake long after the others had fallen asleep.

Flossenberg was not Budakalasz. There was no Lily Gaspar here to bring me all sorts of good food. Here in Flossenberg, I either ate the camp food or starved. But I had resolved that I would not eat unkosher food. I had promised it to my father when we had parted near the train station in Upper Vishiva. And now I was starving. Should I break my promise now, after so many months of faithful compliance? Or should I just starve?

I resisted for two weeks, but then I could not hold out any longer. The next day, after I got my ration of bread, I stood on line to receive a bowl of the thick, greasy soup that was given out every day. I wept as I ate the food and felt the nourishment flow into my body. Never before in my life had a scrap of unkosher meat crossed my lips, and now I was eating unclean food with relish. I half expected the Old Fool to pay me a visit, but he had the good sense to stay away. I knew I had not violated any of the Torah's laws by eating this soup. I knew that when it is a question of life and death, the dietary laws are all suspended. Nonetheless, I felt defeated and unclean, and tears streamed down my face as I ate.

"Why are you so upset, my friend?"

I looked up. Three kind faces were looking down at me.

"Because I finally had to give in," I said. "I had resolved to eat kosher. I had promised my father I would. But I couldn't hold out any more."

The oldest of the three was a slight man with grizzled hair and the look of a scholar. "What are you talking about, my friend?" he said.

"The soup," I said. "I finally gave in and ate the soup."

He smiled at me. "If you thought there was any meat in that soup, you are sadly mistaken. Or perhaps not so sadly." He touched my shoulder. "The three of us also eat only kosher. We checked out the soup. Nothing but water, flour and some pieces of vegetable."

For a moment, I was taken aback. After all that soul-searching, the soup had turned out to be harmless. What irony! Then I started to laugh. I laughed so hard that tears began to run from my eyes once again, and my three new friends laughed along with me. Only when our mirth caught the attention of one of the *kapos* did we bring it to a precipitous halt.

From that day on, I was accepted into their little group, and we formed a deep friendship that warms my heart to this very day, even though we were only together for a few weeks. The man who looked like a scholar, I learned, was a rabbinical judge in a small village not far from Bishtene in the Carpathian region. His name was Tzvi Hersch. The others were Nissen and Shmiel.

"Listen, Maier," Nissen told me, "the soup didn't contain any meat, but according to what I hear, tomorrow we'll start receiving small rations of sausage along with our other rations. The Germans realize that if they don't feed us, they won't get too much work out of us. We have to be careful, but I've already worked it out to exchange my sausage ration for additional bread. You can do the same."

"Of course," I said.

Suddenly, I had a flash of inspiration. But I did not tell it to them immediately. First, I had to think about it.

I recalled that when visiting the latrines my first morning in the camp I had discovered an active little market in operation. For the most part, it was concerned with clothes swapping. The clothing had been issued to us at the bathhouse without any thought to size or fit. The result was often comical, tall people wearing trousers that barely covered their knees and shirts whose sleeves ended at mid-forearm and short people wearing trousers that dragged on the ground and shirtsleeves that covered their hands. Here in the latrines the men came together to swap their clothes for other ones that fit them better.

I myself had been given an enormous shirt and very small trousers, and I was unable to exchange them for better fitting clothing. In the end, I found a sharp stone and cut the sleeves down to size. There was, of course, no way I could stretch the trousers to make them longer, and I had no choice but to walk around with my calves exposed even in the frosty weather.

While trying to exchange my clothes in the latrine marketplace, I noticed that several prisoners had established themselves as camp merchants and seemed to be doing quite a brisk business. One of them in particular, a huge Russian peasant whose name I do not recall, caught my attention. The punishment for camp entrepreneurship was very severe, to say the least, but he was impervious to the danger. I wanted to approach him several times, but I was too terrified to go near him. Others caught dealing had been so viciously beaten that they had practically lost their minds; they wandered about the camp, shadowy husks of former human beings. I was convinced that the Germans allowed them to roam about the camp as an example to the rest of us. And it worked. I, for one, did not want that happening to me. It was a fate worse than death.

Fear was not the only deterrent to my participation in the latrine marketplace. There was also the slight problem that I had no wherewithal. The currency of the marketplace was bread, but since I did not eat the soup, I could not spare even a small piece of bread. I needed to eat every crumb.

Now, however, things had changed. The sausage ration would, of course, be available for exchanges, and if I tried hard, I could probably save some of my bread as well. Moreover, if the four of us pooled our resources we could muster some real business clout. As for the danger, where there was a will there was a way. Something could be worked out. It was time to do some dealing.

I shared my thoughts with my new friends, but they were still puzzled.

"All right, let's say we have extra rations to trade," said Shmiel, "what do we trade them for? Why don't we just trade the sausage for some more bread and eat it?"

"You can't guess?" I asked, savoring the drama of the moment.

They all shook their heads.

"*Tefillin!*" I declared triumphantly. "We can exchange the rations for a pair of *tefillin*."

"Tell us more," said Tzvi Hersch.

"The key is the Russian," I said. "He works in the sorting of the personal belongings from the big pit. There must be dozens of pairs of *tefillin* in the warehouse where they keep everything. I believe he can supply us with a pair of *tefillin*. For the right price, of course."

"So how do we get to the Russian?" asked Nissen. "And how do you know you can trust him? He can just take the rations and report you to the guards. This is a very risky business, you know."

"I know," I said. "I thought about it, and I think I have the answer. You remember the Jewish barber in the bathhouse."

They all nodded. "Well, it appears to me that he is on very good terms with the Russian. I think we should approach the barber to act as the intermediary on this transaction."

"How much do you think it will cost?" asked Shmiel.

I shrugged. "I was thinking of two full rations of bread and one or two rations of sausage. The barber will take maybe a half ration for himself and give the rest to the Russian. That's what I was thinking. What do you say?"

"I guess I would agree to it," said Shmiel. "But try to get it for less. A ration of bread is an immense sum. It's like a bar of gold. Much better. What can you do with gold anyway? You can't eat it."

"It's agreed then?" I said. "I will negotiate with the barber, and we will all share in the expense?"

All three murmured their assent, and it was done.

The next day, as Nissen had predicted, we each received a small ration of sausage. I immediately went to the barber and told him my plan.

"You're crazy," he said. "You want me to risk my life?"

"Not really," I said. "You get on well with the Russian. He won't betray you. And you can trust me. So where is your risk?"

"Don't make me laugh. This thing is full of risk. And besides, how do I know I can trust you?"

"Look, my friend. From the time, they took away my *tefill-in* I've been like a fish out of water. I am desperate for a pair of *tefillin*, so desperate that I'm willing to give up a full ration of bread and two rations of sausage for it. Do you think I would do anything to jeopardize the deal? Would I? Of course not, and you know it. You can trust me."

"You're a good talker, but I'll still be taking a big risk. A full ration of bread you said? And two rations of sausage?"

"That's right. You know as well as I do that a full ration of bread is worth its weight in gold. Even more! You can't eat gold. I say you should take half the bread for yourself and give the Russian the other half and the sausage. I think that's a fair deal all around."

"I'm glad you think so," said the barber. "I don't."

I squinted at him. "What do you mean?"

"I mean the price is far too low. I'm far from sure I'm going to do this crazy deal, but if I do, it has to be worthwhile."

"All right," I said. "One and a half rations of bread, and that's my final offer. Take it or leave it."

The barber chuckled. "For a young fellow, you seem to have more than a little negotiating experience, haven't you? Well, I'll leave it. I'm not interested in your offer."

I began to sweat. "So what do you think is fair?"

"Fair? For risking my life? No price is too high if it means I have to risk my life. Still, I see how important this is to you, so I'll consider it. But the price has to make sense. Four rations of bread and four rations of sausage. That's what it would take if I should even consider doing this deal. Not one crumb less."

"But that's ridiculous," I cried. "How can I get you four rations of bread? Am I supposed to live on air for a week?"

"That's your problem, not mine. Now, if you don't mind, I have things to do. I really can't just stand around and talk to you all day."

"Wait a minute, wait a minute," I said in desperation. "All right, let's say I agree to this outrageous price. Only because the *mitzvah* of *tefillin* is so precious to me. I can't give it all to you at once. I can give you four rations of sausage and one ration of bread when you deliver the *tefillin* and the rest of the bread one week later."

"What do you think I am, a bank? I don't give credit. How do I know you'll pay up, if I get you the *tefillin*?"

"Come on," I pleaded. "Have a heart. Don't you see that I'm doing this because I want to fulfill the *mitzvah* of *tefillin*? If so, what good would stolen *tefillin* be to me? Of course, I'll pay up."

"Well, maybe. I'm still not so sure. All right, give me two rations of bread when I deliver the *tefillin* and two more within three days."

"Done!"

"Very well, when you see me walk into your block, that will be your signal that I've secured a pair of *tefillin* for you. Meet me in the bathhouse the next morning."

When I reported back to my friends, they were at first dismayed by the high price, but they still agreed to bear it equally. We would have to go hungry for a few days, but we would put together the required amount within the required time frame.

Two days later, the barber walked into our block, puttered around a bit and left. Our excitement knew no bounds. The *tefillin* were already in his possession, and we couldn't wait to get our hands on them.

Early the next morning, I met the barber in the bathhouse, as we had agreed. He looked very nervous.

"Did you bring the rations?" he said.

I showed him the sausage and the bread, and he brightened.

"All right," he said. "Let's do it."

I handed him the rations, and he gave me the *tefillin* wrapped in a cloth. Then we parted. I stuffed the *tefillin* into my pocket and proceeded to wash myself. I didn't want anyone to see me coming out of the bathhouse dry, and I also wanted to clean myself in honor of the *mitzvah*, which I would soon be performing.

Back in the block, my friends awaited me eagerly. As soon as they saw my face, they knew I had been successful, and they broke into happy smiles. They offered me a piece of bread, but I refused to eat until after I had put on the *tefillin*. The problem was that the *mitzvah* could not be performed after nightfall. It had to be done during the daytime and, of course, in absolute secrecy, and the supervision was too strict.

We waited the entire day for an opportunity to present itself, but none did. Finally, a few minutes before nightfall, we came up with a plan. One of us would get under the blankets on one of the lower shelves and put on the *tefillin* while the others would sit around together and block him from view. I was given the honor of being the first to put them on. My blood ran cold with the fear of discovery, but I pressed forward nonetheless.

As I climbed under the blanket with the *tefillin* wrapped in their cloth I felt an incredible excitement, as great as any I had ever felt in my life. I touched the *tefillin* and it seemed to me that they were alive in a certain sense. My hands trembled as I reached into the cloth and pulled out the first one to check if it was for the arm or for the head. According to the law, the one for the arm is put on first.

I drew the first one out and examined it. It was for the head. I kissed it and put it aside. Then I reached in and drew out the second one. It, too, was for the head! The Russian, not knowing the difference, had taken two for the head and none for the arm. This was not a full pair of *tefillin*. But I hugged and kissed them anyway. I put one of them on my head, and I said the Shema with great fervor. My happiness was complete.

I took off the *tefillin* and left them unwrapped. Then I climbed out from under the blanket. There was no time for the others to do as I had done. They would have to wait until tomorrow, but their faces gleamed with joy. I told them what had happened, and their joy remained undiminished. They reached under the blanket and, touching the *tefillin* with their trembling fingers, they each said the Shema. It was a moment of transcendent holiness, one of the holiest moments of my life. At that moment, we felt G-d with us. We felt His embrace.

It was worth everything.

Chapter 17

The next day, I told the barber that we had gotten two for the head and none for the arm. He promised to try to get me what I needed to complete the set, and in the meantime, afraid we might inform on him, he returned one ration of bread. We never did get the one for the arm before we left Flossenberg, but we put on the one for the head every chance we got. Each time, we hid under the blanket, and each time, the fear and the exhilaration were the same as on that first day.

Altogether, I spent only a few weeks with my three new friends, all of whom were considerably older than I was. Nonetheless, we became very close. Perhaps being thrown together under such conditions of adversity, never knowing if today will be your last on earth, perhaps this breaks down the barriers between people and lets them connect quickly and profoundly.

Whenever we could steal a few moments, we would sit and talk, usually finding strength in the lessons of the Torah and using them to bolster our faith in the Almighty. We had no books, only our memories, and each of us would repeat any insights and interpretations he could recall or even just the unexplicated sayings of the Sages. Tzvi Hersch, the scholar, excelled at this. When we discussed legal issues, he would often quote dozens of sources from all over the Talmud and the Codes. We were in awe of him.

Tzvi Hersch was also a master at finding a silver lining in even the darkest cloud. He was convinced that in the merit of his suffering he would eventually be reunited with his wife and children. Salvation, he assured us, was just around the corner. Someone pointed out to him that people were dying like flies in the camp and probably in all the other camps as well, but he was not perturbed. On the contrary, didn't we learn that numerous Jews died during the plague of darkness shortly before the Exodus?

When we stood naked in the camp yard for roll call during the driving rain or the freezing cold, when many of us had completely depleted our last reservoirs of strength and endurance, he assured us that all would turn out well. When the great day of our salvation will arrive, he told us, we will be reunited with our families in joy and love, and we will all see in retrospect that everything had been for the good.

His contagious optimism kept us all going, but he had no explanations for why we were being subjected to such torture. Often in the stillness of the night, we talked about these things. What did G-d want from us? What had we done that we deserved such punishment? Had G-d forgotten about us?

"I don't know," Tzvi Hersch said one night. "How can I know what G-d is thinking? But I do know one thing. The ultimate result will be positive. Something very good will come out of this, and we will have been the ones who paid for it with our blood and pain."

"But enough is enough," said Nissen. "How much suffering is needed to bring about this wonderful result? Isn't it time this hell came to an end?"

"Nissen, my friend," said Shmiel, "let's hope we are liberated tomorrow. In the meantime, all we can do is pray."

We sat in a silence for a few minutes, each of us following the train of his own thoughts.

"Speaking about praying," I said, breaking the silence, "it occurs to me that our prayers may be incomplete."

"What do you mean?" asked Nissen. The others also leaned forward, their interest piqued.

"Do you remember what the great sage Rabbi Maier said?" I began. "'When a person is suffering, what does G-d say? He says, 'Oh, my head hurts! Oh, my arm hurts!' G-d suffers along with us, so to speak, whatever that means. So we should pray not only for ourselves but for Him as well, don't you think?"

Tzvi Hersch jumped to his feet, electrified. He hugged me and spun me around. "Maier! Maier! You've found the answer. Now we know why our suffering is so endless. We've only been thinking about ourselves. Have we given a thought to the suffering of the Almighty? Have we prayed for the *Shechinta begalusa*, the Divine Presence that is in exile? How selfish of us! How small-minded! My friends, we have the answer. From now on, we will pray for the Almighty before we pray for ourselves, and you will see. Our salvation will come in a flash."

The next day was a Friday, and we couldn't wait to celebrate the Sabbath with our newfound awareness and sensitivity to the Almighty. That afternoon, a group of barbers entered the block and began shaving the prisoners. They were using razors. My three friends and I exchanged glances, communicating our thoughts without having to say anything.

The Torah forbids shaving with a razor, and in our new exalted state, we didn't want to enter the Sabbath with our faces freshly shaven in a forbidden manner. This was not exactly what we needed if we intended to add new depth and meaning to our relationship with G-d.

Tzvi Hersch inclined his head slightly toward the door, and we all understood. We would slip away and stay out of sight for the next hour. No barber's razor would touch our faces this Friday.

The plan worked well. By the time we returned to the block, the barbers were all gone. Our fellow prisoners were all freshly shorn. Only the four of us had shadowy beards on our faces.

That night, we sat down together to celebrate the Sabbath meal, which consisted of nothing more than a piece of bread and a glass of tepid coffee for each of us. But it was ambrosia. We chewed the bread slowly, sang the old familiar Shabbos tunes and spoke about Torah topics. We were in spiritual ecstasy. I recalled the Sabbath and festival celebrations in Lower Vishiva, and I did not think I had ever reached such a state of spiritual exaltation. The others felt the same.

On Shabbos morning, we had a surprise inspection. We were assembled in the block at eleven o'clock and ordered to stand at attention. A few minutes later, the door opened and the camp commandant, a high SS officer, marched in. A few other SS officers and two of the most vicious kapos in the camp accompanied him.

While the commandant conferred briefly with the *stubalteste*, the block leader, the *kapos* ran up and down the lines to make sure that we were all standing at perfect attention, delivering kicks and blows to those who displayed the slightest signs of slouching.

The commandant turned and fixed us with a harsh stare, his hard eyes boring right through our skin into our innards. A terrified silence descended. No one spoke. No one even breathed aloud. Then he began to walk up and down the rows, his highly polished boots smacking against the wooden floors like thunderclaps in the stillness of the block.

When he came to the four of us, he stopped and frowned. He snapped his fingers at the block leader and summoned him with a slight movement of his head.

"What is the meaning of this, *stubalteste*?" he asked. "Why aren't these men shaven?"

The block leader trembled. "I don't know, sir."

"Do you call this hygiene?"

"No, sir. I'm sorry, sir. I cannot explain how we missed these men."

The commandant turned to stare at us. "Why aren't you men shaven?"

We were too frightened to respond.

"Answer me!"

"We were in the latrine, sir," said Nissen.

"All of you?"

"Y-yes, sir."

The commandant sneered and turned away. "*Stubalteste*, you and the *kapos* will be penalized for this. See that these men get what they deserve. And get them shaven. Right now!"

He spun on his heel and marched out of the block. For two seconds, everyone remained frozen in place. Then the kapos attacked us, screaming and punching wildly in their fury. They dragged us into another room, ordered us to remove our clothing and whipped us mercilessly until we nearly lost consciousness. I worried that Tzvi Hersch, a slight and delicate man, could not endure such brutal punishment. Finally, the violence subsided, but we were unable to return to the block under our own power. Other prisoners had to be brought in to carry us out.

If we thought a respite awaited us, we were sadly mistaken. A barber awaited us, ready to rectify the lapse in hygiene. The *kapos* did not allow him to strop his razor or to lather our faces prior to shaving us. And so, we were shaved dry with a dull and nicked blade. For me in particular, it was exceedingly painful, because I have stiff and wiry hair. Every pass of the blade removed not only hair but also pieces of my skin. My whole face bled profusely, but I suppose it was a blessing in disguise. The blood wet and softened the hairs and made them easier to cut.

When it was all over, we were beaten and bloodied literally from top to bottom. Nonetheless, Tzvi Hersch found his silver lining. "What a kindness the Almighty has shown us," he said. "The barber used a blunt razor so we did not violate the prohibition."

The rest of us just groaned in response.

"I'm not sorry we did it," said Shmiel. "It was worth it for last night."

Indeed, it was.

Thankfully, none of us suffered broken bones or ruptured organs, and in a few days, we were more or less back to our normal debilitated state. The daily routine continued. Hard labor all day and a few hours labored rest in the night. For us, the routine also included a few stolen minutes under the blankets with the *tefillin* on our heads.

One day, towards the end of that week, one of the two kapos who had been penalized because of our little escapade came into the block just when I was under the blanket. As usual, the others were sitting in front of me, blocking me from view.

"What's going on here?" the *kapo* demanded.

"Nothing, sir," said Nissen.

"You're lying! Get out of my way." He pushed them aside and swept the blanket away. For a long moment, we looked at each other, both of us startled. Then he punched me in the face.

Bellowing with rage, he grabbed me and flung me to the ground, ripping the *tefillin* off my head as I fell. He tossed the *tefillin* onto the ground and kicked me repeatedly with his heavy boots. I rolled myself into a ball to protect my head and abdomen, but otherwise, there was no escape. There was not an unprotected part of my body that was not mauled by his boots.

How did he know I was under the blanket? I do not know. Perhaps an informer had told him. Or perhaps it was just my bad fortune that he came in at that moment and thought the scene was suspicious.

When he had fed his rage to the point of satisfaction, he turned to the *tefillin* that were lying on the floor and trampled them with both his feet until they were nothing more than a shapeless black mass. Then he picked them up gingerly, dropped them into the garbage can and left. Watching him do this hurt me more than all the blows of his boots, and I am sure he knew this perfectly well. He had left the best for last.

"So what do you have to say now, Maier?"

It was the Old Fool again. I closed my eyes and turned my head away.

"Can't you see that it's useless, Maier?" he continued. "No matter what you try, it all blows up in your face. G-d is not interested in you, Maier. It's time you realized it. Who knows if you'll ever get out of this alive? But at least you can try to get through without getting beaten to a pulp every other day. And for what? For razor blades? For *tefillin*? Tell me, is it really worth it? Think about yourself, Maier. Take care of yourself. Understand, Maier?"

"You always come just when I've been knocked down, just when I'm depressed," I told him. "Why didn't you come last Friday night? I know why. Because you are a coward. That's why. Try giving me your advice when I'm not hurting and miserable. You know you wouldn't even stand a chance. You would just be wasting your breath. Well, you're wasting your breath now, too. Go away."

He said no more, but he knew he had scored some points. So had I.

Flossenberg was a staging camp. The procedure was that, after about a month, prisoners were sent off to many different labor camps, some established, some temporary nameless camps set up somewhere in a forest or near some other work site. In most cases, prisoners did not know the name of the camp to which they were being transferred. Sometimes, they didn't even find out after they got there. It was a shadowy world with tens of thousands of slave laborers flowing in every direction.

When our time came to be sent off to other camps, I had hoped I would be able to stay with my three new friends, but it was not to be. All prisoners who came to Flossenberg were assigned numbers imprinted on pieces of cloth. With typical German orderliness, everything went according to those numbers. When they assigned prisoners to satellite camps, they did so by the sequence of numbers. Numbers this through that will go to such and such a camp. It didn't matter what kind of people those numbers represented, what their skills and inclinations were. All that mattered was the number, because that's all that people were to them—numbers.

My three friends had come to Flossenberg together and were therefore assigned consecutive numbers. I, however, had come a little later, and my number was of a later sequence. And so our separation was practically guaranteed. They were transferred one day before me. They did not know the name of the camp to which they were being sent, nor did we know if we would ever see each other again.

Our parting from each other was a very emotional scene. We assured each other that all would be well and that we would meet again in happier times when we would be able to look back on our experiences with the wisdom of hindsight. Most important of all, we told each other, we had to remain strong in our faith and our loyalty to the Almighty. Otherwise, we didn't have a chance.

Chapter 18

One day after my friends were shipped out of Flossenberg, I was transferred, along with five thousand other prisoners, to a labor camp called Ohrdruf. We arrived there in the evening when there was still a little light in the winter sky. The camp did not seem to have been built for prisoners. It was actually a cluster of many small buildings that gave the appearance of a government installation or a college residence area.

Apparently, our group had the honor of being the first prisoners to occupy the camp. The welcome we received was nowhere near as atrocious as our reception in Flossenberg, but it still fell far short of warmth and hospitality. We had come to expect brutality and sadism, and we were not disappointed. We even considered it normal.

The blocks were each four stories high, six rooms on each level, thirty men to a room. One *stubalteste*, the room leader, was assigned to each room, and one *kapo* to the entire block. Our *stubalteste* was a rotund Slovak named Otto. He spoke perfect German, and I could see that he enjoyed cordial relations with both the SS officers and the prisoners. I immediately saw that I needed to be on his good side, and I intended to do everything necessary to be there.

I gave Otto my best smile as I entered the block. Considering the condition of my scraped and battered face, my smile must have borne a closer resemblance to a grotesque grimace. Still, it was the best I could muster, and it found its mark. Otto returned my smile, adding a wink into the bargain.

Later that evening, I offered to shine Otto's shoes. He graciously gave me permission, and I spent the better part of the evening making sure his shoes were gleaming and spotless.

My first few days in Ohrdruf I did not join any of the work details. Otto ordered that I remain right there in the block to make sure his things and room were in tiptop condition. But then one of the *kapos* assigned a prisoner to cleaning all the rooms of the privileged, including Otto's, and I was out of a job. The next day, I was assigned to a work detail.

We were awakened at five thirty in the morning. We had some muddy coffee and a piece of bread, and then we began to walk. The work sites were in a forest between ten and twenty kilometers from the camp, and we walked for hours in the freezing cold over icy and snow-covered roads. Our clothes were thin rags, and our shoes were little better than torn slippers. Every once in a while, there was a sudden downpour of frozen rain, but the guards in their slickers did not allow us to seek shelter, forcing us to walk unprotected until the deluge soaked through our pathetic garments right to our skin.

The work site was a clearing in the forest, and our assignment was to fell the trees, cut them into logs and load them onto wagons. It was brutal work, and the cold was unbearably bitter. The deep darkness of the forest beckoned to me, but I knew it only held death. If I was not shot down by the guards or torn apart by their dogs, I would surely perish of cold and hunger in the forest itself.

Logging is exceedingly difficult, especially for inexperienced, emaciated, cold-crazed prisoners. The overseers ran from place to place, shouting orders and directions at their hapless crews, while the guards followed close behind, delivering blows and lashes to encourage quicker and more efficient compliance. From time to time, huge trees trunks would come crashing down where they shouldn't have, crushing anyone, prisoner or guard, who stood in their trajectory.

I sawed and cut and dragged and lifted until I felt my arms and legs would fall off and my lungs and heart would explode. I thought that the harder I worked the less I would feel the cold, but I was wrong. I did not know how I could endure this hellish torture for an entire day.

In the early afternoon, we had a short break. I took my cup of oily brown broth and my piece of bread, and I sat down against a tree trunk. I closed my eyes for a few moments to catch my breath, but I made sure to hold on tightly to my food. The slightest lapse of vigilance, and it would be snatched away and devoured.

I was not unfamiliar with snow-covered forests. In fact, my father's main source of income during the winter months had been from the logging business. He would buy logs from various sources, process them into lumber and sell them to his clients. He worked in a twenty-five-kilometer radius that included the forest-covered hills of Lower Vishiva, Selisz, Sitszel and other villages in the area. It was hard work. He used to go on foot from site to site in the ice and the snow, often leaving the house early in the morning and not returning more dead than alive close to midnight and sometimes later.

During the last few years before the War reached Lower Vishiva, I had begun helping my father in the logging business, and soon, I was scampering over the steep wooded hills and valleys like a mountain goat. I was glad to alleviate some of the pressures from my father, and I enjoyed the feel of the great outdoors and the thrill of the deal. Working together with a Jewish broker from Sighet by the name of Fruchter and a big company called Solvia Products, we purchased unprocessed logs and delivered finished lumber. Before we cut the logs into planks, we usually called in a Jewish lumber consultant named Dushnitz.

Dushnitz was an extraordinary expert. He could just glance at a log and determine all its interior flaws, and he was always right. While he inspected our logs, he allowed me to tag along as his temporary apprentice, and he kept up a steady stream of instruction as he worked. I drank in every word, and soon, he allowed me to make the evaluations in his presence. He corrected me when I was wrong and positively glowed with pleasure when I was right. I was learning.

While my father was making his deals, I tested my new-found expertise in a small side deal of my own in Kechnia, and I made a tidy profit. Between my father and me, we earned enough money to provide very nicely for the Cahan household for the entire winter, but it seemed that carefree leisure was not in our destiny.

As soon as we got home, my father developed an angry red rash on his neck that refused to go away. The doctors in Upper Vishiva were baffled by the rash and could offer no medications for it. There was no choice but to take him to the hospital. My stepmother and I took him to Doctor Barko's private clinic in Sighet where he was operated on not once but twice. My father spent a miserable few weeks in Sighet before he could come home.

About two weeks after we arrived in Sighet, my stepmother's brother Shloime Kalush came from Hust to visit my father.

Uncle Shloime was a hearty man, always looking for the angle, always ready to make a deal. He was also generous; he had donated many of the artifacts in the Lower Vishiva synagogue.

My father lay on his side, moaning softly. My uncle greeted him warmly, took a seat and conversed with his sister for a while. Then he turned back to my father. He obviously had something on his mind.

"I hear you did well this year, Favish," he said.

My father grunted but didn't respond.

"Does that mean yes, my dear brother-in-law?" asked Uncle Shloime.

"He's really not up to this, Shloime," my stepmother said. "They must have pulled a whole liter of pus from his neck."

"Well, it's not in his neck any more, is it?" said Uncle Shloime. "So what does it matter? It's time to look toward the future. I have a deal in the works, Favish. Are you interested?"

My father opened his eyes and gave my uncle a baleful look. "Let's hear."

"Good, so I'll talk, but you listen. You heard of the Veti-Oloiosh Company from Budapest, of course. They are prepared to buy an enormous amount of lumber from me, but I will need an entire forest to supply them. I need your help. We need to find such a forest, cut the trees and process the logs into lumber. I tell you, we will both make a handsome profit. What do you say?"

My father remained silent.

"You don't have to talk, you know," said my uncle. "Just nod if you want to do the deal."

My father rolled over onto his back and winced as the bandage on his neck caught the edge of the pillow. "The Cahan family has a large forest," he said. "In Dragomiresti. Where my father lives. An inheritance from my grandfather Reb Yosef Mordechai Cahan. You can buy it."

"Really?" said Uncle Shloime. "You own a forest? Then why don't you use it?"

"I don't own a forest. My family does. Either we sell it, or it stays as it is. If you want to buy it, I'll get you a decent price."

"Fine. We have what to talk about."

"All right," said my father, and he closed his eyes.

"There's just one more thing. I don't have the experience to undertake such a venture by myself. I need your help. Part of the deal has to be that you manage the work."

A weak smile appeared on my father's face, but it deteriorated into a grimace. "You must be joking. Do I look like I'm in a condition to manage a logging venture?"

Uncle Shloime shrugged. "Another week and you'll be a new man."

"I'll be lucky if I can go home in a week. Forget about me logging for a while. But I have an idea. I'll go into the deal with you, and I'll send you Maier in my place."

I hadn't said one word since the conversation had begun, but now I sat bolt upright.

Uncle Shloime was just as aghast. "Maier? But he's just a young boy!"

"Don't underestimate Maier. He knows wood. He worked together with Dushnitz, and in just a short time, he has learned an incredible amount. I tell you, he knows wood better than I do. Much better."

I was stunned. It was the first time in my life that my father had given me a compliment. Well, if this was what my father wanted me to do, this was what I would do. I was headed to the forest in Dragomiresti.

This particular logging venture turned out to be the worst debacle my father had ever encountered. The problems were endless from the beginning. My presence there from time to time was helpful, but the difficulties appeared insurmountable. The forest was just about inaccessible. The company gave a deposit, but it wasn't enough to fund the operation. The workers, exhausted and unpaid, mutinied and had to be pacified and mollified again and again. Unexpected obstacles cropped up as the work progressed, raising serious doubts as to whether it would ever be completed.

One of the problems was with transporting the logs from the forest to the railroad station about eight kilometers away. Normally, the horses would drag them along the downward-sloping, snow-covered roads. The logs would slide easily, and one horse could usually drag maybe eight or ten logs at a time. This year, however, there had been hardly any snow, and the horses could not drag the logs on the dry roadbed. One hundred men worked in the forest, piling up huge stacks of logs, but there was no way of getting them down to the station.

The company backed out of the agreement, refusing to invest any more money in a venture going nowhere, leaving my father and uncle with a forest full of laborers and horses to feed and no income with which to pay for it. The debt mounted daily, and my father and uncle were on the verge of being wiped out. At the last minute, my father asked me to go back to the work site and see what I could accomplish.

I arrived in the forest to find the workers up in arms. Some of them were ready to attack me physically, since I represented management. I had to get control of the situation quickly. I called an immediate assembly of all the workers.

"Listen to me," I said. "You are right in all your grievances. You have worked hard, and you haven't been paid. You haven't even been fed properly. So what do you want? Do you want to be right? Or do you want to find a way out of this mess? You are not responsible for this. I am not responsible for this. The weather is responsible. If you want to deal with it in a civilized manner, fine. If you give me a little time, I'll try to work out something fair for all of us. Otherwise, I'll just turn around and go home."

Suddenly, it was quiet. They all knew this was their last chance to come away from this job with something for all their efforts, and they did not dare jeopardize it by not cooperating.

I knew I had only one chance to make it work. I spent an hour assessing the situation. It was awful. The first thing I did was send away most of the workers and their animals with a promise that I would send them their wages when the project was completed. Then I took the two foremen and went to inspect the delivery route. The road was rough, rutted and thoroughly dry. Unless it snowed during the night, I could see no way of getting the logs to the station.

Unless.

An interesting idea occurred to me. Although there was no snow, it was nonetheless extremely cold. What if we poured water on the road during the night? In the freezing cold, it would turn to ice, and the road would become slick as a skating rink.

The foremen were doubtful. The ice sheets would certainly make it easier to move the logs, but they would also create risks for the men and horses who were likely to slip on the ice and injure themselves. Moreover, logs would inevitably break loose and come hurtling down the slopes, like missiles destroying everything in their paths. But despite their skepticism, the foremen admitted precautions could be taken.

In the end, we poured water down only one side of the road. We also equipped the horses with special horseshoes for additional traction, and we made sure that all men and animals stayed at least five meters away from the ice chutes we created.

The plan worked like a charm. We poured the water in the beginning of the night when it was coldest, and the roads froze over almost immediately. Then we worked through the night under the full moon. We had only one minor incident and no serious injury, and in a few days, towering stacks of logs we had transported from the forest dwarfed the railroad station.

We were all relieved when the project finally came to a successful conclusion. My father and uncle were effusively grateful to me for saving them from financial ruin, and the Budapest company was pleased to receive delivery before the deadline at a reasonable price. I was happy to have been of help to my father and uncle, and to be free to return to my regular life, and I politely but firmly turned down all the lucrative offers to manage logging crews that came to me after my success in Dragomiresti.

Several short months later, we were driven into the ghetto, and all our strivings and efforts became trivial in retrospect. Looking back, the frightening specter of financial ruin became a laughing matter. Ah, if only our calamities were limited to financial losses. Ah, if only we could lose all our houses and forests and businesses but hold on to the people we loved. Ah, if only we could stay alive.

Ah, if only I could stay alive. This thought reverberated in my mind now as I leaned against the tree at the work site near Ohrdruf. I don't know why I clung so tightly to the cruel nightmare that my life had become, but I did. I ate my food and wondered if the forest in Dragomiresti had been as cold as this one. Perhaps it had, but I had been free and happy and wrapped in layers of warm clothing. Here the cold penetrated my body. Even worse, it penetrated my soul.

A shrill whistle signaled the return to work. I struggled to my feet and returned to my labors. Sometime during the afternoon everything dissolved into a haze, and I don't know how I managed to get through it, to the end of the day.

We started back to the camp well after dark, thousands of us staggering through the frigid forest under the watchful eyes of armed guards and dogs. I did not believe it could get any colder than it had been that day, but it got worse. Much worse. Hundreds of prisoners dropped dead right in the road. The guards just kicked their bodies aside into the trees and left them there. Tomorrow, there would be a new shipment of prisoners to replenish the ranks. And the day after. And the day after. Death was not even a stumble. It was nothing at all.

On the way back, I fell in beside a tall young man by the name of Avrum. We had been together since Hungary, and he was in my block in Ohrdruf. Although we were not particularly close, I liked him a lot. He was a fine person, and he absolutely never complained about his plight. I was concerned about him. He was coughing and wheezing terribly, and I thought his lungs had been damaged. It wouldn't have been surprising, in the least. The wonder was that it hadn't happened to all of us yet.

I talked to him soothingly along the way, and I steadied him whenever he stumbled. If he had fallen to the ground, the guards would have told me to leave him there to die.

It was almost eleven o'clock when we returned to the camp. We were given some warm food and sent to our blocks. We curled up on the floor and were fast asleep as soon as our eyes closed. A short while later, I awoke with a start. Avrum was having a coughing fit, but he was still asleep. I covered him with my blanket and went back to sleep.

At five o'clock we were awakened once again, and the macabre routine started all over again. I realized that this was not forced labor. It was execution. How many such days could a human being endure before he expired? Three? Five? It could not be much more.

We reached the forest work site in a blizzard. The trees drowned in snowdrifts, and overladen branches fell on our heads. Without gloves on our hands, we had to cut down the trees, sweep the snow from the logs and load them into wagons. But the difficulties of working in such a snowstorm were too great, and the system broke down. Trees fell where they shouldn't have. Wagons snapped their axles or got stuck in drifts. Horses broke loose. It was pandemonium.

After two hours, the SS officer in charge called a halt to the work and ordered all of us to line up in the clearing.

"We have a problem here," he declared. "You men are not only lazy, you are also a bunch of bumbling fools. If you are not careful, you will get us all killed. We need more overseers, men who have experience with logging or at least some kind of outdoor work. Overseers will be given special privileges, more food and warm clothing. Anyone who can serve as an overseer is ordered to step forward right now!"

Maybe four or five men stepped forward, hardly a significant number with a labor force numbering in the thousands.

The officer was clearly displeased.

"You dirty, sniveling Jews," he hissed. "Do you know what you all are? A bunch of parasites, sucking the blood of the German people. Have any of you ever plowed a field? Have any of you ever built a house? No, all you can do is peddle and steal. Look at yourselves. What kind of people are you?"

We all stood there shivering in silence. Even the guards were shivering inside their coats.

"I want more overseers right now! Anyone who has any experience in carpentry, step forward!"

A few more men ventured forward, but still the officer was not satisfied. He strode through the ranks of the prisoners, stopping every once in a while to question someone. I did not know if he chose his candidates at random or if he had some indication that they could be of use to him.

Presently, he came to me.

"What is your name?" he asked me.

"Maier Cahan."

"Where are you from?"

"Lower Vishiva in Hungary."

"Plenty of forests in that district, aren't there?"

"Yes, sir."

"I saw you swing a pretty good axe this morning. Where did you learn to do that?"

"I didn't learn anywhere, sir. I just did what I was told to do."

"Are you cold, Cahan?"

"Yes, sir."

"Are you hungry?"

"Yes, sir."

"Would you like a coat and some food?"

"Yes, sir."

"Do you want to be an overseer? You will get food and a coat."

That morning and the day before, I had seen what overseers had to do to earn their privileges. Under the best of circumstances, they had to drive their men relentlessly to produce the quotas expected of them. Under the worst of circumstances, they had to do worse.

"I am not qualified, sir," I replied.

"What is your occupation?" he asked. I noticed that snowflakes had settled on his eyelashes.

"I am a bookkeeper."

The officer gave me a sharp look. Then he spat on the ground and walked away.

I knew I might very well have just signed my death warrant, but I had no regrets. I did not want to be a *kapo*.

Chapter 19

The next morning, we were awakened at five o'clock as usual. As we gathered in the central plaza for roll call, it occurred to me that this marked my third day on work detail in the forest. I did not think I could possibly make it through to the end of the winter. I did not even think I could make it through to the end of next week.

Avrum was standing a few rows away. I caught his eye, and we exchanged smiles. I was glad to see that he looked a little improved, but I wondered how long it could last. A ten-kilometer hike in sub-freezing weather would not be very therapeutic in his condition.

One morning, the camp commandant graced us with his presence. After roll call, he made a few announcements, the most significant coming at the end. "We are looking for craftsmen. Carpenters, plumbers, locksmiths. If you qualify remain in your place after dismissal. Everyone else proceed to your work details."

This was my chance, I realized. From this minute on, I was a locksmith. Why not? First of all, I might be able to pick up some things from watching the other locksmiths and maybe even do a credible job. If worse came to worst, I would be found out and sent back to the forest. In the meantime, I would have spared myself a day or two of work. Wasn't that worth a lot? After all, what could they do to me, shoot me for claiming to be a locksmith? There was a greater danger in not claiming to be a locksmith and going back to the forest.

I looked around to see if the SS officer from the work site was anywhere nearby. He wasn't, and I breathed a sigh of relief. Yesterday, I had been a bookkeeper. Today, I was a locksmith.

Actually, I did have a tiny bit of experience in locksmithing. Sort of. Back in Lower Vishiva, whenever any of the locks in our house broke or jammed I was the one who tried to fix them. True, most of the time I only succeeded in breaking them completely, but every once in a while, I would really fix it. Yes, I decided, I was most definitely a locksmith.

All the craftsmen, and I among them, remained standing in the central plaza after all the rest had marched off toward the forest. We were left standing there for the entire morning with no idea of what to do, shivering in the cold but warmed by the knowledge that we were not in the forest. At noon, two SS officers and the camp commandant appeared. One of the officers, a tiny rooster of a man with tiny wire-rimmed glasses and a large notebook, recorded our names and occupations in neat columns. Then the commandant told us to return to our blocks and await instructions.

I did not know what form our assignments would take and how difficult they would be, but it could not possibly be anywhere near as dreadful as logging in the forest. Besides, I had already profited tremendously from my new profession. I had gained an entire day without work of any sort. That day was one of the most precious gifts I ever received in my life, and I thanked G-d for it from the bottom of my heart. I was able to wash myself and rest my battered body, and I caught up on some restorative sleep.

It is amazing how everything in life is comparative. Had I been forced to spend an idle day in Ohrdruf one year earlier, wearing camp clothing, eating camp food, sleeping on the cold floor, I would have felt violated, but after two days in the forest, a day in Ohrdruf was a slice of heaven.

The following morning, the craftsmen were assembled in the plaza after the others left for the forest. I found myself assigned to a small group together with four other locksmiths. Our group leader was none other than Otto, the *stubalteste* of my block.

"Well, well, Cahan," he greeted me. "Why did you keep your skills a secret from us? The others in our little group told us a long time ago that they were locksmiths, but you never mentioned it."

"It slipped my mind," I said.

Otto laughed and slapped me on the back. "Let's get going."

We set off down the road accompanied by a single SS officer.

As if to underscore my good fortune, the sky cleared, and the sun shone warm through the frigid air. For the first time in a long while, I felt a spring in my step and a blithe lift in my heart. But then my thoughts turned to my friend Avrum coughing and wheezing in the snow-covered mountains, and I felt guilty.

We turned into a narrow country lane bordered on both sides by thick hedges of wildberry-laden bushes. The large, purple, plump berries, unlike any I had ever seen, made my mouth salivate and my empty stomach rumble. Surreptitiously, I snatched a handful and stuffed them into my mouth. They were delicious. I immediately thought of

Avrum. What a treat these berries would be for him after returning from another day in the forest. I grabbed another handful and shoved them into my pocket.

Within minutes, I collapsed to the ground with such painful convulsions that I thought I was going to die. I gasped for air, the world spinning before my eyes, and then I vomited. I turned over onto my knees and heaved again and again until my mouth stung with bile. The convulsions subsided, and I returned to the land of the living. Quickly, I emptied my pocket of the berries. I looked up and saw that two other locksmiths had also tasted the forbidden fruit and were still lying convulsed on the ground. Otto and the SS officer were staring at us with a sort of detached concern. I struggled to my feet and shook my head to clear it. I was fine. The others, however, were not so fine. Otto helped them to their feet, and with great effort, they stumbled along until we reached the work site, which was not too far away.

Our destination was a new house that had been built for a high-ranking SS officer. Wartime shortages had slowed the progress of the construction, and the officer was getting impatient. Our job, although we were officially locksmiths, was to fix and complete the piping of the house. There may have been shortages in plumbing materials, but there was no shortage of labor. On the contrary, there seemed to be an endless supply in Ohrdruf.

When we got to the house, the two stricken locksmiths collapsed incapacitated on the floor. The three remaining locksmiths, myself included, would have to pick up the slack.

The work was not very hard, nor was it very complicated. The first order of business was to repair the hot water pipes, which were leaking badly. But we were locksmiths not plumbers. Otto offered to help, but he was useless. Even the SS officer got his hands dirty trying to fix the pipes, but he was no better at it than the rest of us.

Seeing that no one knew what to do, I volunteered to do it myself. Many years before, when I was a young child in the *cheder* of Lower Vishiva, I used to come to school early, before the *rebbe* arrived, to watch Fishel the tinsmith putter with the plumbing and solder the cracks in the large tin pots used for boiling water. I supposed that this could be considered plumbing experience, and I decided to attempt the repair. I took apart the leaking pipe and scraped it clean of the accumulated rust. After fitting it back together, I wrapped them tightly in long filaments of lead, and with a iron heated in the fire, I melted the lead into place. The pipe now sported large gelatinous blobs around the joints, a sight that would have undoubtedly offended any self-respecting plumber, but the pipe no longer leaked.

"Well done, Cahan," Otto said and slapped me on the back. "Great job."

The SS officer bent over the pipes and examined them closely. "Truly an expert job," he commented with a touch of sarcasm. "It seems you are a man of many talents, Cahan. First a locksmith, now a plumber. Perhaps you are also a good shoemaker, eh? I need my other boots repaired. Do you think you could do that as well, Cahan?"

He was mocking me, but at least he had not mentioned bookkeeper among my many talents. Apparently, he was not aware that I had rejected an offer of becoming an overseer in the logging operation by claiming to be a bookkeeper.

"I could fix your boots, sir," I said, allowing myself a small liberty, "if you will allow me to melt lead on them."

The officer gave me a mirthless smile and walked away.

For nearly two weeks, I was a locksmith. I took for myself all those tasks that did not require any special expertise and left the other work for the real experts. I also paid close attention to everything going on around me, and after a while, I actually did learn a thing or two about locksmithing. Otto and the SS officer easily saw through my pretense. But they kept me on because I made myself extremely useful to the work detail. I did all the simpler tasks quickly and efficiently, and I was rapidly learning the craft itself. Furthermore, Otto had taken a liking to me. And so, I remained with the work detail until the assignment came to an end.

Otto promised to conscript me for the next assignment for expert craftsmen. In the meantime, it was back to the forest again. I sank into despair, but I consoled myself that it would be just for a short while. Otto would get me out. As soon as this thought crossed my mind, I was overcome by guilt. What was I doing? Putting my faith in Otto the Slovak? Did he hold my fate in his hands? How foolish of me. Only G-d controlled my fate. If I expected to survive, I would have to place my faith in Him. I apologized silently and went to sleep.

The next morning, I was awakened at five, and a half-hour later, I was trudging off to work beside my friend Avrum. Somehow, he had survived the two weeks during which I had been a locksmith. His coughing was less violent, but still persistent and ominously deep. He had been thin before, but now he had become grotesquely gaunt. He had even lost weight in his head, which was now just a skin-covered skull. But his will to live was as strong as ever, and he never gave up hope.

On our long trek to the forest, we helped each other say the prayers. Words we had said every day for years and years, words that had been as familiar to us as our own names were beginning to slip away, and we helped each other fill in the gaps in our memories. We succeeded in completing the prayers, and we delighted in the accomplishment.

The work site was as hellish as it had been two weeks before. Even worse, if such a thing were possible. During my stint as a locksmith, the weather had broken for a while. The temperature had even crept above freezing for a few days, but now it plunged to mind-numbing depths. Men fell dead right in middle of the work area. Their bodies were dragged away and piled in stacks near the road. I don't know what they did with these bodies, but they were gone the next morning, making room for stacks of fresh victims.

On my second day back in the forest, I saw Avrum bend over suddenly during lunch break, and I hurried to his side, terrified that he was on the verge of collapse. There was a man lying on the ground, a wasted shadow of a man, and he was trying to speak. Avrum was leaning over to listen.

"What is it?" I heard Avrum say. "Is there something I can get you? A drink of water?"

The man shook his head, irritated and frustrated. He opened his mouth again to speak, but no sounds emerged. He lifted his left hand and pointed to his right side.

"Do you have a pain?" asked Avrum.

The man shook his head again. He lay back eyes closed, lips moving imperceptibly. After a few moments, he opened his eyes. They held a look of resignation and such profound peace that I knew he was halfway to the next world. He seemed to pull himself back with a great effort, and with an even greater effort, he reached into his pocket and brought out an object wrapped in rags. With a trembling hand, he extended it towards Avrum.

"You want me to take this?" said Avrum.

The man nodded, closed his eyes and was still. Dead.

Avrum looked up and saw me. We exchanged glances but no words. He shoved the object into his pocket and shuffled back to his place.

I saw Avrum again towards the end of the day. He joined me on the assembly ground, and we waited to be counted before the long walk back to the camp.

"Maier, do you know what was in the package?" he asked, his eyes glittering with excitement.

"How would I know? A loaf of bread?"

"Don't mock me. It was a pair of *tefillin!*"

"What!"

"That's right, Maier. Somehow this fellow hid or acquired a pair of *tefillin* right under the noses of the Nazis. How hard it must have been for him to keep them and take care of them! He must have had a holy soul. He knew he was dying, and his greatest concern was to make sure that his *tefillin* passed into Jewish hands. He struggled against death until he saw the *tefillin* safely in my hands, then he closed his eyes and died."

"Amazing," I said.

"Maier, think of what this means." He was so ecstatic that his shoulders straightened and his cheeks seemed to fill out. "We have *tefillin*. We can do the *mitzvah* again with our own pair of *tefillin*. I checked. It's a full pair, one for the head and one for the arm."

"Did you know the man, Avrum?"

"No, I didn't. I think we exchanged two or three words one time, but other than that, nothing. Maier, I have such mixed feelings. I don't know if I should dance for joy because we now have *tefillin* or cry for the poor, holy fellow who just died in front of our eyes."

I embraced Avrum and said, "Let's do both."

And we did.

Walking back to the camp a little later, we passed that day's stack of corpses piled helter skelter at the roadside. There was still a faint glimmer of daylight remaining, and I could see the contorted faces and the vacant eyes of the dead. I searched for our departed friend, but I could not find him. He must have been somewhere under the pile.

The next day, we put on the *tefillin* in the forest during the lunch break. There were no guards posted in the trees behind the latrine; anyone escaping into the forest knew he would be dead before the next morning. We slipped into the trees and stood behind the trunk of a massive oak. My only concern was that our place of concealment should not be betrayed by Avrum's racking coughs, which were becoming progressively worse.

Avrum wanted me to go first, but I would not hear of it. They were his *tefillin*. We both managed to say the Shema while wearing *tefillin* before the whistle signaled the end of the break. I thought back to the *tefillin* I had put on in Flossenberg, and I felt the same exhilaration.

I could not stop thinking about the *tefillin* as I worked through the brutal afternoon. I thought about the man who had given them to Avrum, and I blessed him. I thought about the wonderful feeling of being wrapped in the holy *tefillin*, and I recognized the feeling as being very complex. The *tefillin* were my connection to my past, to my identity, to my father. They gave me comfort. The *tefillin* were also our own small victory over our tormentors, as if to say, "You can torture us, kill us, work us to death, but you will never overcome us. We are invincible."

Two days later, Avrum collapsed during the morning roll call. I ran to him, but the SS officer struck me in the head and chased me away. With my ears ringing, I watched two prisoners lift Avrum by the arms and drag him away to the hospital.

Hospital. What a joke. It was no more than a shack containing a few beds. The job of the doctor on duty was to be on the lookout for outbreaks of epidemics, not to heal or waste medicines on the half-dead prisoners brought to him every day. The prisoners were allowed to stay in the beds for a day or two. Either they recovered and returned to work. Or they died.

The next day in the forest, I thought I would die. The cold was incredible, and my arms and legs felt like blocks of ice that were not really part of my body. Loneliness and worry for Avrum just made the conditions even more unbearable. I thought frequently about the man who had given Avrum the *tefillin*. I considered him fortunate, and I wondered if by the end of the day I too would be on the roadside stack of corpses.

The following morning, Otto called me aside.

"Cahan," he said, "we are organizing another work detail for locksmiths. Do you want to join?"

I would have laughed if all my face muscles hadn't been so sore. Did I want to join? Did I want life over death? "I think so," I said.

"Do you need a day or two to think about it?"

"Absolutely not. I definitely want to join."

"Good. We will be taxing your locksmithing skills to the maximum."

"Oh," I said. "Well, that's just fine."

Otto laughed and slapped me on the back. "Don't worry, Cahan. We'll put you to good use. in the meantime, you have a few hours off. I'll see you in the plaza at noon."

My heart broke as I watched the men march off to the forest. I knew that many of them would not return. And for those that lived to work another day, it was also only a matter of time before they too would perish.

When they were gone, I went to the hospital to visit Avrum. He was lying on a narrow cot in a cubicle, separated from the other sick and wounded, by a screen. He was wide awake, but too weak to move. I covered him with a blanket.

"Good morning, Maier," he whispered. "What brings you here?"

"I came to see you."

"Really? Did they give you a pass from work just to visit me?"

"I've been transferred, Avrum. I'm a locksmith again. When you go back to the forest, I won't be with you. I'm sorry."

"Don't be sorry. Why should we both suffer?" He sighed. "Besides, who knows if I will ever go back to the forest?"

"Stop it, Avrum! Don't talk like that. If you've survived this long, you'll make it through to the end. The war is almost over, you know."

"Well, for those people piled by the side of the road, it's over already. But you're right. Let's not talk about dark things.

The doctor comes in during the afternoon. No one comes here in the morning. The *tefillin* are on a small stool behind my bed. Let's put them on."

I helped him put on the *tefillin*, and as soon as he said the Shema, I took them off. After I had done the same myself, I put the *tefillin* back on the stool. No one had come in to disturb us, just as Avrum predicted, but we didn't want to take unnecessary chances.

Before taking leave of Avrum, I gave him part of my bread ration. I didn't think they would waste bread on a useless patient in the hospital.

At noon, we assembled in the plaza for the work detail. In addition to the locksmiths, there were also carpenters, plumbers and blacksmiths. Our assignment was to renovate one of the outlying buildings right here in the camp. The work required skills that I did not have, but Otto gave me many tasks that were very useful. I brought buckets of coal from the coal storage shed. I also brought wood and other building materials. And at the end of the day's work, I cleaned up all the tools neatly and stored them away. It was a good day.

In the morning, I was the first to arrive at the building. I brought out the tools from storage and distributed them to the appropriate craftsmen. I also ran to fetch buckets of coals and building materials. In between, I learned through observation how to duplicate keys, and I made myself useful doing that. In short, I did whatever I could to make myself indispensable.

We made a lot of progress that day, and Otto rewarded us with early dismissal and an extra ration of bread. Immediately, I headed to the hospital. I wanted to see how my friend Avrum was faring, and I also wanted to give him my extra bread. He needed it much more than I did.

The doctor was talking to an SS officer near the front door of the hospital, and I thought it more prudent to wait until they went away. After about fifteen minutes, they left. Holding the bread tightly, I went inside.

Avrum's bed was empty.

"Avrum!" I burst out. "Where are you?"

No answer.

I covered my face with my hands and began to weep. Just then, there was a light tap on the screen near the bed.

"Are you looking for your friend?" I heard a voice call out.

I walked around the screen and saw a young man, his head swathed in a bandage streaked with blood and grime.

"Do you know where he is?" I asked, afraid to hear the answer.

"Your friend passed away in middle of the night. I heard him die. They took him away in the morning. I'm sorry."

I had not expected Avrum to live even this long, but now that he was dead, I was shocked. I felt as if part of me had died. Somehow, I had considered the discovery of the *tefillin* a portent of good things. It had given me hope, and it had invigorated Avrum. But it was just too much to expect. His lungs had wasted away, and he had been unable to hold on.

Then my thoughts turned to the *tefillin*. Where were they? I went back to Avrum's bed and checked the small stool behind it.

The *tefillin* were gone.

Chapter 20

Part of my job was lugging the heavy buckets from the coal shed, but I never complained. I knew I was on this work detail under false pretenses, and I dared not do or say anything that would jeopardize my already precarious position.

One day, I had to fight my way through a furious icy wind with the empty buckets banging against my knees. I arrived at the shed exhausted and decided to seek shelter inside for a few minutes before returning to the building site. There was a narrow aisle between the piles of coal, but I had never been deep enough to notice it. I had scooped my bucketfuls of coal from the doorway and left right away. There was no reason to linger at the coal shed. Now, with the wind howling behind me, I made my way tentatively between the mounds of coal, seeking a place to sit and rest.

A door awaited me behind the coal. I put my hand on the knob, turned it slowly and pulled the door open.

I felt as if I had stepped into a royal treasurehouse. I saw a good-sized pantry illuminated by a tiny window near the ceiling. A single bulb hung from a wire in the center of the pantry, but I did not dare switch it on. Even in the dim light I could see that I had stumbled into a treasure trove. The shelves were stocked with loaves of fragrant bread, potatoes, tubs of margarine, sugar cane, even strawberry jam. I could not believe my good fortune.

First of all, I had myself a small feast, then rearranged everything so that no one would notice anything missing. Then I sat down to think about the next step. Here was my chance, I decided, to become not only indispensable to my group, not only invaluable, but actually priceless.

Quickly, I filled half of each coal bucket with delicious food and covered it with coals. Then I again removed all traces of my intrusion and returned to my group.

Just as I expected, Otto and the others were overjoyed at my discovery, and from that day on I became an important person. My skills were no longer questioned, and I was freed from all my menial jobs. All I had to do was bring the coal and, of course, what lay under it. In fact, I spent more time cooking and baking that smithing locks, but no one minded. I also distributed some of my delicacies to others in the camp, both prisoners and supervisors, and I accumulated many favors owed to me. This went on for several weeks.

One fine day, I came to the coal shed with my empty buckets, as always. I looked around, and when I saw no one, I entered the shed and went to the pantry in the back, as always. One thing, however, was different. There was a great big padlock on the door of the pantry, bigger than any I had ever seen in my life. The point was loud and clear. The party was over.

This in itself would not have been so terrible for me. I could not expect to go on feasting forever. I gained weight and recovered my strength and color, and I would survive a return to the bread and water on which I had subsisted for so long. The problem was much more serious. Without my special status as provider for the entire group, I knew that my days as a locksmith were numbered.

A few days later, my fears materialized. I was relieved of my duties in the locksmithing work detail and reassigned to the forest. Nonetheless, I was thankful to the Almighty for giving a respite of a few weeks, an opportunity to restore my body and my soul and brace myself for the ordeals of the future.

Back in the forest again, I was given a lighter assignment than I had had before. It cost me a number of favors owed to me, but it was well worth it. But if the work was easier, the problems came from a different direction. I caught a terrible cold and soon I was coughing uncontrollably. I thought of Avrum coughing his lungs out and shuddered. As the days progressed, I lost all the weight I had gained, and I became debilitated and lethargic. At least, I thought, I had been in good physical condition to begin with. If this cold had struck me a few weeks earlier, I would probably be sitting beside Avrum in the next world.

Thankfully, the Almighty did not leave me in this situation for too long. After a short while, a group of laborers was sent off from Ohrdruf to a different work camp at Krawinkel. I was part of the group.

In Krawinkel, conditions were a little better. The work site was in a bunker not too far from the camp, and although the work was hard, we were at least protected from the elements. Furthermore, sick prisoners, if their condition was serious enough, were occasionally excused from work, but they forfeited their rations.

On my first day in the camp, I saw a man about forty years old walking some distance away. He looked familiar, but I couldn't quite place him. There was something about his walk, his carriage, the tilt of his head. I walked over and extended out my hand in greeting. Instantly, we recognized each other.

"Uncle Shloime!"

"Maier!"

We embraced and wept bitter tears on each other's shoulders. I could not believe what had become of my Uncle Shloime, my stepmother's brother. I recalled all the times he had visited us in Lower Vishiva, well-dressed, prosperous, dispensing donations and favors, right and left. I recalled his expansive manner and supreme confidence as he sat in my father's hospital room in Sighet and talked about his logging venture. And now he was reduced to a gaunt scarecrow that bore only a faint resemblance to his former self. Oh, how the mighty had fallen!

It did not take me long to discover that Uncle Shloime still had plenty of his old skills. As a rule, prisoners in Krawinkel were given only half their ration in the morning. The other half was distributed at the work site. This was done to encourage the prisoners to go to work and not claim to be sick, and for the most part, it worked. Uncle Shloime, however, was very often able to arrange that he receive his full ration and still be excused from work. He had not lost his touch.

As for myself, I really was very sick, and I was content to live on half rations for most of my first week in camp in order to recuperate. Half rations were not enough to still my hunger. Full rations barely were. But I managed to get some potato peels from the kitchen, and those kept me going. By the end of the week, my cough was gone, and I was slowly regaining my strength.

Less than a week later, I was separated from Uncle Shloime. He remained in Krawinkel, while I was transferred out. My new camp was just a large collection of tents in a field somewhere. I never learned its name. In fact, I don't even know if it had one.

The tent camp was very cold. The wind blew in through the openings in the canvas and practically froze the blood in my veins. It was also infested with lice. To make matters worse, since there was no plumbing, the water supply was reserved for drinking, leaving hardly any water available for washing. The lice seemed to know this, and they feasted on us mercilessly.

Every morning, I had to choose between the cold and the lice, and I always chose the cold. I would go outside, undress in the freezing cold and, teeth chattering, wash down my body with handfuls of snow until I was completely deloused. I also scrubbed and cleaned my clothing as best I could. This gave me some relief for a while. Not long after I dressed, however, the lice in my clothing found me and once again began their feast.

One morning, I noticed a familiar-looking young man going through the same delousing ritual that I was. Could it be Herschel Pollack, my old friend from Lower Vishiva?

"Herschel?" I ventured.

He looked at me, and his eyes widened. "Maier! Is it really you?"

We hugged each other, laughing and crying at the same time.

"I recognized your voice, Maier," he said. "That's how I knew it was you. I can't believe that this is the same Maier, so handsome, like a beautiful flower in bloom."

Well, it was a good thing Herschel couldn't see that he didn't look like much of a rose himself. "Herschel, you look great," I said.

He broke into a great big smile. "You really mean it?"

"Would I say it if I didn't mean it?" And that was the end of that.

Our workday usually began at five o'clock in the morning. We walked a few kilometers to a mine where we were divided into two groups. One group worked in the shafts, digging for ore. The other worked outside, loading the ore onto wagons along with other tasks.

The mine had about twenty shafts. The one in which I worked was identified as Position Number 15. Large groups of prisoners from the tent camp worked every one of the other shafts as well.

With the war going so badly for the Germans, as all of us knew, why was it so important to work so diligently in the mines? Rumor had it that the Germans were desperately looking for an ore called uranium, and that Hitler intended to use it for a secret weapon against the Allies.

I was assigned to the detail that worked inside the mineshaft. My job was to use a power drill to bore into the walls in the hopes of uncovering lodes of ore. After a few days, I thought I would collapse. The dust and the sulfur fumes choked my lungs, sending me into cough spasms even worse than the ones I had suffered through in Ohrdruf. The pressure underground affected my ears, and I was unable to keep my balance. I had to do something, if I was to survive.

An idea came to me. I would ask one of the prisoners in the outside group to alternate with me day by day. Inside, it was hard to breathe. Outside, on the other hand, it was absolutely freezing but the air was fresh. One day at a time of each was bearable.

It was incredibly cold the next morning, and the first man I approached was glad to change places with me. I knew he would have second thoughts by the end of the day, but tomorrow he would be back in the fresh but frigid air. It was a good deal for both, for me certainly. In a short while, I felt better, and my cough practically disappeared.

What would have happened to me if my cough had persisted? I do not know for sure, but I can well imagine, especially after what happened a few days later. We went down into the mine shaft as usual, all eighteen of us on the inside detail. As I picked up my drill, I heard a dull boom, and then a large rock came hurtling down at me and sent me sprawling several meters away from the mine shaft.

A second boom, this time a deafening explosion, followed the first, and suddenly the entire ceiling over the mine shaft caved in, burying all of us in rocks and debris. I lay there in a daze, my legs covered with broken timbers and rocks, but I was alive. Of the other prisoners, all of whom were in the shaft at the time of the explosion, fifteen were instantly killed by the impact or were buried alive and suffocated to death.

When the other prisoners came down to extricate the survivors, they had to amputate the legs of two of them, in order to get them out. I doubt that they administered anesthetics. As for me, I got away with many bad bruises and a terrible case of fright. They carried the three of us out and set us down on the ground near the mine entrance. I floated in and out of consciousness.

Meanwhile, in the chaos caused by the mine explosion, one of the prisoners had run away, and guards with tracking dogs set off in hot pursuit. From where I sat, I could see the SS officer in charge of our detail pacing back and forth, his face glowering with fury, as he awaited their return.

It did not take long for the guards to return with the prisoner in tow. The officer grunted with satisfaction.

"Undress him," he ordered.

The guards stripped the prisoner and stepped back. He was shivering. I did not know if it was from fear or from the cold.

"Set the dogs on him!" the officer shouted.

The guards released the dogs, and they leaped on the hapless prisoner. He screamed and struggled, but the dogs ripped at his exposed flesh, practically tearing him limb from limb, until his spurting blood formed a puddle around the vicious scene. His heart must have given out, because he suddenly fell limp. The dogs barked at the lifeless body, their tails wagging, as if begging it to come back to life so that they could continue their sport. Then they turned and loped back to the guards, panting with their tongues hanging out, their fangs stained crimson.

Having completed this business to his satisfaction, the officer turned and walked toward us.

"What happened to these men?" he asked one of the junior officers.

"To get these two out," he replied, "we had to amputate their legs."

"I see," said the officer. He pulled his pistol from his holster and shot each of them in the center of the forehead. "We have no use for Jewish amputees."

He turned to me. "And what about you?"

I struggled to my feet. "Only a few bruises, sir," I said. "I'm fine."

My head throbbed, my back was on fire, and I had a hard time keeping my balance. But I stayed on my feet until I was out of his sight, then I collapsed against a wall and closed my eyes. In my mind, the grisly scenes replayed themselves over and over again, the escapee torn apart by dogs and the poor amputees, forced to suffer so much during their rescue, only to be rewarded with a bullet in the head. So much suffering. How could one man be expected to witness so much suffering? I wept.

For the next two days, I could barely move. I did not report for work. Instead, I stayed in bed to rest and recuperate from my ordeal. No one objected. When I tried to stay back from work on the third day, however, I was sent off to roll call with a barrage of kicks and blows. The ones who had it best, I decided as I stumbled along in a fog of pain, were the prisoners who were killed instantly when the mine collapsed.

When we got to the mine, I discovered that I had been assigned to the outside detail. As usual, it was extremely cold, and I thought that, in my weakened condition, I would be better off inside the mine than outside. Normally, I would have approached someone from the inside detail and asked him to exchange places with me for the day, but I simply did not feel up to it. It took a great effort just to remain standing on my feet. I decided to attach myself to the inside detail and hope for the best. It was a big mistake.

An hour after we began to work, someone decided to count the outside detail and found there were only fifteen men instead of sixteen. Apparently, a prisoner had escaped. The guards and their dogs jumped to the ready, eager for the chase. But first they had to determine how many others, if any, had escaped. The alarm was immediately sounded. All work was called to halt, and a full head count was ordered.

Our detail was called out from the mine and told to line up against the wall. A scowling SS officer was counting the heads of the work details. Finally, it was our turn. The officer jabbed at us through the air with his finger.

"Seventeen!" he exclaimed in surprise; he had expected a short count. "Why are there seventeen men in your detail? There should be only sixteen. Why is there an extra man? The one who doesn't belong here, step forward and identify yourself!"

I took a few steps forward and hung my head.

"Well, at least we have now accounted for the missing prisoner," said the officer, pacing back and forth. He seemed more relieved than annoyed. "What is your name?

"Maier Cahan, sir."

"Why were you with a different detail?"

"It was too cold outside," I said. "I was the only survivor from the mine that caved in three days ago, sir, and I have still not recovered completely. I thought I would work inside where it is not as cold. I know I should have told someone. I'm sorry."

The officer had lost interest in me. He turned to the head *kapo* impatiently and said, "Take care of this." Then he left.

The head *kapo*, a brutish Pole whom we called Haman, brandished a heavy stick at me.

"You dirty Jew!" he screamed. "Do you realize what you've done? Because of you, the entire group had to stop working for a good fifteen minutes. Over a hundred hours lost! And all because of you were worried about the cold. You filthy piece of garbage!"

I don't know if he expected me to feel remorse for causing a work stoppage. Actually, I felt quite good about it. I considered myself fortunate to have struck even a small a blow against the Reich.

Haman must have seen my lack of remorse written on my face, because he suddenly attacked me viciously. Knocking me to the ground, kicking me and striking at me mercilessly with his heavy stick. It was a nightmare. I skittered around on the ground to avoid his blows, but he kept charging at me from all directions, swinging his stick without a thought for where it might land.

When I could take no more, I stuck my foot between his feet and sent him sprawling flat on his face. Howling with pain and fury, he scrambled to his feet, his face marked by abrasions, blood running from his nose.

"You did this deliberately!" he yelled at me.

"No! It was an accident. Believe me!"

He picked up his stick and came after me. "Liar!"

I gathered that he didn't believe me, and it crossed my mind that I had finally reached the end. Haman was about to kill me.

But he didn't. His nose had swelled to twice the size, and blood poured from it profusely. He tried to staunch it, but the flow did not stop.

"Try lying on your back and lifting your left arm," I offered helpfully.

He glowered at me and did as I suggested, and after a minute or two, the flow subsided.

"You dirty Jew," he said to me. "I'll get you for this yet. I'll bring you up on charges to the commandant and have you shot. In the meantime, get back to work!"

I lived in abject fear for a few days, but Haman never did mention the episode again, not to me, not to the commandant. Why did he decide to let the matter go? I really don't know. Perhaps he was too embarrassed about being tripped up by a lowly prisoner. Perhaps he reconsidered and decided that the vicious beating I had endured at his hand was punishment enough for my transgressions. Or perhaps it was just another of the many miracles that saw me through these years alive.

Chapter 21

The weeks dragged by lethargically. I lost more weight and grew weaker with every passing day. I lived in such a blurred state that I was almost unaware of the grueling work and the icy weather. Presently, the cold gave way to a hint of springtime. I thought about our balmy Passovers in Lower Vishiva, of the smiling faces of my beloved family, and I wept. For a short while, I considered trying to observe Passover right here in the camp, but I knew it was impossible. I had lost track of the calendar, and besides, I could not survive without bread for eight days.

Rumors about the war were rampant in the camp. We heard that the Allies were pushing the Germans back on all sides and that the end of the war was imminent. I don't know how the information penetrated to the prisoners, but it did.

Perhaps it came from guards who had read the handwriting on the wall and wanted to curry favor with the prisoners.

There were two schools of thought among the prisoners about what to expect from the Germans with their backs against the wall. Some were optimistic, thinking that fear of the Allies would make the Germans more lenient towards us, but others were convinced they would wipe us out at the last minute. I tended to side with the optimists. The pessimistic view was simply too awful to consider.

Soon we were hearing reports that the Allies had crossed into Germany itself both from the east and the west and were driving toward Berlin, capturing huge chunks of territory. The Germans were in retreat on all fronts. What did this mean for us? We did not know.

One day, the orders came to break camp and retreat. Where were we headed? We didn't know, and I don't think the officers knew either. All we knew was that we were marching away from the fighting, away from the approaching Allies. Germany was hanging on by a hair, hoping desperately that Hitler's promise of a secret weapon of mass destruction would materialize before the final collapse. One way or another, the war would be over in a matter of weeks, but it was highly questionable as to whether we would survive until the end.

As the days progressed, numerous prisoners from other camps in the area joined us. I couldn't understand why the Germans were making such an effort to take us along in their retreat. It must have been a logistic nightmare for them to transport and guard so many prisoners. Just the food alone must have been a serious undertaking. Granted that we only got a few morsels each day, but multiply that by many thousands and it becomes a very significant amount. Why didn't they just shoot us and then retreat? I didn't know the answer then, nor do I know it now. Perhaps their orders to retreat had not given them specific instructions about the prisoners, and therefore, they were forced to take us along.

There were thousands of us streaming along the roads to nowhere. Except for a few periods of rest during the day, we were forced to march at a killing pace. Haman, the Polish *kapo*, walked beside us like an angry shepherd, striking with his stick at anyone who dared falter in his stride. The guards fired at anyone who even looked like he was contemplating a run for freedom or simply stepped out of line.

On many occasions, I felt I could not go on. My head wanted to continue, but my body, wasted by hunger and fatigue, refused to cooperate. Only the thought of the certain bullet that awaited me kept me going.

In the evenings we slept under the open sky, exposed to the cold wind and the pouring rain. To build up our morale, Herschel and I would talk about the wonderful life that awaited us, after we would be liberated. Herschel talked about being reunited with his wife and children, but I did not speak about my family. I feared that no one remained, neither in my family, nor in Herschel's, but I said nothing. I let him savor his fantasies.

One day, I was assigned the singular privilege of carrying a heavy bucket of fruit jam together with another prisoner on the march. If the day before I had thought my suffering was at its worst, it was because I hadn't yet known about today. On top of everything, I was ravenously hungry, and I keep thinking about the jam I was carrying. Finally, I could control myself no longer. I glanced around to see if anyone was watching me, then I lifted the lid, scooped out a handful of the jam and stuffed it into my mouth. It was delicious.

Less than a minute later, my stomach rebelled violently. Apparently, it wasn't accustomed to such a heavy dose of sugar. A jolt of pain shot through my abdomen, and I was forced to double over. I tried desperately to keep walking, because I knew what awaited me if I stopped. But I couldn't. In horror, I felt myself falling to the ground. Instantly, two guards appeared at my side. One of them grabbed me by the arm and dragged me out of the line to the side of the road. The other pulled out his pistol.

It was the end. This time there would be no escape. As I said the Shema, the confession of faith that would purify my soul for its journey, the image of my two younger brothers, Hersch Meilech and Yidel Eber, flashed before my eyes. Their hands were outstretched to me, and they were saying, "Maier, where have been so long? We were waiting for you!"

I heard the click of the pistol being cocked, and I squinched my eyes shut, bracing myself for the bullet that was about to tear into my skull.

"Halt!" I heard the commandant shout. "Rest!"

Unaware of this little drama playing itself out at the side of the road, he had called for a short rest break. The guard replaced his pistol in its holster and walked away, like a worker from an assembly line when the lunch bell rings. It meant absolutely nothing to him that he had just been about to snuff out the life of a human being, to tear body and soul apart forever.

My last-second reprieve from death had not reprieved me from my abdominal cramps. I writhed on the ground in agony, unable to sit or stand or do anything else at all but writhe. I had only a few minutes more to recover, since the rest stops rarely lasted more than a quarter hour. My friends took turns massaging my stomach. But the minutes ticked by inexorably, and my cramps did not subside. Try as I might, I was simply unable to walk on my own power. I needed time, and there was none. Death stared me in the face.

Fifteen minutes passed, then a half-hour, but the order to march was not given. Presently, we heard we were waiting for another group of prisoners to join us. There were also whispers that the destination to which we were headed had been captured by the Allies and that the officers were awaiting new orders. Be that as it may, the Almighty had sent me the time I needed. By the time we were ready to march, I was back among the living.

By the time we stopped for the night, we were a multitude of prisoners brought together from different camps. We slept in a vast open field, thousands of us stretched out upon the ground under the stars. The perimeter of the field was heavily guarded lest some prisoner dare to make a break for freedom.

Herschel and I found ourselves in a corner of the field pitted with stones and gnarled roots. The ground did not make for very comfortable bedding, but what could we do? I lay down and tried to find a comfortable position.

"Maier, we can't sleep here," said Herschel. "We won't get a minute of rest. Let's find a different spot."

"Are you joking, Herschel? Do you see how crowded this field is? We could walk all over the field and not find anything."

"I don't agree. Look over that rise. The ground looks comfortable, and it doesn't look so crowded. I'm sure we could find an open piece of soft ground over there."

"I'm not moving," I said. "I need every minute of sleep I can get."

"Well, have it your way. I'm going over there. I'll see you in the morning. We'll see who is better rested."

Through half-closed eyes, I watched Herschel walk off to find a better place. From afar, I saw him locate a spot and lie down. I was happy for him.

Suddenly, I saw muzzle flashes and heard the rat-tat-tat of machine gun fire. Shouts and screams rose heavenward in an ever increasing crescendo of torment and death. All around me, men were screaming and dying. A stream of bullets stitched the ground just a few meters from where I lay, leaving death and havoc in its wake. I closed my eyes and burrowed down, pressing myself against the rocky soil, as if that would somehow help me escape the bullets. The fusillade passed on to other parts of the field, but I remained where I was.

Two hands grabbed me and spun me around.

"Maier! Are you alive?" Herschel screamed into my ear.

I opened my eyes. "Just barely," I said.

He lay down beside me, and we huddled together in fear as sporadic firing continued to rake the killing fields. Then it was over.

For a few long moments, an eerie, deathly silence quivered in the air. Then the silence burst open, and a cascade of wails and screams came pouring out. I lay there listening in shocked wonderment to the sounds of agony, until I felt a hand over my mouth.

"Sh!" Herschel whispered in my ear. "It is over. We are alive."

Only then did I realize that I had been screaming at the top of my lungs. I closed my eyes and wept silently, and presently, I fell into a dreamless sleep.

I awoke with the first light, and the memory of what had transpired the previous night made me sit bolt upright. Herschel was still asleep beside me. I looked out over the fields and saw thousands of reclining men, but I could not tell which were asleep and which were dead. Here and there, I heard the faint whimpers of those wounded or deranged by the German attack. I put my hand over my mouth to make sure I was not among them.

Herschel opened his eyes. He sat up, looked around and shuddered. Then he took a closer look at me.

"Maier, are you all right?" he asked. "Are you wounded?"

"No, I'm fine."

"Your clothes are covered with blood," he said.

I looked behind me. The man lying next to me had been ripped open by the bullets, and his blood must have spurted all over me. In fact, some of it had even gotten onto Herschel's clothes.

The horizon glowed pink, and the men in the field began to stir and take stock of themselves and their surroundings. By the time the sun clambered over the horizon, we knew that only a few hundred of us, at the most, had survived the night.

A squad of SS men entered the field from the far side and made their way methodically across, shooting all the wounded they encountered. My heart pounded wildly in my chest as they drew closer.

About forty meters away, an SS man stopped near a man sitting on the ground. His left shoulder was covered with blood.

"Are you wounded?" said the German.

The man jumped to his feet, his left arm hanging limp by his side. "No sir, I am fine. Please let me live. I can walk a hundred kilometers without any problem. I can work. I can do anything."

"Your arm?"

"Oh, it's nothing, sir. Only a slight scratch. It will be—"

A bullet in his forehead interrupted his sentence.

"No wounded," the German said to the falling body, and he continued on towards us.

Herschel and I were standing at attention when he came to us. He gave Herschel a passing glance, then he looked at me with dead blue eyes.

"Are you wounded?" he asked.

"No, sir."

"There is blood on your clothing."

"It's not mine. It's from the man next to me."

"You were not hit?"

"No, sir. Look!" I jumped up and down and waved my hands in the air. "You see, sir? I am fine. The blood is not mine."

"Go to the assembly on the north side. Both of you. *Schnell!*"

To get to the north side, we had to cross almost the entire field. Herschel and I picked our way between the bodies. It was a nightmare. Halfway there, something off to my right caught my attention. I peered across the grisly tableau, but all I saw was death.

Then I saw it. Three bodies lying together. There was something about them. I walked over to investigate and recognized Tzvi Hersch, Nissen and Shmiel, my beloved friends from Flossenberg. I thought my heart would burst with pain and grief. I squatted on the ground and wept and wept until I had no tears left. I felt Herschel's hand on my shoulder.

"We have to go, Maier," he said. "We'll talk later, if there is a later."

We marched aimlessly for days, five abreast, first in one direction then another, as our destinations fell to the Allies one by one. We had virtually nothing to eat, only the few scraps we were able to beg from bystanders who watched us from the roadside. I grew so weak that I could hardly put one foot in front of the other.

One day, a German farmer drove a wagon full of sugar cane across the road in front of us. The prisoners lunged forward and grabbed the sticks. I was too weak to push through to the wagon. Suddenly, the guards opened fire on the prisoners pressed against the wagon.

"Stop!" shouted the farmer. "They are welcome to it! Stop the killing!"

But the killing did not stop. The guards continue to fire until the ground was littered with corpses. Fifty men from my own group died near the sugar cane wagon. The other groups also suffered heavy casualties. My weakened condition had saved me.

A few sticks had rolled away from the wagon and come to a stop on the ground at my feet. I looked down at them with hungry eyes, but I did not dare bend down to pick them up.

We continued on, and the next day we arrived at Buchenwald, a pitiful remnant of the multitude of prisoners that had set out on the journey. Only the ranks of the guards and the *kapos* had remained intact. Haman the Polish *kapo* was still as robust and vicious as ever, as were all the others.

Buchenwald was a huge, meticulously organized detention camp, built to house two hundred thousand prisoners. They put us into barracks and gave us a little food, barely enough to fill the cavities in our teeth, but better than nothing. We slept squashed together on wooden shelves but, compared to sleeping in the fields, it was luxury. We went to sleep hungry, hoping that the next morning we would be mustered for work and given something to eat.

But the morning brought a rude awakening. Haman and the other *kapos* came charging into the barracks, clubs swinging, screaming and shouting at us to get outside immediately. That was our breakfast.

We staggered outside, weakened by fatigue and hunger, barely dragging ourselves from step to step. The Germans were organizing groups to be sent out onto the road. I suppose they realized they could no longer force these poor shadows of men to go, unless they offered some inducement. And they did. Each man who agreed to go out was given two loaves of bread, margarine and even some fruit jam. Those who remained received nothing at all. That was the choice, starvation or the road.

I chose starvation. I knew the war would be over in days if not hours. There were perils in either choice, and in case of doubt, our Sages taught us that it is best to sit tight and do nothing. I would rather wait it out with nothing to eat in Buchenwald than take my chances on the road. Herschel wasn't sure.

"Maier!"

I looked up, and my heart leaped. "Uncle Shloime!" I shouted, or at least I meant it to be a shout. It came out as no more than a hoarse whisper.

"Maier, look at you!" he said with tears in his eyes. "But at least you're alive. Just a little while longer, and we'll be free."

"I'm Herschel Pollack from Lower Vishiva," Herschel introduced himself. "You must be Reb Shloime Kalush."

"That's right," said Uncle Shloime. "I remember you, young fellow. I'm glad the two of you were together. A friend makes all the difference."

"Well, I don't know how long we'll be together," said Herschel. "I'm considering going on the road, while Maier wants to stay. How about you? Are you taking the food and going on the road?"

Uncle Shloime gave me a sharp glance. "Of course, I'm taking the offer. Maier, have you lost your senses? If you stay here, you'll starve to death. There is no food in this camp. On the road, at least you will have what to eat. At least, you will have a chance to survive!"

I shook my head. "I'm staying right here. I'm going to find a corner somewhere in which to hide and lie still as much as I can, until we are liberated. If I die of starvation, so be it."

Uncle Shloime became agitated. "Do you have any idea how long it will take until we are liberated? It could take weeks! Can you live without food for weeks?"

"Uncle Shloime, I've had too many brushes with the Angel of Death on the road. I'm staying here. Whatever happens, happens."

"Well, I'm not. How about you, Herschel?"

Herschel looked down and chewed on his knuckles. "I'll stay with Maier," he said at last.

Uncle Shloime hugged both of us, and we tearfully said our farewells. Then he went to get his loaves of bread. I never heard from Uncle Shloime again, nor from any of the other men that went out of the camp for the two loaves of bread. I often wonder if he suffered much, and if he had the opportunity to enjoy his bread and jam before the Germans murdered him.

In the end, I suppose I survived because I had become so debilitated in Ohrdruf, working in the forest in the freezing cold. I had come to Ohrdruf as a strong young man, but I had left broken and drained of vitality. Had I been stronger I might have considered going out on the road for those two loaves of bread, but I was too weak even to consider it.

Every day in Buchenwald, I endured beatings by the *kapos* who wanted us to go out on the road, but I among many thousands of others remained listlessly rooted to our places. Only a bullet to the head would dislodge us, and for some reason, it didn't come.

But they gave us no food, and people all around us were dying of starvation. For the first few days, we would slip in among the new arrivals, since they were each given a bowl of soup. It was really not much more than water, but for us it was a full meal.

One day, Haman the *kapo* caught sight of me among the new arrivals. He swung his stick at my hand, breaking my bone and knocking the bowl to the ground. The empty bowl hurt me more than my injured hand. I picked up the bowl with my good hand and licked it dry. From that day on, however, they were on the lookout for Herschel and me, and we had to find other means of securing something to eat.

Herschel and I became expert at foraging for food. I would go out in the middle of the night to search for scraps, sometimes coming back with only a few blades of grass. One night, I found some grains of rice on the ground that must have spilled from a leaking sack, and Herschel found some potato peels. We had a feast.

The next night, I went out to forage again and saw a few guards digging behind the barracks and running wire in the ground. I didn't think they were repairing the telephones or the electrical service. What they were doing reminded me of our work in the mines, and I was sure they were laying explosives.

I went straight back and reported to Herschel. He did not seem overly concerned, and we let the matter lapse. As it turned out, I had been right. After the liberation, the SS officers in the camp used the explosives in their defense, claiming that they had disobeyed their orders to blow up the camp and kill all the remaining prisoners.

The mood in the camp changed imperceptibly. The Germans continued to bark at us, but they sounded like dogs without teeth. The *kapos* disappeared from sight altogether. We all awaited the final countdown. Days, hours, minutes.

On the last day of my captivity, I was sitting on the ground not far from the camp gate, trying to still my hunger by escaping into my fantasy world. The sound of explosions brought me out of my reverie in a cold sweat. I was sure that the demolition of the camp had begun, that my life would be snatched from me at the very last moment.

But I was wrong. I looked up and saw American soldiers inside the camp gate, surrounded by jubilant prisoners; the explosions had obviously come from fighting outside the camp.

I was free.

Chapter 22

Freedom. After such a long time in captivity, dehumanized, demoralized, defeated, we were free again. Our first thought was for food, but there wasn't very much in the camp. All we found was honey and sugar, which we stuffed into our mouths by the handful.

With the hunger in their stomachs somewhat stilled, many prisoners went on a rampage. Some broke open the armories, grabbed weapons and went off in search of their tormentors. Others found stores of uniforms and put them on. Living skeletons with black SS uniforms draped over them like tents, paraded around the camp. The peaked caps with the death's head emblems sat incongruously on their heads, held up only by their ears, from falling over their eyes.

I went into the armory and picked up a rifle, but it was so heavy that I lost my balance and fell. There was a commotion outside, and I went out to investigate. A group of screaming prisoners had cornered Haman, the Polish *kapo*, and had shoved his head into a bucket filled with water. He heaved and struggled, but they piled on and prevented him from breaking free. I also leaned against the pile, although I don't know how much it helped. After two or three minutes, his body went limp. He was dead.

We had exacted vengeance, but it was strangely unsatisfactory. Killing Haman did not even the score for all the torment and the death he had caused. No amount of vengeance could even the score for any of the horrors perpetrated against the Jewish people these last few years. Of course, the criminals would have to be brought to justice, but there would be no satisfaction in it for me, no vindication. I had seen the face of pure evil, and all I wanted to do was put the experience behind me.

Two days after our liberation, I came down with very high fever. The doctor diagnosed my illness as typhus, a very deadly disease. I was emaciated, and my blood pressure was ridiculously low. But my heartbeat was surprisingly strong. I had a slim chance of recovery. I spent the next few weeks in the hospital, watching typhus patients all around me, dying like flies. I passed in and out of delirium for days on end, but ultimately, the fever broke, and the long, slow process of recovery began.

After I regained a semblance of my former health, I joined a transport leaving Buchenwald for Transylvania, which was now no longer Hungary but Romania again. I stopped over in Budapest to sign in at the central registry of survivors and to make inquiries about my family and the Gaspars. There was no information, and I decided to wait in Budapest for a while, often visiting the registry several times a day in case someone turned up during the previous few hours. It was inconceivable to me that I would be the only one left alive. Why me?

One day, the secretary had news for me. There was still no word of the Gaspars or my sister Chaya and her little daughter, but my four younger sisters were alive and well and back home in Lower Vishiva. The whole family had been taken to Auschwitz. At the selection, my sisters were sent to work, and my parents and two little brothers to the gas chambers. The news was like a stab in my heart. I had grieved for my parents for a year, always hoping to be reunited with them but never expecting it to happen. But all along it had been only a nightmare, and now it had become part of my reality, an unmendable rent in the fabric of my life. But the news that my sisters had survived was like a ray of sunshine bursting through a dark cloud. I did not know if I should dance for joy or cry. I did both.

It was time to leave Budapest and return to Lower Vishiva to be reunited with my sisters. But I decided to linger on for a few days in case I might hear some news of my sister or the Gaspars. Budapest was full of returning survivors, and I went to the meeting halls, synagogues and all the other places where the survivors congregated, questioning, listening, hoping for an answer but dreading to hear it.

In a small luncheonette, I met an old acquaintance from Grossverdan. His eyes lit up when he saw me. We embraced and sat down to have a cup of coffee together.

"Do you know anything about my sister Chaya?" I asked.

The man looked down and sighed.

"Oh my G-d!" I cried out. "Oh my G-d! She is dead, isn't she?"

The man nodded.

"And the child?" I asked superfluously.

"Also."

I burst into tears. My own beloved sister, the sweet companion of my childhood, the person I loved more than any other in the whole world, gone. My grief was overwhelming, and I wept like a baby right there in the luncheonette. The other patrons gave me looks of sympathy, but they were not dismayed. It was a commonplace occurrence.

"Tell me about it," I said when I recovered my composure.

"There is not that much to tell. She used the money you left her to join a group that was being smuggled across the border. But her baby started crying, and they sent her back. She was taken to Auschwitz along with her child. I was on the same transport. She carried herself like a queen, and she doted on the child. During the selection, one of the guards tried to take away the baby and give her to an older woman, so that your sister could go to work and survive. But your sister would not part from her child. We begged her to save herself. The child was going to die anyway. Why should she die as well? But she wouldn't hear of it. I saw her and the child being led off to the gas chambers. I never saw her again."

That night, I wandered the streets of Budapest for hours. The hurt was unbearable. I had held out such hope for Chaya's survival. I had hoped she was in Romania or perhaps even Palestine. I had imagined us reunited on a sunny day, her glowing face wreathed in smiles, her rosy-cheeked little daughter holding her hand ever so tightly. I could not accept her death. It was as if part of my heart had been ripped away, leaving a jagged hole. I did not think I could ever become whole again.

The next day was a Friday. I decided to leave Budapest early Sunday morning. Death surrounded me in the capital city, while life awaited me in Lower Vishiva. It was time to go.

On Shabbos, I walked to the synagogue alone. All around me there was a new stirring. I was reminded of a hurricane tearing apart a town and leaving it little more than a mass of rubble. But after the hurricane passes, the people hiding in the cellars and under the tables come out one by one to assess the damage, and to talk and console each other. There is something hopeful and uplifting about such a scene because, amid all the debris, there is still life. There is still a future.

In the vestibule of the synagogue, I saw a woman of about sixty, holding lit candles in her hand and crying. She did not appear to be Jewish. It was very strange.

"Madame, can I help you?" I said.

"I wanted to put candles in the synagogue, but they won't let me."

"Are you Jewish?" I ventured.

She shook her head. "No, I'm not. Last February, my husband, Katona Janos, and three Jews, a man and two women, were shot for providing forged documents to Jewish refugees."

My heart skipped a beat. Three Jews, a man and two women. Providing forged documents to refugees. Shot. Oh my G-d! Could it be?

"Anyway," she continued, "last night I found a sealed letter among my husband's papers. It was addressed to me, and he wrote, among many other things, that his mother was Jewish. I came here to light a candle in the synagogue in his memory, but they won't let me."

"Don't be offended," I said. "It's just that we don't light candles on the Sabbath day, only at night. Don't worry. I'll light candles tonight in your husband's memory. All right?"

She wiped her eyes and nodded. "Remember. Katona Janos."

"I'll remember. About those Jews that were shot together with your husband. Do you know their names?"

"No, I don't. They used to come in middle of the night. The man would sometimes spend the whole night in the cellar with my husband, but they didn't let me in. Everything was very hush-hush. When the police came, they searched the whole house and found nothing. But then they went down to the cellar and found the trapdoor into the secret room. They found everything, presses, photographic equipment, plates, official seals, blank Swedish papers and all sorts of other forged documents. Then they arrested all of them."

I took a deep breath. "Can you describe them? Your husband's Jewish friends?"

"Not really. I never got a good look at them. Why? Do you think they were your relatives?"

"They may have been."

"I think I heard my husband call the man Miki," she said.

Miki. Short for Miklos. Miklos Gaspar. Much as I dreaded the thought, I knew it had to be them.

"Please," I said. "Can you tell me anything else? Anything at all?"

She gave me a speculative look. "My cousin is a policeman. He saw the execution. Do you want to talk to him?"

"Would he talk to me?"

"If I ask him to."

"Please."

"Come with me. He lives three blocks away."

Her cousin was an elderly man with thick white hair and a bushy white mustache. At first, he was reluctant to speak to a stranger, but he relented.

"There was nothing I could do for my cousin," he began. "Or for his Jewish friends. It was terrible. One two three, and it was over. They called me to come at six-thirty in the morning to the courtyard of the military tribunal. I guess they didn't know that I was related to Janos by marriage."

He lit his pipe and puffed on it.

"So what happened?" I prompted.

"First, they read the order. 'The court has ruled that Katona Janos, along with his confederates, Gaspar Miklos—"

I cried out in horror, interrupting him. I knew it was coming, but I was shocked nonetheless. "I'm sorry," I said. "Please continue."

"Those were your relatives, weren't they?"

I nodded.

"I am so sorry. 'The court has ruled that Katona Janos, along with his confederates, Gaspar Miklos, Gaspar Bella and Gaspar Lily, are guilty of sabotage against the war effort of the Hungarian people, because they provided forged documents to help Jews avoid their duty of serving in labor battalions in Germany. It is the verdict of the courts that they be shot.' The officer in command asked them if they had a final statement to make." He paused.

"Well, did they?"

"Gaspar Miklos did. He said, 'You Hungarian murderers will pay dearly, for spilling innocent blood. You know we didn't do this for profit. We didn't earn even one pengo from our efforts. We just did it to help those innocent people you condemned to annihilation. We tried to save them from your bloodstained hands.'"

"Did anyone else say anything?"

"Not right away. The officer gave them three minutes to bid farewell to their G-d. Gaspar Lily spoke up. 'We don't have to bid farewell to our G-d. We're not parting from Him. In a few minutes, we are going to meet our beloved G-d.'"

"Good for Lily."

"By the way, is your name Maier?"

"Yes, it is. How did you know?"

"You see, they were standing against the wall, and the firing squad was ready. I walked over to offer each of them a blindfold. They declined. Janos asked me to beg forgiveness of his wife for the heartache he had caused her. Gaspar Lily also had a message for me. 'You look like a kind man,' she said. 'If you ever meet our Maier, send him our best regards and tell him that he was on our minds until the last moment. Tell him to remember us always. Will you do this?' I promised, and she smiled. I turned around and walked away without looking back. I heard the order given. I heard the shots ring out. I heard the bodies fall."

That was the end of it. He had nothing more to say. Mrs. Katona was crying again, and so was I. At last, I knew about the Gaspars.

The next morning, I was at the train station early. I bought a ticket for Lower Vishiva with a connection in Grossverdan. I had to say good-bye to my sister Chaya where she had lived.

Frangefan Street, where my sister had lived, was in ruins, the buildings deserted, the windows smashed, and the doors off their hinges. My sister's apartment had been thoroughly vandalized. The floor was strewn with broken glass. Shredded books were scattered everywhere, along with personal papers, letters and photographs trampled under heel and rendered unrecognizable by the rains that had poured in through the gaping windows. I rummaged through the debris of my sister's life, seeking some fragment that had survived, something that would connect us for the very last time.

After a half-hour, I found a crumpled photograph under a pile of rubbish. I straightened the creases and rubbed it with my sleeve to remove the caked mud and the dirt, and presently, an image emerged. It was my sister hugging her baby to her heart and smiling from ear to ear—the picture of perfect happiness.

"Oh my poor, pure, beautiful sister!" I cried out. "Oh my aching heart!"

I kissed the photograph and burst into tears. I had cried often during the previous year. I had cried in pain, in agony, in frustration, and in sorrow. But now I cried with an emotion I could not identify. Perhaps I could say it was a sense that I myself had died a little through all my suffering and the loss of my most beloved, and that for the rest of my life I would only be a shadow of what I should have been.

I slipped the photograph into my pocket, squared my shoulders and left.

Epilogue

Many years passed. I returned to Romania and married my wife Ila. We had children. In 1961, we moved to Antwerp, Belgium, and I became successful in the diamond business. I had friends and social position. I had grandchildren. But I never forgot my family that had perished in the Holocaust, not for a single day.

For many years, I dreamed of writing a Torah scroll in the memory of my beloved family who had no headstones or even graves. On 18 May, 1988, the dream came true. The ceremony took place in Bnei Brak, Israel, in the synagogue of the Seretter Rebbe. The Hebrew date was 2 Sivan, the *yahrzeit* of his grandfather, the holy Vizhnitzer Rebbe, the Ahavas Yisrael.

The auther in his later years

With my three sons, Meshulem Favish, Yehudah and Menachem standing beside me, I filled in the final letters the scribe had left for us. In a moment of tremendous emotion, I dedicated the completion of the holy Torah scroll to the memory of my father, my mother, my stepmother, my sister Chaya, her daughter and my little brothers Hersch Meilech and Yidel Eber. My hands shook as I filled in the outlined letters, but my heart was bursting with happiness. Separated by the chasm between life and death, I had nonetheless given them a gift of timeless value. It was the greatest day of my life.

The completed Torah scroll was paraded through the streets. Family members, dignitaries and friends took turns carrying it. People danced around it, as a band played the exquisitely beautiful songs of Vizhnitz. I carried the Torah for a long time, tearfully hugging and kissing it with all my might. I thought about the people I had lost and the suffering I had endured, and I realized that only this precious Torah formed an eternal bond between me and the rest of my family and people, that only the Torah defined who and what we are, that only my profound faith and trust in the Almighty gave all I had experienced some semblance of meaning. There is so much in the world we cannot fathom. So many questions that must remain unresolved. But if we have true faith in the Almighty, then we know there are answers, that all is not for naught, even though it seems to make no sense. And sometimes that just has to be enough.

After the Torah scroll was escorted into the synagogue and majestically installed in the Holy Ark, there was a special banquet in honor of the occasion. The Rebbe and other speakers thrilled us with words of wisdom and inspiration. We feasted and sang the songs of Vizhnitz until midnight. It was pure ecstasy.

The hour grew late, and my head felt as if it would float away.

"Maier, think about it for a minute," a familiar voice said to me. It was the Old Fool. "All these beloved people to whom you've dedicated this Torah scroll, why did they deserve to die? Wouldn't it have been better if they were all alive to share this celebration with you today? Better for them and better for you. For whom is it better that they are dead? For whom is it better that they suffered so horribly?"

For a moment, my anger flared, but then I leaned back and listened to the strains of the music. In my mind, I was once again dancing in the street, holding on tightly to the Torah and crying like a child, and I no longer heard the Old Fool. Life, I decided, was a choice between anger and joy. I chose joy.

Appendix

The Decimation of the Cahan Family

(The names of the author and his immediate pre-war family are in boldface.)

Meir Cahan,

the author, and his wife Ila remained in Romania until 1961 when they emigrated to Antwerp, Belgium. He passed away on 28 October 1996

☐ His son Meshulem Feivish (Favi), born in Romania, and his wife Civia, live in Brooklyn. They have three children, Batsheva, Daliah and Dovid.

☐ His son Yehuda, born in Romania, and his wife Faygie, live in Denver, Colorado, where he is the *rav*. They have 5 children, Miriam, Esther, Sora, Moshe and Yaakov.

☐ His son Menachem (Mendy), born in Antwerp, lives in Tel Aviv.

R' Meshulem Feivish Cahan,

father of the author, and his second wife, the former Etil Kalush of Munkacz, perished in Auschwitz.

☐ R' Meshulem Feivish's father, R' Yankel Cahan, expired in the cattle car on the way to Auschwitz.

☐ His brother R' Shaul Aryeh and his family survived and settled in Bnei Brak after the war.

☐ His brother R' Eizik Tzvi, who lived in Antwerp with his wife and children, was deported from Belgium. One son Avrohom (Bumi) and one daughter Reji survived.

- His brother R' Ephraim Fishel was sent to forced labor in the Ukraine and never returned.
- His sister Nissel, who lived in Teitch, and her husband, were deported to Auschwitz and killed.
- His sister Chava Yuta and her husband R' Shmuel Hersh had four daughters and one son, who later married the auther's sister Chaya. Chava Yuta passed away before the war. Her entire family was killed .....
- His sister Esther, her husband R' Pinchas Halpert and their children, emigrated and settled in Bnei Brak in the 1930s.
- His sister Chantze Ratza married R' Yitzchak Halpert and had many daughters and one son. All were killed, except for the son, who survived and settled in Eretz Yisrael.
- His sister Devora and her husband were killed.
- His sister Rivka and one daughter perished in Auschwitz. Her husband R' Shaul Fishman and their older daughter survived, eventually settling in Eretz Yisrael.
- His sister Etya and her husband Eliyahu Ganz emigrated to Cuba.

Alta Etieh Cahan,
mother of the author, died when he was a child of two.
- Alta Etieh's father, R' Hershel Cahan, brother of her father-in-law R' Yankel Cahan, was deported from the ghetto to Auschwitz and perished.
- Her mother, Chantze Cahan, daughter of R' Meir Ganz, was deported from the ghetto to Auschwitz and perished.
- Her brother Meshulam Feivish Cahan and his wife Chana Reiza were killed. Two of their sons survived. One married the auther's sister Rickel; they

settled in Eretz Yisrael and had two children. The other raised a family in the United States.

☐ Her brother Yehuda Cahan and his wife Esther were killed. They were survived by a son, who settled in Antwerp, and a daughter, who settled in Eretz Yisrael.

☐ Her brother Dovid Cahan's wife, two sons and a daughter were killed. He survived, as did his son Meir, who settled and raised a family in Manchester, England.

☐ Her brother Meir Cahan, his wife and children all perished in Auschwitz.

☐ Her sister Sarah, her husband R' Feivush Cahan, *dayan* in Lower Vishiva, and her children were killed.

Etil Cahan,

the auther's stepmother, second wife of R' Meshulem Feivush Cahan, perished in Auschwitz.

☐ Etil's father, R' Mordechai Kalush of Munkacz, was killed.

☐ Her mother, Perel Kalush, was killed.

☐ Her brother Hersch Meilech was killed

☐ Her brother Feivel survived and settled in Tel Aviv. His only son was killed in Auschwitz.

☐ Her brother Yaakov survived and settled in Eretz Yisrael. He had two sons and a daughter.

☐ Her sister Hentsha and her husband R' Elya Shlomovitz were killed .. . . .

☐ Her sister Rachel was killed . . .

Chaya,

full sister of the author, and her daughter Etya perished in Auschwitz. Her husband R' Yosef Meir Weiss was sent to forced labor in the Ukraine and never returned.

Hersch Meilech Cahan,

half brother of the author, perished in Auschwitz.

Yehuda Eber Cahan,

half brother of the author, perished in Auschwitz.

Alta Sarah,

half sister of the author, her husband Aryeh Rabinowitz and one son Amir and one daughter Anat live in Eretz Yisrael.

Rickel,

half sister of the author, and her husband Yosef Cahan raised a daughter Edna and a son Shraga Feivish in Romania after the war and then all emigrated to Eretz Yisrael.

Charna Rachel,

half sister of the author, and her husband Shlomo Chanan settled in Eretz Yisrael and had two sons, Doron and Yaron.

Esther,

half sister of the author, emigrated to Eretz Yisrael where she married Moshe (Mundik) Tamir and had three sons. Ben-Ami (died in Yom Kippur war), Rami, Arnon.